A More Perfect Union

DOCUMENTS IN U.S. HISTORY

SIXTH EDITION

Volume 2: Since 1865

Paul F. Boller, Jr.

Professor Emeritus, Texas Christian University

Ronald Story

University of Massachusetts, Amherst

HOUGHTON MIFFLIN COMPANY

Boston   New York

Sponsoring Editor: Sally Constable
Development Editor: Lisa Kalner Williams
Editorial Assistant: Kisha Mitchell
Associate Project Editor: Teresa Huang
Editorial Assistant: Jake Perry
Senior Art and Design Coordinator: Jill Haber
Senior Photo Editor: Jennifer Meyer Dare
Senior Composition Buyer: Sarah Ambrose
Senior Manufacturing Coordinator: Priscilla J. Bailey
Senior Marketing Manager: Sandra McGuire
Marketing Associate: Ilana Gordon

Cover image: Seal of the President of the United States. Office of the Photographer/
The White House, Washington, D.C. Background: The Day of Infamy Speech by President Franklin Delano Roosevelt, FDR Library, Hyde Park, N.Y.

Printed in the U.S.A.

Library of Congress Catalog Card Number: 2004105966

ISBN: 0-618-43684-7

56789-MP-08

Contents

CHAPTER THREE

★

Industry, Expansion, and Reform

CHAPTER FOUR

★

Crisis and Hope

CHAPTER FIVE

★

Protracted Conflict

★

CHAPTER SIX

Movements for Change

CHAPTER SEVEN

★

Modern Times

PREFACE

Our two-volume reader, *A More Perfect Union: Documents in U.S. History*, presents students with the original words of speeches and testimony, political and legal writings, and literature that have reflected, precipitated, and implemented pivotal events of the past four centuries. The readings in Volume 1 cover the era from first settlement to Reconstruction. Volume 2 begins with the post–Civil War period and concludes with selections that relate to recent history. We are pleased with the reception that *A More Perfect Union* has received, and we have worked toward refining the contents of this new edition.

Changes to the Sixth Edition

More than a third of the material is new to this edition. New selections in Volume 1 include, for example, poems by Anne Bradstreet, a Great Awakening sermon by Jonathan Edwards, a resolution by Boston journeymen carpenters, and a fresh selection from *Uncle Tom's Cabin*. Among the new selections in Volume 2 are statements by Samuel Gompers on the rights of labor, Theodore Roosevelt on the Monroe Doctrine, and Senator Sam Ervin on Richard Nixon's impeachment proceedings, as well as labor organizing songs from the 1930s.

Goal and Format

The readings in these volumes represent a blend of social and political history, along with some cultural and economic trends, suitable for introductory courses in American history. We made our selections with three thoughts in mind. First, we looked for famous documents with a lustrous place in the American tradition—the Gettysburg Address, for example, or Franklin D. Roosevelt's First Inaugural Address. These we chose for their great mythic quality, as expressions of fundamental sentiments with which students should be familiar. Second, we looked for writings that caused something to happen or had an impact when they appeared. Examples include the Virginia slave statutes, the Emancipation Proclamation, and Earl Warren's opinion in *Brown v. Board of Education of Topeka*—all of them influential pieces, some of them famous as well. Third, we looked for documents that seem to reflect important attitudes or developments. Into this group fall the writings of Upton Sinclair on industrial Chicago and of Martin Luther King, Jr., on Vietnam. In this category, where the need for careful selection from a wide field was most apparent, we looked especially for thoughtful pieces with a measure of fame and influence. Horace Mann's statement on schools reflected common attitudes; it also caused something to happen and is a well-known reform statement. We have also tried to mix a few unusual items into the stew, as with the "Report of the Joint Committee on Reconstruction" and a statement by the Catholic bishops on parochial schools.

We have edited severely in places, mostly when the document is long or contains extraneous material or obscure references. We have also, in some cases, modernized spelling and punctuation.

Each document has a lengthy headnote that summarizes the relevant trends of the era, provides a specific setting for the document, and sketches the life of the author. In addition, "Questions to Consider" guide students through the prose and suggest ways of thinking about the selections.

Acknowledgements

We would like to thank the following people who reviewed the sixth edition manuscript for one or both volumes: Jonathan M. Atkins, Berry College; Lorri Glover, University of Tennessee; Carol Sue Humphrey, Oklahoma Baptist University; Steven E. Siry, Baldwin-Wallace College; and Andrew McMichael, Western Kentucky University.

We would also like to thank the following people who reviewed the manuscript in prior editions: John K. Alexander, University of Cincinnati; June G. Alexander, University of Cincinnati; Judith L. Demark, Northern Michigan University; Kurk Dorsey, University of New Hampshire; Paul G. Faler, University of Massachusetts at Boston; Harvey Green, Northeastern University; Richard H. Peterson, San Diego State University; Ben Rader, University of Nebraska at Lincoln; C. Elizabeth Raymond, University of Nevada–Reno; Thomas Templeton Taylor, Wittenberg University; and John Scott Wilson, University of South Carolina.

We owe a debt of gratitude to Kisha Mitchell, our editorial assistant, and to Teresa Huang, our associate project editor, for this edition. We also wish to express our appreciation to the editorial staff of Houghton Mifflin Company for their hard and conscientious work in producing these volumes.

P. F. B.
R. S.

A More Perfect Union

Tennessee Klansman in full regalia. A Tennessee Klansman in full regalia designed to put fear into the hearts of freedmen and Republicans, and to disguise the identity of the wearer from federal officers and judges. This man would have also carried rope, possibly a club, and almost certainly a firearm, probably a rifled musket from the war years. (Tennessee State Museum)

CHAPTER ONE

Reconstructing the Union

1

UNITY

Despite Congress's seizure of control over Reconstruction policy and Ulysses S. Grant's defeat of Andrew Johnson for the presidency in 1868, Radical Reconstruction—the garrisoning of the South, the disfranchisement of former rebels, and the control of Southern state governments by Republican votes—did not last long in most places. During President Grant's first term of office, the white-dominated Democratic Party gained control of North Carolina, Tennessee, and Virginia, the three ex-Confederate states with the lowest percentage of black population. During Grant's second term, Democrats seized control of Alabama, Arkansas, Georgia, Mississippi, and Texas. That left Republican governments (and federal troops) in Florida, Louisiana, and South Carolina, three states with large black populations.

Those states mattered greatly in national politics. During the election of 1876 both parties resorted to fraud. Two sets of electoral returns came in from the three states, and it was necessary for Congress to set up an electoral commission to decide whether Rutherford B. Hayes, the Republican candidate, or Samuel J. Tilden, the Democratic standard bearer, had won. By a strict party vote of 8 to 7, the commission awarded all 20 disputed electoral votes to the Republicans. Hayes became president, with 185 votes to Tilden's 184. In the end, Southern Democrats reached a compromise with Northern Republicans. The Democrats agreed to accept the commission's decision and the Republicans promised to withdraw the remaining federal troops from the South. In April 1877, the last federal soldiers left the South. Solid Democratic control—and stepped-up measures to disfranchise black voters—quickly followed.

Although political maneuvering was important in finally killing Republican Reconstruction, the underlying reason it died was simply that Northerners were losing the will to suppress an increasingly violent white South. The nation's approaching centennial celebration in 1876 triggered an especially strong outpouring of sentiment in favor of improving sectional feelings by withdrawing the troops, even if withdrawal meant the resurgence of the Democratic Party. That, in turn, would permit an overdue rebonding of the century-old republic. The following unsigned editorial ran in the August 1875 issue of *Scribner's Monthly,* an influential, generally Republican, New York magazine. It expressed, with unusual eloquence, this emotional yearning for peace.

Questions to Consider. What was the occasion of the *Scribner's* editorial? Was this a natural time to consider troop withdrawals? What, in the view of the editor, was the major accomplishment of the Civil War? What specific political theory had been tested and defeated? When addressing the "men of the South," was the editor speaking to all Southern men? What did the phrase "brotherly sympathy" mean? Was it naive or was it realistic for the writer to think that the upcoming centennial could "heal all the old wounds" and "reconcile all the old differences"? Would Abraham Lincoln have agreed with the spirit of this editorial?

★═══★═══★

What the Centennial Ought to Accomplish (1875)

SCRIBNER'S MONTHLY

We are to have grand doings next year. There is to be an Exposition. There are to be speeches, and songs, and processions, and elaborate ceremonies and general rejoicings. Cannon are to be fired, flags are to be floated, and the eagle is expected to scream while he dips the tip of either pinion in the Atlantic and the Pacific, and sprinkles the land with a new baptism of freedom. The national oratory will exhaust the figures of speech in patriotic glorification, while the effete civilizations of the Old World, and the despots of the East, tottering upon their tumbling thrones, will rub their eyes and sleepily inquire, "What's the row?" The Centennial is expected to celebrate in a fitting way—somewhat dimly apprehended, it is true—the birth of a nation.

Well, the object is a good one. When the old colonies declared themselves free, they took a grand step in the march of progress; but now, before we begin our celebration of this event, would it not be well for us to inquire whether we have a nation? In a large number of the States of this country there exists not only a belief that the United States do not constitute a nation, but a theory of State rights which forbids that they ever shall become one. We hear about the perturbed condition of the Southern mind. We hear it said that multitudes there are just as disloyal as they were during the civil war. This, we believe, we are justified in denying. Before the war they had a theory of

Miss Liberty's torch. A display at the great 1876 Centennial Exposition, Philadelphia. (Library of Congress)

State rights. They fought to establish that theory, and they now speak of the result as "the lost cause." They are not actively in rebellion, and they do not propose to be. They do not hope for the re-establishment of slavery. They fought bravely and well to establish their theory, but the majority was against them; and if the result of the war emphasized any fact, it was that *en masse* the people of the United States constitute a nation—indivisible in con-

stituents, in interest, in destiny. The result of the war was without significance, if it did not mean that the United States constitute a nation which cannot be divided; which will not permit itself to be divided; which is integral,
indissoluble, indestructible. We do not care what theories of State rights are
entertained outside of this. State rights, in all the States, should be jealously
guarded, and, by all legitimate means, defended. New York should be as jeal-
ous of her State prerogatives as South Carolina or Louisiana; but this theory
which makes of the Union a rope of sand, and of the States a collection of
petty nationalities that can at liberty drop the bands which hold them together, is forever exploded. It has been tested at the point of the bayonet. It
went down in blood, and went down for all time. Its adherents may mourn
over the fact, as we can never cease to mourn over the events which accompanied it, over the sad, incalculable cost to them and to those who opposed
them. The great point with them is to recognize the fact that, for richer or
poorer, in sickness and health, until death do us part, these United States constitute a nation; that we are to live, grow, prosper, and suffer together, united
by bands that cannot be sundered.

Unless this fact is fully recognized throughout the Union, our Centennial
will be but a hollow mockery. If we are to celebrate anything worth celebrating, it is the birth of a nation. If we are to celebrate anything worth celebrating,
it should be by the whole heart and united voice of the nation. If we can make
the Centennial an occasion for emphasizing the great lesson of the war, and
universally assenting to the results of the war, it will, indeed, be worth all the
money expended upon and the time devoted to it. If around the old Altars of
Liberty we cannot rejoin our hands in brotherly affection and national loyalty, let us spike the cannon that will only proclaim our weakness, put our
flags at half-mast, smother our eagles, eat our ashes, and wait for our American aloe to give us a better blossoming.

A few weeks ago, Mr. Jefferson Davis, the ex-President of the Confederacy,
was reported to have exhorted an audience to which he was speaking to be
as loyal to the old flag of the Union now as they were during the Mexican
War. If the South could know what music there was in these words to Northern ears—how grateful we were to their old chief for them—it would appreciate the strength of our longing for a complete restoration of the national
feeling that existed when Northern and Southern blood mingled in common
sacrifice on Mexican soil. This national feeling, this national pride, this brotherly sympathy *must be restored;* and accursed be any Northern or Southern
man, whether in power or out of power, whether politician, theorizer, carpet-
bagger, president-maker or plunderer, who puts obstacles in the way of such
a restoration. Men of the South, we want you. Men of the South, we long for
the restoration of your peace and your prosperity. We would see your cities
thriving, your homes happy, your plantations teeming with plenteous har-
vests, your schools overflowing, your wisest statesmen leading you, and all
causes and all memories of discord wiped out forever. You do not believe
this? Then you do not know the heart of the North. Have you cause of

complaint against the politicians? Alas! so have we. Help us, as loving and loyal American citizens, to make our politicians better. Only remember and believe that there is nothing that the North wants so much to-day, as your recognition of the fact that the old relations between you and us are forever restored—that your hope, your pride, your policy, and your destiny are one with ours. Our children will grow up to despise our childishness, if we cannot do away with our personal hates so far, that in the cause of an established nationality we may join hands under the old flag.

To bring about this reunion of the two sections of the country in the old fellowship, should be the leading object of the approaching Centennial. A celebration of the national birth, begun, carried on, and finished by a section, would be a mockery and a shame. The nations of the world might well point at it the finger of scorn. The money expended upon it were better sunk in the sea, or devoted to repairing the waste places of the war. Men of the South, it is for you to say whether your magnanimity is equal to your valor—whether you are as reasonable as you are brave, and whether, like your old chief, you accept that definite and irreversible result of the war which makes you and yours forever members of the great American nation with us. Let us see to it, North and South, that the Centennial heals all the old wounds, reconciles all the old differences, and furnishes the occasion for such a reunion of the great American nationality, as shall make our celebration an expression of fraternal good-will among all sections and all States, and a corner-stone over which shall be reared a new temple to national freedom, concord, peace, and prosperity.

2

SUBJUGATION

Frederick Douglass regarded the Declaration of Independence as a "watchword of freedom." But he was tempted to turn it to the wall, he said, because its human rights principles were so shamelessly violated. A former slave himself, Douglass knew what he was talking about. Douglass thought that enslaving blacks fettered whites as well and that the United States would never be truly free until it ended chattel slavery. During the Civil War, he had several conversations with Lincoln, urging him to make emancipation his major aim. He also put unremitting pressure on the Union army to accept black volunteers, and after resistance to admitting blacks into the army gave way, he toured the country encouraging blacks to enlist and imploring the government to treat black and white soldiers equally in matters of pay and promotion.

Douglass had great hopes for his fellow blacks after the Civil War. He demanded they be given full rights—political, legal, educational, and economic—as citizens. He also wanted to see the wall of separation between the races crumble and see "the colored people of this country, enjoying the same freedom [as whites], voting at the same ballot-box, using the same cartridge-box, going to the same schools, attending the same churches, travelling in the same street cars, in the same railroad cars, on the same steam-boats, proud of the same country, fighting the same war, and enjoying the same peace and all its advantages." He regarded the Republican Party as the "party of progress, justice and freedom" and at election time took to the stump and rallied black votes for the party. He was rewarded for these services by appointment as marshal of the District of Columbia in 1877, as recorder of deeds for the District in 1881, and as minister to Haiti in 1889. But he was also asked by Republican leaders to keep a low profile, was omitted from White House guest lists, and was excluded from presidential receptions even though one duty of the District marshal was to introduce the guests at White House state occasions.

Douglass was puzzled and then upset by the increasing indifference of Republican leaders to conditions among blacks after the Civil War. In 1883 he attended a convention of blacks in Louisville, Kentucky, which met to discuss their plight and reaffirm their demand for full civil rights. In his keynote address, which is reprinted here, Douglass vividly portrayed the discrimination and persecution his people encountered, but he continued to believe that "prejudice, with all its malign accomplishments, may yet be removed by peaceful means."

Born into slavery in Maryland in 1817, Frederick Augustus Washington Bailey learned to read and write despite efforts to keep him illiterate. In 1838 he managed to escape to freedom and adopted the name Frederick Douglass. Shortly afterward he became associated with William Lloyd Garrison and developed into such an articulate spokesman for the antislavery cause that people doubted he had ever been a slave. In 1845 he published his *Narrative of the Life of Frederick Douglass, an American Slave,* naming names, places, dates, and precise events to convince people he had been born in bondage. Douglass continued to be an articulate spokesman for the black cause throughout his life. Shortly before his death in 1895 a college student asked him what a young black could do to help the cause. Douglass is supposed to have told him, "Agitate! Agitate! Agitate!"

Questions to Consider. In the following address Douglass was speaking to a convention of blacks in Louisville, but his appeal was primarily to American whites. How did he try to convince them that blacks deserved the same rights and opportunities as all Americans? How powerful did he think the color line was? What outrages against his people did he report? What was his attitude toward the Republican Party, which he had so faithfully served? Were the grievances he cited largely economic or were they social and political in nature?

★━━★━━★

Address to the Louisville Convention (1883)

FREDERICK DOUGLASS

Born on American soil in common with yourselves, deriving our bodies and our minds from its dust, centuries having passed away since our ancestors were torn from the shores of Africa, we, like yourselves, hold ourselves to be in every sense Americans, and that we may, therefore, venture to speak to you in a tone not lower than that which becomes earnest men and American citizens. Having watered your soil with our tears, enriched it with our blood, performed its roughest labor in time of peace, defended it against enemies in time of war, and at all times been loyal and true to its best interests, we deem

Philip Foner, ed., *The Life and Writings of Frederick Douglass* (4 v., International Publishers, New York, 1955), IV: 373–392. Reprinted by permission.

Frederick Douglass. Douglass's greatest work came before and during the Civil War. One of the most eloquent and magnetic of all the abolitionist leaders, he contributed enormously to the antislavery cause. During the Civil War he pressed hard for the enlistment of blacks to fight in the Union armies on an equal footing with whites. After the war he continued his efforts for civil rights, including black suffrage. For his services to the Republican Party he received appointments as secretary to the Santo Domingo commission, marshal and recorder of deeds for the District of Columbia, and U.S. minister to Haiti. (National Portrait Gallery, Smithsonian Institution/Art Resource, NY)

it no arrogance or presumption to manifest now a common concern with you for its welfare, prosperity, honor and glory. . . .

It is our lot to live among a people whose laws, traditions, and prejudices have been against us for centuries, and from these they are not yet free. To assume that they are free from these evils simply because they have changed their laws is to assume what is utterly unreasonable and contrary to facts. Large bodies move slowly. Individuals may be converted on the instant and change their whole course of life. Nations never. Time and events are required for the conversion of nations. Not even the character of a great political organization can be changed by a new platform. It will be the same old snake though in a new skin. Though we have had war, reconstruction and abolition as a nation, we still linger in the shadow and blight of an extinct institution. Though the colored man is no longer subject to be bought and sold, he is still surrounded by an adverse sentiment which fetters all his movements. In his downward course he meets with no resistance, but his course upward is resented and resisted at every step of his progress. If he comes in ignorance, rags, and wretchedness, he conforms to the popular belief of his character, and in that character he is welcome. But if he shall come as a gentleman, a scholar, and a statesman, he is hailed as a contradiction to the national faith concerning his race, and his coming is resented as impudence. In the one case he may provoke contempt and derision, but in the other he is an affront to pride, and provokes malice. Let him do what he will, there is at present, therefore, no escape for him. The color line meets him everywhere, and in a measure shuts him out from all respectable and profitable trades and callings. In spite of all your religion and laws he is a rejected man.

He is rejected by trade unions, of every trade, and refused work while he lives, and burial when he dies, and yet he is asked to forget his color, and forget that which everybody else remembers. If he offers himself to a builder as a mechanic, to a client as a lawyer, to a patient as a physician, to a college as a professor, to a firm as a clerk, to a Government Department as an agent, or an officer, he is sternly met on the color line, and his claim to consideration in some way is disputed on the ground of color.

Not even our churches, whose members profess to follow the despised Nazarene, whose home, when on earth, was among the lowly and despised, have yet conquered this feeling of color madness, and what is true of our churches is also true of our courts of law. Neither is free from this all-pervading atmosphere of color hate. The one describes the Deity as impartial, no respecter of persons, and the other the Goddess of Justice as blindfolded, with sword by her side and scales in her hand held evenly between high and low, rich and low, white and black, but both are the images of American imagination, rather than American practices.

Taking advantage of the general disposition in this country to impute crime to color, white men *color* their faces to commit crime and wash off the hated color to escape punishment. In many places where the commission of crime is alleged against one of our color, the ordinary processes of law are set aside as too slow for the impetuous justice of the infuriated populace. They take the law into their own bloody hands and proceed to whip, stab, shoot, hang, or burn the alleged culprit, without the intervention of courts, counsel, judges, juries, or witnesses. In such cases it is not the business of the accusers to prove guilt, but it is for the accused to prove his innocence, a thing hard for him to do in these infernal Lynch courts. A man accused, surprised, frightened, and captured by a motley crowd, dragged with a rope about his neck in midnight-darkness to the nearest tree, and told in the coarsest terms of profanity to prepare for death, would be more than human if he did not, in his terror-stricken appearance, more confirm suspicion of guilt than the contrary. Worse still, in the presence of such hell-black outrages, the pulpit is usually dumb, and the press in the neighborhood is silent or openly takes side with the mob. There are occasional cases in which white men are lynched, but one sparrow does not make a summer. Every one knows that what is called Lynch law is peculiarly the law for colored people and for nobody else. If there were no other grievance than this horrible and barbarous Lynch law custom, we should be justified in assembling, as we have now done, to expose and denounce it. But this is not all. Even now, after twenty years of so-called emancipation, we are subject to lawless raids of midnight riders, who, with blackened faces, invade our homes and perpetrate the foulest of crimes upon us and our families. This condition of things is too flagrant and notorious to require specifications or proof. Thus in all the relations of life and death we are met by the color line.

While we recognize the color line as a hurtful force, a mountain barrier to our progress, wounding our bleeding feet with its flinty rocks at every step, we do not despair. We are a hopeful people. This convention is a proof of our faith in you, in reason, in truth and justice—our belief that prejudice, with all its malign accomplishments, may yet be removed by peaceful means; that, assisted by time and events and the growing enlightenment of both races, the color line will ultimately become harmless. When this shall come it will then only be used, as it should be, to distinguish one variety of the human family from another. It will cease to have any civil, political, or moral significance, and colored conventions will then be dispensed with as anachronisms, wholly out of place, but not till then. Do not marvel that we are discouraged. The faith within us has a rational basis, and is confirmed by facts. When we consider how deep-seated this feeling against us is; the long centuries it has been forming; the forces of avarice which have been marshaled to sustain it; how the language and literature of the country have been pervaded with it; how the church, the press, the play-house, and other influences of the country have been arrayed in its support, the progress toward its extinction must be considered vast and wonderful. . . .

We do not believe, as we are often told, that the Negro is the ugly child of the national family, and the more he is kept out of sight the better it will be for him. You know that liberty given is never so precious as liberty sought for and fought for. The man outraged is the man to make the outcry. Depend upon it, men will not care much for a people who do not care for themselves. Our meeting here was opposed by some of our members, because it would disturb the peace of the Republican party. The suggestion came from coward lips and misapprehended the character of that party. If the Republican party cannot stand a demand for justice and fair play, it ought to go down. We were men before that party was born, and our manhood is more sacred than any party can be. Parties were made for men, not men for parties.

The colored people of the South are the laboring people of the South. The labor of a country is the source of its wealth; without the colored laborer to-day the South would be a howling wilderness, given up to bats, owls, wolves, and bears. He was the source of its wealth before the war, and has been the source of its prosperity since the war. He almost alone is visible in her fields, with implements of toil in his hands, and laboriously using them to-day.

Let us look candidly at the matter. While we see and hear that the South is more prosperous than it ever was before and rapidly recovering from the waste of war, while we read that it raises more cotton, sugar, rice, tobacco, corn, and other valuable products than it ever produced before, how happens it, we sternly ask, that the houses of its laborers are miserable huts, that their clothes are rags, and their food the coarsest and scantiest? How happens it that the land-owner is becoming richer and the laborer poorer?

The implication is irresistible—that where the landlord is prosperous the laborer ought to share his prosperity, and whenever and wherever we find this is not the case there is manifestly wrong somewhere. . . .

Flagrant as have been the outrages committed upon colored citizens in respect to their civil rights, more flagrant, shocking, and scandalous still have been the outrages committed upon our political rights by means of bulldozing and Kukluxing, Mississippi plans, fraudulent courts, tissue ballots, and the like devices. Three States in which the colored people outnumber the white population are without colored representation and their political voice suppressed. The colored citizens in those States are virtually disfranchised, the Constitution held in utter contempt and its provisions nullified. This has been done in the face of the Republican party and successive Republican administrations. . . .

This is no question of party. It is a question of law and government. It is a question whether men shall be protected by law, or be left to the mercy of cyclones of anarchy and bloodshed. It is whether the Government or the mob shall rule this land; whether the promises solemnly made to us in the constitution be manfully kept or meanly and flagrantly broken. Upon this vital point we ask the whole people of the United States to take notice that whatever of political power we have shall be exerted for no man of any party who will not, in advance of election, promise to use every power given him by the

Government, State or National, to make the black man's path to the ballot-box as straight, smooth and safe as that of any other American citizen. . . .

We hold it to be self-evident that no class or color should be the exclusive rulers of this country. If there is such a ruling class, there must of course be a subject class, and when this condition is once established this Government of the people, by the people, and for the people, will have perished from the earth.

Miss Liberty welcoming a family of Jewish immigrants. (YIVO Institute for Jewish Research)

CHAPTER TWO

Minorities

3

CHEYENNE AUTUMN

Conflict between whites and Indians began with the first colonial landings and continued undiminished into the late nineteenth century. At that time the United States finally completed its conquest of the continent and extended its authority over all the lands formerly belonging to the Indians. After the Civil War, as whites began moving in large numbers along the new rail lines into areas west of the Mississippi River, the U.S. Army fought a series of wars against the larger and more combative of the Indian nations, notably the Comanche, the Apache, the Kiowa, the Cheyenne, and the Sioux. The Indians won occasional victories, such as the one over the former Civil War general George A. Custer at the Little Bighorn in 1876, but most of the time they fell victim to the superior organization, supplies, and firepower of the whites. The slaughter by the white people of the vast buffalo herds on which the Indians had based their lives—thirteen million buffalo had been killed by 1883—virtually assured the crushing of the tribes.

The Plains Indians were confined almost entirely to reservations, large tracts of land where, with the protection and economic aid of the Indian Office, it was thought that they might continue their nomadic, communal ways. But this policy was a failure. Tribal ranks, already severely depleted by the Plains wars, were further thinned by the growing scarcity of buffalo. Moreover, large tribes were often divided on widely scattered reservations, where resident (white) Indian agents usually proved unwilling or unable to prevent looting by settlers and the theft of funds earmarked for Indian assistance.

This excerpt from Helen Hunt Jackson's *A Century of Dishonor* illustrates the plight of the Cheyenne, who had been separated into two reservations, one in Oklahoma and the other in Montana-Wyoming, and had been victims of one of the period's most brutal massacres, at Sand Creek, Colorado, in 1864. *A Century of Dishonor* helped move government policy from subjugation and control of Indians toward their acculturation into white society by way of education and individual land ownership. An 1887 act of Congress distributed reservation lands as Indian farming plots and also released millions of acres for white settlement. The last major military clash between the government and the Indians came with the slaughter of scores of Sioux families in 1890 at Wounded Knee, South Dakota.

Helen Hunt Jackson, born in Amherst, Massachusetts, in 1830, was the daughter of a professor and a childhood friend of poet Emily Dickinson. After the death in 1863 of Jackson's first husband, a Union army officer, she earned her living by writing poems, stories, and travel pieces. In 1872 she moved to Colorado, where she married a financier, grew concerned over the plight of the Indians, and wrote *A Century of Dishonor,* published in 1881, which she sent to every member of Congress at her own expense. Jackson soon became a best-selling novelist and a forceful advocate for the new policy of Indian assimilation. Her life embodied two great ironies. Though an Indian sympathizer, she was married to a man who helped build the railroads that destroyed the habitat of the Plains tribes. And even though she was a famous writer, much of her early work remained wrapped in obscurity because sexual prejudice had sometimes forced her to assume masculine pen names. She died in San Francisco, at the peak of her fame, in 1885.

Questions to Consider. How knowledgeable does Helen Hunt Jackson seem to have been about the ways and conditions of the Cheyennes and Arapahoes? According to this sketch, what was the most severe danger they faced? What was her attitude toward the Indians' violent efforts to resist the demands of the Department of the Interior and the army? Which of the agencies involved with the Indians—the Interior and the army—seemed to Jackson to be most understanding of the circumstances of the Cheyenne? Why did *A Century of Dishonor* strike so positive a chord among readers, including U.S. Senators?

★═══★═══★

A Century of Dishonor (1881)

HELEN HUNT JACKSON

The winter of 1877 and summer of 1878 were terrible seasons for the Cheyennes. Their fall hunt had proved unsuccessful. Indians from other reservations had hunted the ground over before them, and driven the buffalo off; and the Cheyennes made their way home again in straggling parties, destitute and hungry. Their agent reports that the result of this hunt has clearly proved that "in the future the Indian must rely on tilling the ground

Helen Hunt Jackson, *A Century of Dishonor* (Harper and Brothers, New York, 1881), 92–102.

as the principal means of support; and if this conviction can be firmly established, the greatest obstacle to advancement in agriculture will be overcome. With the buffalo gone, and their pony herds being constantly decimated by the inroads of horse-thieves, they must soon adopt, in all its varieties, the way of the white man."

The ration allowed to these Indians is reported as being "reduced and insufficient," and the small sums they have been able to earn by selling buffalo-hides are said to have been "of material assistance" to them in "supplementing" this ration. But in this year there have been sold only $657 worth of skins by the Cheyennes and Arapahoes together. In 1876 they sold $17,600 worth. Here is a falling off enough to cause very great suffering in a little community of five thousand people. But this was only the beginning of their troubles. The summer proved one of unusual heat. Extreme heat, chills and fever, and "a reduced and insufficient ration," all combined, resulted in an amount of sickness heart-rending to read of. "It is no exaggerated estimate," says the agent, "to place the number of sick people on the reservation at two thousand. Many deaths occurred which might have been obviated had there been a proper supply of anti-malarial remedies at hand. Hundreds applying for treatment have been refused medicine."

The Northern Cheyennes grew more and more restless and unhappy. "In council and elsewhere they profess an intense desire to be sent North, where they say they will settle down as the others have done," says the report; adding, with an obtuseness which is inexplicable, that "no difference has been made in the treatment of the Indians," but that the "compliance" of these Northern Cheyennes has been "of an entirely different nature from that of the other Indians," and that it may be "necessary in the future to compel what so far we have been unable to effect by kindness and appeal to their better natures."

If it is "an appeal to men's better natures" to remove them by force from a healthful Northern climate, which they love and thrive in, to a malarial Southern one, where they are struck down by chills and fever—refuse them medicine which can combat chills and fever, and finally starve them—there indeed, might be said to have been most forcible appeals made to the "better natures" of these Northern Cheyennes. What might have been predicted followed.

Early in the autumn, after this terrible summer, a band of some three hundred of these Northern Cheyennes took the desperate step of running off and attempting to make their way back to Dakota. They were pursued, fought desperately, but were finally overpowered, and surrendered. They surrendered, however, only on the condition that they should be taken to Dakota. They were unanimous in declaring that they would rather die than go back to the Indian Territory. This was nothing more, in fact, than saying that they would rather die by bullets than of chills and fever and starvation.

These Indians were taken to Fort Robinson, Nebraska. Here they were confined as prisoners of war, and held subject to the orders of the Department of the Interior. The department was informed of the Indians' determination never to be taken back alive to Indian Territory. The army officers in charge reiterated these statements, and implored the department to permit them to remain at the North; but it was of no avail. Orders came—explicit, repeated, finally stern—insisting on the return of these Indians to their agency. The commanding officer at Fort Robinson has been censured severely for the course he pursued in his effort to carry out those orders. It is difficult to see what else he could have done, except to have resigned his post. He could not take three hundred Indians by sheer brute force and carry them hundreds of miles, especially when they were so desperate that they had broken up the iron stoves in their quarters, and wrought and twisted them into weapons with which to resist. He thought perhaps he could starve them into submission. He stopped the issue of food; he also stopped the issue of fuel to them. It was midwinter; the mercury froze in that month at Fort Robinson. At the end of two days he asked the Indians to let their women and children come out that he might feed them. Not a woman would come out. On the night of the fourth day—or, according to some accounts, the sixth—these starving, freezing Indians broke prison, overpowered the guards, and fled, carrying their women and children with them. They held the pursuing troops at bay for several days; finally made a last stand in a deep ravine, and were shot down—men, women, and children together. Out of the whole band there were left alive some fifty women and children and seven men, who, having been confined in another part of the fort, had not had the good fortune to share in this outbreak and meet their death in the ravine. These, with their wives and children, were sent to Fort Leavenworth to be put in prison; the men to be tried for murders committed in their skirmishes in Kansas on their way to the north. Red Cloud, a Sioux chief, came to Fort Robinson immediately after this massacre and entreated to be allowed to take the Cheyenne widows and orphans into his tribe to be cared for. The Government, therefore, kindly permitted twenty-two Cheyenne widows and thirty-two Cheyenne children—many of them orphans—to be received into the band of the Ogallalla Sioux.

An attempt was made by the Commissioner of Indian Affairs, in his Report for 1879, to show by tables and figures that these Indians were not starving at the time of their flight from Indian Territory. The attempt only redounded to his own disgrace; it being proved, by the testimony given by a former clerk of the Indian Bureau before the Senate committee appointed to investigate the case of the Northern Cheyennes, that the commissioner had been guilty of absolute dishonesty in his estimates, and that the quantity of beef actually issued to the Cheyenne Agency was hundreds of pounds less than he had reported it, and that the Indians were actually, as they had claimed, "starving."

The testimony given before this committee by some of the Cheyenne prisoners themselves is heart-rending. One must have a callous heart who can read it unmoved.

When asked by Senator [John T.] Morgan [of Alabama], "Did you ever really suffer from hunger?" one of the chiefs replied. "We were always hungry; we never had enough. When they that were sick once in awhile felt as though they could eat something, we had nothing to give them."

"Did you not go out on the plains sometimes and hunt buffalo, with the consent of the agent?"

"We went out on a buffalo-hunt, and nearly starved while out; we could not find any buffalo hardly; we could hardly get back with our ponies; we had to kill a good many of our ponies to eat, to save ourselves from starving."

"How many children got sick and died?"

"Between the fall of 1877 and 1878 we lost fifty children. A great many of our finest young men died, as well as many women."

"Old Crow," a chief who served faithfully as Indian scout and ally under General [George] Crook [commander of Far Western troops since 1868] for years, said: "I did not feel like doing anything for awhile, because I had no heart. I did not want to be in this country. I was all the time wanting to get back to the better country where I was born, and where my children are buried, and where my mother and sister yet live. So I have laid in my lodge most of the time with nothing to think about but that, and the affair up north at Fort Robinson, and my relatives and friends who were killed there. But now I feel as though, if I had a wagon and a horse or two, and some land, I would try to work. If I had something, so that I could do something, I might not think so much about these other things. As it is now, I feel as though I would just as soon be asleep with the rest."

The wife of one of the chiefs confined at Fort Leavenworth testified before the committee as follows: "The main thing I complained of was that we didn't get enough to eat; my children nearly starved to death; then sickness came, and there was nothing good for them to eat; for a long time the most they had to eat was corn-meal and salt. Three or four children died every day for awhile, and that frightened us."

When asked if there were anything she would like to say to the committee, the poor woman replied: "I wish you would do what you can to get my husband released. I am very poor here, and do not know what is to become of me. If he were released he would come down here, and we would live together quietly, and do no harm to anybody, and make no trouble. But I should never get over my desire to get back north; I should always want to get back where my children were born, and died, and were buried. That country is better than this in every respect. There is plenty of good, cool water there—pure water—while here the water is not good. It is not hot there, nor so sickly: Are you going where my husband is? Can you tell when he is likely to be released?" . . .

It is stated also that there was not sufficient clothing to furnish each Indian with a warm suit of clothing, "as promised by the treaty," and that, "by reference to official correspondence, the fact is established that the Cheyennes and Arapahoes are judged as having no legal rights to any lands, having forfeited their treaty reservation by a failure to settle thereon," and their "present reservation not having been, as yet, confirmed by Congress. Inasmuch as the Indians fully understood, and were assured that this reservation was given to them in lieu of their treaty reservation, and have commenced farming in the belief that there was no uncertainty about the matter it is but common justice that definite action be had at an early day, securing to them what is their right."

It would seem that there could be found nowhere in the melancholy record of the experiences of our Indians a more glaring instance of confused multiplication of injustices than this. The Cheyennes were pursued and slain for venturing to leave this very reservation, which, it appears, is not their reservation at all, and they have no legal right to it. Are there any words to fitly characterize such treatment as this from a great, powerful, rich nation, to a handful of helpless people?

4

CATHOLICISM IN AMERICA

In the seventeenth century Catholics found a brief refuge from persecution in Maryland, which was established by Catholics and attracted Catholic settlers, including some who accumulated substantial holdings of land and slaves. Elsewhere in overwhelmingly Protestant British North America, there was widespread discrimination against Catholics in politics and office-holding and therefore trade relations and imperial preferment. By 1700 this was the pattern even in Maryland, now dominated by adherents to the Church of England. But during the Revolutionary and early national era, faith in reason and suspicion of established churches led to greater religious pluralism on the one hand and a reduction of state support for Protestant churches on the other. Both these trends benefited various evangelical denominations. But they also benefited Catholics, who, even though they were a small minority, could now practice their religion openly and feel like Americans rather than outcasts.

As long as Catholics remained a small minority, they experienced relatively little hostility. This changed in the mid-nineteenth century with the arrival of millions of poor Catholic immigrants from Ireland and Germany and eventually from Italy and Eastern Europe. The consequences were twofold. Protestants were alarmed at the sudden appearance of huge numbers of newcomers whose patriotism was untested and whose religion centered on devotion to a foreign authority, the papacy. Anti-Catholic rioting occurred in Boston and other places; evangelists thundered against the Catholic menace; whole political parties arose over the issue of keeping America for Americans. Catholics meanwhile struggled not only to maintain amicable relations with Protestant leaders but to find ways to build churches, appoint priests, and educate the youth of an immigrant population that seemed to be increasing exponentially.

Schools were a special and abiding concern. Catholics, like most Americans, were committed to sound education for their children, and some—perhaps as many as half—took immediate advantage of the American public school system, which their taxes supported and which was probably the best in the world at that time. But American schools were secular. In some places, they were tinged with Protestantism. Catholic leaders therefore considered them unsuited to a population striving to retain its faith and moved early on to erect a system of parish, or "parochial," Catholic education that would parallel the public schools. By the 1880s, Catholics constituted some twenty percent of the entire American population, with more arriving yearly. In 1884 the Third Plenary Council of American Bishops, meeting in Baltimore, addressed this challenge directly. Excerpts from the Council's Statement of Parochial Education follow.

Questions to Consider. What basic arguments did the bishops use in urging more and better parochial schools in America? What seemed to be their chief concerns? To what extent did the bishops order rather than simply exhort American Catholics to build and send their children to Catholic schools? What were the economic and social implications of the bishops' directive on education? What strains might this have placed on Catholic family finances or on the relations of Catholics with their Protestant neighbors? Did the bishops seem to think of Catholic education as a temporary solution to the problem of Americanization or as a permanent institutional framework against even larger forces? What does the bishops' statement suggest about how they perceived the whole process of "Americanization"?

★══★══★

The Catholic Bishops on Parochial Education (1884)

Education, in order to foster civilization, must foster religion. Now the three great educational agencies are the home, the Church, and the school. These mold men and shape society. Therefore, each of them, to do its part well, must foster religion. But many, unfortunately, while avowing that religion should be the light and the atmosphere of the home and of the Church, are content to see it excluded from the school, and even advocate as the best school system that which necessarily excludes religion. Few surely will deny that childhood and youth are the periods of life when the character ought especially to be subjected to religious influences.

. . . The school is an important factor in the forming of childhood and youth—so important that its influence often outweighs that of home and Church. It cannot, therefore, be desirable or advantageous that religion should be excluded from the school. On the contrary, it ought, therefore, to be

Hugh J. Nolan, ed., *Pastoral Letters of the U.S. Catholic Bishops* (Washington, 1984), I: 224–225.

one of the chief agencies for molding the young life to all that is true and vir-
tuous, and holy. To shut religion out of the school, and keep it for home and
the Church, is, logically, to train up a generation that will consider religion
good for home and the Church, but not for the practical business of real life.
But a more false and pretentious notion could not be imagined. Religion, in
order to elevate a people, should inspire their whole life and rule their relations with one another. A life is not dwarfed, but ennobled by being lived in
the presence of God. Therefore, the school, which principally gives the
knowledge fitting for practical life, ought to be pre-eminently under the holy
influence of religion. From the shelter of home and school, the youth must
soon go out into the busy ways of trade or traffic or professional practice. In
all these, the principles of religion should animate and direct him. But he
cannot expect to learn these principles in the workshop or the office or the
counting-room. Therefore, let him be well and thoroughly imbued with them
by the joint influences of home and school, before he is launched out on the
dangerous sea of life.

All denominations of Christians are now awakening to this great truth,
which the Catholic Church has never ceased to maintain. Reason and experience are forcing them to recognize that the only practical way to secure a
Christian people, is to give the youth a Christian education. The avowed enemies of Christianity in some European countries are banishing religion from
the schools, in order gradually to eliminate it from among the people. In this
they are logical, and we may well profit by the lesson. Hence, the cry for
Christian education is going up from all religious bodies throughout the
land. And this is no narrowness and "sectarianism" on their part; it is an honest and logical endeavor to preserve Christian truth and morality among the
people by fostering religion in the young. Nor is it any antagonism to the
state; on the contrary, it is an honest endeavor to give to the state better citizens, by making them better Christians. The friends of Christian education
do not condemn the state for not imparting religious instruction in the public schools as they are now organized; because they well know it does not lie
within the province of the state to teach religion. They simply follow their
conscience by sending their students to denominational schools, where religion can have its rightful place and influence.

Two objects, therefore, dear brethren, we have in view, to multiply our
schools, and to perfect them. We must multiply them, till every Catholic
child in the land shall have within his reach the means of education. There is
still much to do ere this be attained. There are still thousands of Catholic children in the United States deprived of the benefit of a Catholic school. Pastors
and parents should not rest till this defect be remedied. No parish is complete till it has schools adequate to the needs of its children, and the pastor
and people of such a parish should feel that they have not accomplished their
entire duty until the want is supplied.

But then, we must also perfect our schools. We repudiate the idea that the
Catholic school need be in any respect inferior to any other school whatso-

ever. And if hitherto, in some places, our people have acted on the principle that it is better to have an imperfect Catholic school than to have none, let them now push their praiseworthy ambitions still further, and not relax their efforts till their schools be elevated to the highest educational excellence. And we implore parents not to hasten to take their children from school, but to give them all the time and all the advantages that they have the capacity to profit by, so that, in after life, their children may "rise up and call them blessed."

5

NEWCOMERS

The sprawling city was as fundamental a fact of life as the great West or the bitter South in the late nineteenth century, and most Americans found it simultaneously exciting and unsettling. Cities were exciting because they symbolized prosperity and progress, cardinal virtues of the country for decades if not centuries. These urban centers were full of good and novel things to buy and do in a land lusting to do both. But cities were also unsettling—seething (so it seemed) with greedy landlords, corrupt politicians, and radical workers. Most unsettling of all, they were populated by foreigners, not "real" Americans—immigrants from a dozen lands, speaking as many languages and exhibiting as many objectionable habits. These newcomers spilled out from the waterfronts of New York, Baltimore, or Chicago into vast impoverished tenement districts that strained not only public morality but also public order and public health. They may have been lovers of liberty "yearning to be free," as it said on the Statue of Liberty, but they were also "huddled masses."

For most Americans, New York City—the country's largest city and chief port of European debarkation—was the epitome of the immigrant city. No U.S. city could claim more foreign-born inhabitants or more crowded housing conditions. Relatively little open space remained for new residential or business construction. But New York was more than an immigrant center; it was also the publishing and literary capital of the United States. By 1890, hundreds of reporters and writers lived in the city, working for dozens of newspapers and magazines, not counting the foreign-language press. When the United States developed an appetite for urban coverage, New York had a thriving industry to supply it.

Jacob Riis, a Danish immigrant, was a pioneer in the field of urban exposé journalism. Riis, who arrived in New York in 1870, wandered in semipoverty for several years before becoming a city police reporter, first for the *New York Tribune,* then for the *Evening Sun.* His beat was the Lower East Side, a teeming immigrant district. For twenty-two years, until 1899, his office was directly across from police headquarters.

Here, he wrote, "I was to find my lifework." But Riis was more than a reporter; he became a reformer, determined not only to describe slum life but to improve it. His goal was partly to establish better building codes, but chiefly to ensure that all immigrants learned English and were assimilated thoroughly into American life. This path, after all, was the one that Jacob Riis himself had followed. *How the Other Half Lives,* which first appeared as a series of newspaper essays (one of which is excerpted below), was a weapon in Riis's crusade.

Jacob Riis, born in Ribe, Denmark, in 1849, was educated by his father and became an apprentice carpenter before emigrating to the United States in 1870. By 1890 he had become one of the best-known, most colorful newspapermen in New York. *How the Other Half Lives,* which Riis illustrated with startling photographs of slum conditions, made him a byword in the nation as well. Among its readers was another budding reformer and member of the New York City police board—Theodore Roosevelt, who befriended Riis, accompanied him on forays into the slums, and supported his reform efforts. Riis carried on his crusade in later books, including several on immigrant children, and saw significant improvements in slum schools and recreational facilities. He died in Barre, Massachusetts, in 1914.

Questions to Consider. Modern readers will instantly notice Riis's constant use of stereotypes in discussing various immigrant groups. Why might an intelligent, sympathetic reporter of the 1890s resort to such stereotypes? How could such an author be seen (as Riis was) as a champion of liberal social reform? Riis was a reporter, not a social scientist. Are his descriptions and explanations of group social mobility persuasive? When he explains why immigrant groups tend to form separate enclaves, is he persuasive?

★━━★━━★

How the Other Half Lives (1890)

JACOB RIIS

When once I asked the agent of a notorious Fourth Ward alley how many people might be living in it I was told: One hundred and forty families, one hundred Irish, thirty-eight Italian, and two that spoke the German tongue. Barring the agent herself there was not a native-born individual in the court. The answer was characteristic of the cosmopolitan character of lower New

Jacob Riis, *How the Other Half Lives* (Scribner's, New York, 1907), 14–21.

Bandit's Roost, Mulberry Street, Manhattan. Jacob Riis took this photograph of the toughest, most dangerous denizens of the Lower East Side in 1890, about the time he enlisted the assistance of Theodore Roosevelt, then chairman of the New York Police Commission. (Museum of the City of New York)

York, very nearly so of the whole of it, wherever it runs to alleys and courts. One may find for the asking an Italian, a German, a French, African, Spanish, Bohemian, Russian, Scandinavian, Jewish, and Chinese colony. Even the Arab, who peddles "holy earth" from the Battery as a direct importation from Jerusalem, has his exclusive preserves at the lower end of Washington Street. The one thing you shall vainly ask for in the chief city of America is a distinctively American community. . . .

They are not here. In their place has come this queer conglomerate mass of heterogeneous elements, ever striving and working like whiskey and water in one glass, and with the like result: final union and a prevailing taint of whiskey. The once unwelcome Irishman has been followed in his turn by the Italian, the Russian Jew, and the Chinaman, and has himself taken a hand at opposition, quite as bitter and quite as ineffectual, against these later hordes.

Wherever these have gone they have crowded him out, possessing the block, the street, the ward with their denser swarms. But the Irishman's revenge is complete. Victorious in defeat over his recent as over his more ancient foe, the one who opposed his coming no less than the one who drove him out, he dictates to both their politics, and, secure in possession of the offices, returns the native his greeting with interest, while collecting the rents of the Italian whose house he has bought with the profits of his saloon. . . .

In justice to the Irish landlord it must be said that like an apt pupil he was merely showing forth the result of the schooling he had received, reenacting, in his own way, the scheme of the tenements. It is only his frankness that shocks. The Irishman does not naturally take kindly to tenement life, though with characteristic versatility he adapts himself to its conditions at once. It does violence, nevertheless, to the best that is in him, and for that very reason of all who come within its sphere soonest corrupts him. The result is a sediment, the product of more than a generation in the city's slums, that, as distinguished from the larger body of his class, justly ranks at the foot of tenement dwellers, the so-called "low Irish." . . .

An impulse toward better things there certainly is. The German ragpicker of thirty years ago, quite as low in the scale as his Italian successor, is the thrifty tradesman or prosperous farmer of today.

The Italian scavenger of our time is fast graduating into exclusive control of the corner fruit-stands, while his black-eyed boy monopolizes the boot-blacking industry in which a few years ago he was an intruder. The Irish hod-carrier in the second generation has become a bricklayer, if not the Alderman of his ward, while the Chinese coolie is in almost exclusive possession of the laundry business. The reason is obvious. The poorest immigrant comes here with the purpose and ambition to better himself and, given half a chance, might be reasonably expected to make the most of it. To the false plea that he prefers the squalid homes in which his kind are housed there could be no better answer. . . .

As emigration from east to west follows the latitude, so does the foreign influx in New York distribute itself along certain well-defined lines that waver and break only under the stronger pressure of a more gregarious race or the encroachments of inexorable business. A feeling of dependence upon mutual effort, natural to strangers in a strange land, unacquainted with its language and customs, sufficiently accounts for this.

The Irishman is the true cosmopolitan immigrant. All-pervading, he shares his lodging with perfect impartiality with the Italian, the Greek, and the "Dutchman," yielding only to sheer force of numbers, and objects equally to them all. A map of the city, colored to designate nationalities, would show more stripes than on the skin of a zebra, and more colors than any rainbow. The city on such a map would fall into two great halves, green for the Irish prevailing in the West Side tenement districts, and blue for the Germans on the East Side. But intermingled with these ground colors would be an odd variety of tints that would give the whole the appearance of an extraordinary crazy-quilt. From down in the Sixth Ward, upon the site of the old Collect Pond that in the days of the fathers drained the hills which are no more, the red of the Italian would be seen forcing its way northward along the line of Mulberry Street to the quarter of the French purple on Bleecker Street and South Fifth Avenue, to lose itself and reappear, after a lapse of miles, in the "Little Italy" of Harlem, east of Second Avenue. Dashes of red, sharply defined, would be seen strung through the Annexed District, northward to the city line. On the West Side the red would be seen overrunning the old Africa of Thompson Street, pushing the black of the negro rapidly uptown, against querulous but unavailing protests, occupying his home, his church, his trade, and all with merciless impartiality.

Hardly less aggressive than the Italian, the Russian and Polish Jew, having overrun the district between Rivington and Division Streets, east of the Bowery, to the point of suffocation, is filling the tenements of the old Seventh Ward to the river front, and disputing with the Italian every foot of available space in the back alleys of Mulberry Street. The two races, differing hopelessly in much, have this in common: they carry their slums with them wherever they go, if allowed to do it. Little Italy already rivals its parent, the "Bend," in foulness. Other nationalities that begin at the bottom make a fresh start when crowded up the ladder. Happily both are manageable, the one by rabbinical, the other by the civil law. Between the dull gray of the Jew, his favorite color, and the Italian red, would be seen squeezed in on the map a sharp streak of yellow, marking the narrow boundaries of Chinatown. Dovetailed in with the German population, the poor but thrifty Bohemian might be picked out by the sombre hue of his life as of his philosophy, struggling against heavy odds in the big human bee-hives of the East Side. Colonies of his people extend northward, with long lapses of space, from below the Cooper Institute more than three miles. The Bohemian is the only foreigner with any considerable representation in the city who counts no wealthy man of his race, none who has not to work hard for a living, or has got beyond the reach of the tenement.

Down near the Battery the West Side emerald would be soiled by a dirty stain, spreading rapidly like a splash of ink on a sheet of blotting paper, headquarters of the Arab tribe, that in a single year has swelled from the original dozen to twelve hundred, intent, every mother's son, on trade and barter. Dots and dashes of color here and there would show where the Finnish sailors worship their djumala (God), the Greek pedlars the ancient name of their race, and the Swiss the goddess of thrift. And so on to the end of the long register, all toiling together in the galling fetters of the tenement. Were the question raised who makes the most of life thus mortgaged, who resists most stubbornly its levelling tendency—knows how to drag even the barracks upward a part of the way at least toward the ideal plane of the home—the palm must be unhesitatingly awarded the Teuton. The Italian and the poor Jew rise only by compulsion. The Chinaman does not rise at all; here, as at home, he simply remains stationary. The Irishman's genius runs to public affairs rather than domestic life; wherever he is mustered in force the saloon is the gorgeous centre of political activity. The German struggles vainly to learn his trick; his Teutonic wit is too heavy, and the political ladder he raises from his saloon usually too short or too clumsy to reach the desired goal. The best part of his life is lived at home, and he makes himself a home independent of the surroundings, giving the lie to the saying, unhappily become a maxim of social truth, that pauperism and drunkenness naturally grow in the tenements. He makes the most of his tenement, and it should be added that whenever and as soon as he can save up money enough, he gets out and never crosses the threshold of one again.

6

From Another Shore

In 1882, Congress passed the Chinese Exclusion Act, prohibiting Chinese workers from entering this country for a period of ten years. As the date of expiration approached, however, pressure from powerful sources mounted for renewing the law. Leading the fight was the Immigration Committee of the House of Representatives, under the chairmanship of Representative Herman Stump of Maryland, who produced a stream of witnesses describing how the Chinese used drugs, committed crimes, and lusted after American women. Stump distilled the most important parts of this testimony in the report, reprinted below, that accompanied the committee's recommendation that the exclusion act be renewed.

The committee and its witnesses were persuasive. Not only did Congress extend the law for another ten years, but in 1893 President Grover Cleveland named Representative Stump superintendent of immigration. The exclusion act and Stump's appointment in turn set the stage for a treaty between the United States and China, signed in 1894, barring the immigration of Chinese laborers for ten years from the date of the exchange of ratifications. Those who had left the United States were permitted to return, provided they had wives, children, parents, or property worth $1,000 in this country. The treaty gave China the right to exclude American workers (of which there were none in China), but not American merchants and officials (who were numerous and important there). Chinese were thus all but barred from American soil, even as the Statue of Liberty (a gift of France) was unveiled in 1886 to welcome immigrants from Europe.

By 1900, Japanese workers, too, were entering the United States in sizable numbers; outcries against the "yellow peril" were again raised in the West. The so-called Gentleman's Agreement of 1907 between Washington and Tokyo instantly reduced the flow of unskilled Japanese laborers into the United States.

Questions to Consider. The congressional report of 1892 argued that the Chinese presence in the United States was a threat to American "institutions." What institutions did the Immigration Committee seem most concerned about? Why does the report mention the "vegetable"

diets of the Chinese? One aim of the committee was evidently to reduce the "smuggling" of Chinese aliens into the country. Why might
such smuggling have taken place, and why did immigration officers
seem unable to prevent it? The committee based much of its argument
on the idea that the Chinese either could not or would not assimilate.
Assuming that this lack of assimilation was a genuine problem, what
alternatives might the committee have explored besides exclusion?

★▬▬★▬▬★

Congressional Report on Chinese Immigration (1892)

There is urgent necessity for prompt legislation on the subject of Chinese immigration. The exclusion act approved May 6, 1882, and its supplement ex-
pires by limitation of time on May 6, 1892, and after that time there will be no
law to prevent the Chinese hordes from invading our country in number so
vast, as soon to outnumber the present population of our flourishing States
on the Pacific slope. . . .

The popular demand for legislation excluding the Chinese from this country is urgent and imperative and almost universal. Their presence here is inim-
ical to our institutions and is deemed injurious and a source of danger. They
are a distinct race, saving from their earnings a few hundred dollars and returning to China. This they succeed in doing in from five to ten years by living
in the most miserable manner, when in cities and towns in crowded tenement houses, surrounded by dirt, filth, corruption, pollution, and prostitution;
and gambling houses and opium joints abound. When used as cooks, farmhands, servants, and gardeners, they are more cleanly in habits and manners.
They, as a rule, have no families here; all are men, save a few women, usually
prostitutes. They have no attachment to our country, its laws or its institutions,
nor are they interested in its prosperity. They never assimilate with our people,
our manners, tastes, religion, or ideas. With us they have nothing in common.

Living on the cheapest diet (mostly vegetable), wearing the poorest clothing, with no family to support, they enter the field of labor in competition with
the American workman. In San Francisco, and in fact throughout the whole
Pacific slope, we learn from the testimony heretofore alluded to, that the Chinamen have invaded almost every branch of industry; manufacturers of ci-
gars, cigar boxes, brooms, tailors, laundrymen, cooks, servants, farmhands,
fishermen, miners and all departments of manual labor, for wages and prices
at which white men and women could not support themselves and those dependent upon them. Recently this was a new country, and the Chinese may

Congressional Record, October 1892.

Chinese American merchant. A late-nineteenth-century Chinese American dry goods store, San Francisco. (University of California at Berkeley, Bancroft Library)

have been a necessity at one time, but now our own people are fast filling up and developing this rich and highly favored land, and American citizens will not and can not afford to stand idly by and see this undesirable race carry away the fruits of the labor which justly belongs to them. A war of races would soon be inaugurated; several times it has broken out, and bloodshed has followed. The town of Tacoma, in 1887, banished some 3,000 Chinamen on twenty-four hours' notice, and no Chinaman has ever been permitted to return.

Our people are willing, however, that those now here may remain, protected by the laws which they do not appreciate or obey, provided strong provision be made that no more shall be allowed to come, and that the smuggling of Chinese across the frontiers be scrupulously guarded against, so that gradually, by voluntary departures, death by sickness, accident, or old age, this race may be eliminated from this country, and the white race fill their places without inconvenience to our own people or to the Chinese, and thus a desirable change be happily and peacefully accomplished. It was thought that the exclusion act of 1882 would bring about this result; but it now appears that although at San Francisco the departures largely exceed the arrivals, yet the business of smuggling Chinese persons across the lines from the British Possessions and Mexico has so greatly increased that the number of arrivals now exceed the departures. This must be effectually stopped.

7

NEW SOUTH, OLD SOUTH

Following the Civil War, the South suffered two ordeals: racism and poverty. The problem of race touched all Southerners, from oppressed former slaves to anxious white farmers and city dwellers. Poverty, especially the bleak agricultural poverty characteristic of the South, intensified the already severe problem of race. These twin cauldrons finally boiled over in the 1890s, when more than one hundred and fifty blacks were lynched per year, and collapsing farm prices drove many thousands of families—black and white—into bankruptcy.

The Cotton States Exposition of Industry and the Arts, held in Atlanta in 1895, was designed to address the problem of poverty. Mainly the brainchild of Atlanta publishers and bankers, the exposition made much of the prospects for railroad expansion, iron and textile manufacturing, and lumber and tobacco processing. It was hoped their success would reduce the South's unhappy dependence on agriculture and tie the region to the rest of industrial America. But the explosive issue of race also loomed. To address it, the exposition organizers, almost as an afterthought, invited Booker T. Washington, head of the Tuskegee Institute, a black vocational school in Tuskegee, Alabama, to speak to the mostly white exposition gathering. The exposition produced only a slight effect on Southern industrialization—manufacturing did not become widespread there until the 1920s and industrial prosperity has barely arrived even today. Washington's speech, however, was of major importance. His moderate message, accommodating tone, and stress on business and hard work generally pleased his listeners, who marked him as a worthy spokesman for his race. His reputation soon spread to the white North and to blacks as well. Thus, almost overnight, Washington became a prominent figure whose message mattered to everyone, especially in the South.

Not everyone agreed with Washington's approach. Black intellectuals and reformers still found their inspiration in Frederick Douglass, the great abolitionist and stalwart of Radical Reconstruction and equal rights. In their eyes, Washington's acceptance of disfranchisement and segregation seemed a betrayal. They thought his refusal to condemn lynching was a surrender and viewed his influence as mostly negative.

One of the most forceful of these critics was Ida B. Wells, a Chicago woman born to Mississippi slaves. Wells's *A Red Record,* excerpted below, told the gruesome story of antiblack violence in the South in persuasive, compelling terms. It thus formed an important counterpoint to Washington's conservative views.

Ida B. Wells was born a slave in Holly Springs, Mississippi, in 1862. She was educated in a freedmen's school, became a teacher herself, and eventually moved to Memphis, Tennessee, where she taught school and attended Fisk University. She turned to journalism in 1891 after losing her teaching post for refusing to give up her seat in a "whites-only" railroad car. When she wrote against antiblack violence, whites retaliated by burning her newspaper office. She left the South in 1892, in time marrying Ferdinand Barnett, a prominent black Chicagoan. A tireless writer and speaker for both women's and black's rights, Wells encouraged the Niagara Movement, a 1909 initiative of W. E. B. Du Bois and other militants opposed to the Tuskegee Machine. She refused to support its successor organization, the National Association for the Advancement of Colored People (NAACP), on the grounds that it was too moderate. She died in Chicago in 1931.

Questions to Consider. Why did Ida B. Wells go to such enormous pains in *A Red Record* to establish the record, from white sources, of antiblack atrocities in the post–Civil War South? For whom does she appear to have been writing? Were there models elsewhere in American society for this kind of "exposé" journalism? In this excerpt, she also takes care to refute the arguments given by white Southerners to justify the violence. Do these passages constitute an attack on paternalism—male chauvinism—as well as on racism? If Wells wrote, as she said, "in no spirit of vindictiveness," why did whites burn her newspaper office for printing similar stories? Was vindictiveness inherent in the material, bound inevitably to provoke outrage and assault? What strategies did Wells devise to avoid this?

A Red Record (1895)

IDA B. WELLS

Not all nor nearly all of the murders done by white men, during the past thirty years in the South, have come to light, but the statistics as gathered and

Ida B. Wells, *A Red Record: Tabulated Statistics and Alleged Causes of Lynchings in the United States, 1892–1893–1894* (Chicago, n.d.), 9–15, 20, 43, 45–48.

Four sharecroppers hanging from a tree in Russellville, Kentucky, 1908. Their "crime" was to express sympathy for a black man who had killed his white employer in self-defense. Thousands of black lynching victims died the same way, prompting the anti-lynching crusade of Ida B. Wells and other reformers. (Gilman Paper Company Collection)

preserved by white men, and which have not been questioned, show that during these years more than ten thousand Negroes have been killed in cold blood, without the formality of judicial trial and legal execution. And yet, as evidence of the absolute impunity with which the white man dares to kill a Negro, the same record shows that during all these years, and for all these murders only three white men have been tried, convicted, and executed. As no white man has been lynched for the murder of colored people, these three executions are the only instances of the death penalty being visited upon white men for murdering Negroes.

Naturally enough the commission of these crimes began to tell upon the public conscience, and the Southern white man, as a tribute to the nineteenth century civilization, was in a manner compelled to give excuses for his barbarism.

The first excuse given to the civilized world for the murder of unoffending Negroes was the necessity of the white man to repress and stamp out alleged "race riots." For years immediately succeeding the war there was an appalling slaughter of colored people, and the wires usually conveyed to northern people and the world the intelligence, first, that an insurrection was being planned by Negroes, which, a few hours later, would prove to have been vigorously resisted by white men, and controlled with a resulting loss of several killed and wounded. It was always a remarkable feature in these insurrections and riots that only Negroes were killed during the rioting, and that all the white men escaped unharmed. . . .

Then came the second excuse, which had its birth during the turbulent times of reconstruction. By an amendment to the Constitution the Negro was given the right of franchise, and, theoretically at least, his ballot became his invaluable emblem of citizenship. In a government "of the people, for the people, and by the people," the Negro's vote became an important factor in all matters of state and national politics. But this did not last long. The southern white man would not consider that the Negro had any right which a white man was bound to respect, and the idea of a republican form of government in the southern states grew into general contempt.

The white man's victory soon became complete by fraud, violence, intimidation and murder. The franchise vouchsafed to the Negro grew to be a "barren ideality," and regardless of numbers, the colored people found themselves voiceless in the councils of those whose duty it was to rule. With no longer the fear of "Negro Domination" before their eyes, the white man's second excuse became valueless. With the Southern governments all subverted and the Negro actually eliminated from all participation in state and national elections, there could be no longer an excuse for killing Negroes to prevent "Negro Domination."

Brutality still continued; Negroes were whipped, scourged, exiled, shot and hung whenever and wherever it pleased the white man so to treat them, and as the civilized world with increasing persistency held the white people of the South to account for its outlawry, the murderers invented the third excuse—that Negroes had to be killed to avenge their assaults upon women. There could be framed no possible excuse more harmful to the Negro and more unanswerable if true in its sufficiency for the white man.

Humanity abhors the assailant of womanhood, and this charge upon the Negro at once placed him beyond the pale of human sympathy. With such unanimity, earnestness, and apparent candor was this charge made and reiterated that the world has accepted the story that the Negro is a monster which the Southern white man has painted him. . . .

A word as to the charge itself. In considering the third reason assigned by the Southern white people for the butchery of blacks, the question must be asked, what the white man means when he charges the black man with rape. Does he mean the crime which the statutes of the civilized states describe as such? Not by any means. With the Southern white man, any mésalliance existing between a white woman and a black man is a sufficient foundation for the charge of rape. The Southern white man says that it is impossible for a voluntary alliance to exist between a white woman and a colored man, and therefore, the fact of an alliance is a proof of force. In numerous instances where colored men have been lynched on the charge of rape, it was positively known at the time of lynching, and indisputably proven after the victim's death, that the relationship sustained between the man and woman was voluntary and clandestine, and that in no court of law could even the charge of assault have been successfully maintained.

It was for the assertion of this fact, in the defense of her own race, that the writer hereof became an exile; her property destroyed and her return to her home forbidden under penalty of death. . . .

But threats cannot suppress the truth, and while the Negro suffers the soul deformity, resultant from two and a half centuries of slavery, he is no more guilty of this vilest of all vile charges than the white man who would blacken his name.

During all the years of slavery, no such charge was ever made, not even during the dark days of the rebellion, when the white man, following the fortunes of war went to do battle for the maintenance of slavery. While the master was away fighting to forge the fetters upon the slave, he left his wife and children with no protectors save the Negroes themselves. And yet during those years of trust and peril, no Negro proved recreant to his trust and no white man returned to a home that had been despoiled.

Likewise during the period of alleged "insurrection," and alarming "race riots," it never occurred to the white man, that his wife and children were in danger of assault. Nor in the Reconstruction era, when the hue and cry was against "Negro Domination," was there ever a thought that the domination would ever contaminate a fireside or strike to death the virtue of womanhood. . . .

In his remarkable apology for lynching, Bishop Haygood, of Georgia, says: "No race, not the most savage, tolerates the rape of women, but it may be said without reflection upon any other people that the Southern people are now and always have been most sensitive concerning the honor of their women—their mothers, wives, sisters and daughters." It is not the purpose of this defense to say one word against the white women of the South. Such need not be said, but it is their misfortune that the chivalrous white men of that section, in order to escape the deserved execration of the civilized world, should shield themselves by their cowardly and infamously false excuse, and call into question that very honor about which their distinguished priestly apologist claims they are most sensitive. To justify their own barbarism they assume a chivalry which they do not possess. . . .

When emancipation came to the Negroes, there arose in the northern part of the United States an almost divine sentiment among the noblest, purest and best white women of the North, who felt called to a mission to educate and Christianize the millions of southern ex-slaves. From every nook and corner of the North, brave young white women answered that call and left their cultured homes, their happy associations and their lives of ease, and with heroic determination went to the South to carry light and truth to the benighted blacks. It was a heroism no less than that which calls for volunteers for India, Africa, and the Isles of the sea. To educate their unfortunate charges; to teach them the Christian virtues and to inspire in them the moral sentiments manifest in their own lives, these young women braved dangers whose record reads more like fiction than fact. They became social outlaws in the South. The peculiar sensitiveness of the southern white men for women, never shed its protecting influence about them. No friendly word from their own race cheered them in their work; no hospitable doors gave them the companionship like that from which they had come. No chivalrous white man doffed his hat in honor or respect. They were "Nigger teachers"— unpardonable offenders in the social ethics of the South, and were insulted, persecuted and ostracized, not by Negroes, but by the white manhood which boasts of its chivalry toward women.

And yet these northern women worked on, year after year, unselfishly, with a heroism which amounted almost to martyrdom. Threading their way through dense forests, working in schoolhouse, in the cabin and in the church, thrown at all times and in all places among the unfortunate and lowly Negroes, whom they had come to find and to serve, these northern women, thousands and thousands of them, have spent more than a quarter of a century in giving to the colored people their splendid lessons for home and heart and soul. Without protection, save that which innocence gives to every good woman, they went about their work, fearing no assault and suffering none. . . . Before the world adjudges the Negro a moral monster, a vicious assailant of womanhood and a menace to the sacred precints of home, the colored people ask the consideration of the silent record of gratitude, respect, protection, and devotion of the millions of the race in the South, to the thousands of northern white women who have served as teachers and missionaries since the war. . . .

These pages are written in no spirit of vindictiveness, for all who give the subject consideration must concede that far too serious is the condition of that civilized government in which the spirit of unrestrained outlawry constantly increases in violence, and casts its blight over a continually growing area of territory. We plead not for the colored people alone, but for all victims of the terrible injustice which puts men and women to death without form of law. During the year 1894, there were 132 persons executed in the United States by due form of law, while in the same year, 197 persons were put to death by mobs who gave the victims no opportunity to make a lawful defense. No comment need be made upon a condition of public sentiment responsible for such alarming results.

8

PATRIOTISM

Most modern nations have adopted national songs and flags and pledges mainly in order to unify far-flung regions and contending political factions. The United States was no different, particularly after the savage sectional conflicts of the 1860s and the massive waves of nineteenth-century immigration. The current Pledge of Allegiance first appeared in 1892 in *The Youth's Companion,* a leading family magazine of the time, in connection with the celebration of Columbus Day in the public schools. Its author was Francis Bellamy, a former Baptist minister and a staff member of *The Youth's Companion.* The original pledge, used in the schools on October 12, 1892, by proclamation of President Benjamin Harrison, appears below.

Several interesting changes to the Pledge were incorporated in later years. In 1923 the First National Flag Conference, held in Washington under the auspices of the American Legion and the Daughters of the American Revolution, substituted the phrase "the Flag of the United States" for the words "my flag." In 1924 the same group added "of America" after "States." The Pledge remained unofficial until 1942, when Congress included it as a unifying war measure in the United States Flag Code; the title became official in 1945. The final change in wording came in 1954, at the height of the Cold War, when President Dwight Eisenhower endorsed the addition of the words "under God" right after "one nation."

The more militaristic "Star-Spangled Banner," written by Francis Scott Key during the War of 1812, became the country's unofficial national anthem at the end of the Spanish-American War. In 1916, as World War I approached, President Woodrow Wilson ordered the armed services to play it; and Congress finally designated it the national anthem in 1931. But even though intended to help forge national unity in a time of conflict, "The Star-Spangled Banner" did not touch the hearts of every group equally. In particular, it did not touch the hearts of African Americans, who had not come to North America of their own volition, had endured centuries of slavery and decades of lynching, and by the turn of the century were losing virtually all political rights and economic standing. Experiencing the pain of such exclusion, in 1900 James Weldon Johnson wrote a song, reprinted below, for a celebration of Lincoln's birthday in a black (segregated) school in Jacksonville, Florida. Set to music by Johnson's brother, J. Rosamond Johnson, the song grew in popularity over the next twenty years until it became what Johnson called it—the "Negro National Hymn," or anthem. Little known among Americans of non-African descent, the Negro National Anthem was sung at virtually every significant black gathering of the twentieth century.

Francis Bellamy was a Baptist minister and Christian Socialist whose Pledge of Allegiance reflected the utopian socialist ideas of his cousin, Edward Bellamy. Francis Bellamy joined the staff of *The Youth's Companion,* where his oath first appeared, in 1891 after his Boston congregation forced him out of his pulpit for preaching socialism. After his retirement to Florida, Bellamy stopped attending church because of the racial bigotry he witnessed. His daughter later said that her father would have disliked the addition of "under God," which changed the Pledge into a public prayer as well as a patriotic oath. He died in 1931 at the age of seventy-six.

James Weldon Johnson was born in 1871 in Florida. He attended Atlanta University for both high school and college because his hometown of Jacksonville had no high school that allowed African Americans. He studied law and became the first black American admitted to the Florida bar; he also began writing songs with his brother, J. Rosamond. Eventually the pair moved to New York City to pursue musical and literary careers. A lifelong Republican and member of the new National Association for the Advancement of Colored People (NAACP), Johnson held minor diplomatic posts in the Caribbean under Presidents Theodore Roosevelt and William Howard Taft and became a key figure in the renowned Harlem Renaissance of the 1920s. He taught creative writing at Fisk University in Nashville from 1930 until his death in an auto accident in 1938.

Questions to Consider. To what extent did the phrasing of Bellamy's original Pledge of Allegiance in 1892 seem to reflect his socialist ideals? Why didn't he make socialism an even larger part of the anthem? Why did he focus so much on reverence for the American flag? Did his writing make it easier to recite the Pledge as part of a public ceremony? Why might it have taken so long for Congress to make the Pledge official? Did the addition of the words "under God" in the 1950s change the meaning of the Pledge, as Bellamy's daughter thought?

In "Lift Every Voice and Sing," the so-called Negro National Anthem, what was the dominant attitude? To what extent was it appropriate to build references to the unhappy experiences of African Americans into the song? Did Johnson expect white Americans to know about and sing the song? Was it an anthem of despair or of hope? How did the song differ from the official "Star-Spangled Banner" sung by white America? Was it a "hymn," as Johnson originally called it, or an "anthem"? Why did it become so popular in black communities?

★━━★━━★

The Pledge of Allegiance (1892)

FRANCIS BELLAMY

I pledge allegiance to my Flag,
And to the Republic for which it stands:
One nation indivisible,
With Liberty and Justice for all.

★━━★━━★

Lift Every Voice and Sing (1900)

JAMES WELDON JOHNSON

Lift every voice and sing
Till earth and heaven ring,
Ring with the harmonies of Liberty;
Let our rejoicing rise
High as the listening skies,
Let it resound loud as the rolling seas.
Sing a song full of the faith that the dark past has taught us,
Sing a song full of the hope that the present has brought us,
Facing the rising sun of our new day begun,
Let us march on till victory is won.

Stony the road we trod,
Bitter the chastening rod,
Felt in the days when hope unborn had died;
Yet with a steady beat,
Have not our weary feet
Come to the place for which our fathers sighed?

John W. Baer, *The Pledge of Allegiance* (Free State Press, Annapolis, 1992).

Julian Bond and Sandra Kathryn Wilson, eds., *Lift Every Voice and Sing* (Random House, New York, 2000), 3–4.

We have come over a way that with tears has been watered,
We have come treading our path through the blood of the slaughtered,
Out from the gloomy past,
Till now we stand at last
Where the white gleam of our bright star is cast.

God of our weary years,
God of our silent tears,
Thou who hast brought us thus far on the way;
Thou who has by Thy might
Led us into the light.
Keep us forever in the path, we pray.
Lest our feet stray from the places, our God, where we met Thee,
Lest our hearts, drunk with the wine of the world, we forget Thee,
Shadowed beneath Thy hand,
May we forever stand,
True to our God
True to our native land.

9

BEARING GIFTS

Nativist bigotry was widespread in turn-of-the-century America, attaching itself with special force to immigrants from Eastern or Catholic Europe and perhaps most venomously to Jews. Anti-Semitism was a powerful current from czarist Russia to the democratic United States in the late nineteenth century, intensifying in the United States with the beginning of large-scale Jewish immigration in the 1880s. Thereafter, anti-Semitism emerged in all regions, classes, and parties. Resort hotels and exclusive men's clubs barred Jewish businessmen, and upper-class colleges established quota systems. Small-town Midwesterners and Southern farmers criticized not just Wall Street bankers but international Jewish bankers. Radical writers like Jack London cast a racist net that snared Jews as well as blacks. Even urban Catholic immigrants, who themselves experienced religious and nativist discrimination, harassed the "Christ-killers" and "Shylocks" who shared their ethnic slums.

Spokespersons for the various immigrant groups labored hard to counter nativist bigotry. They challenged stereotypes where they could, chiefly by publicizing their group's successes, including successful examples of Americanization. They also tried to portray the group's distinctive characteristics in positive terms, stressing how the country would benefit from Italian musical genius, for example, or Polish religious fervor. The Jewish community had no finer advocate than Mary Antin, a young writer and political activist whose speech before a New York convention of the General Federation of Women's Clubs is excerpted below.

Mary Antin was born in Russia in 1881 and emigrated with her parents to the United States in 1894. When she was still a teenager, Antin wrote her first book—in Yiddish—about the Jewish immigrant experience. After studying at Teachers College and Barnard College in New York City, she published *The Promised Land* (1912), perhaps our most beautiful version of the immigrant saga. An ardent socialist and union supporter, Antin continued to write and lecture on the subject of immigration; she was a notable opponent of congressional efforts to pass restrictive immigration laws. She died in Suffern, New York, on May 15, 1949.

Questions to Consider. Why didn't Mary Antin argue for the value of Jewish immigration by offering case studies, as immigrant defenders sometimes did, of successful individual Jews? What point was she trying to make by implicitly reinforcing a stereotype about Jews—that as a group they produced a disproportionate number of scholars, lawyers, and debaters? How did she attempt to connect the discussion about Jews and the law with her discussion later about the organization of the clothing industry? Was she right to argue that the passion for justice was fundamental to being a Jew, so that Jews were, in a sense, heirs to the "Spirit of '76" and therefore naturally American? What were the "false gods" Antin referred to in her final sentence?

★━━★━━★

Russian Jews (1916)

MARY ANTIN

On the whole the Russian immigrant in this country is the Jewish immigrant, since we are the most numerous group out of Russia. But to speak for the Jews—the most misunderstood people in the whole of history—ten minutes, in which to clear away 2,000 years of misunderstanding! Your President has probably in this instance, as in other instances, been guided by some inspiration, the source of which none of us may know. I was called by name long before your President notified me that she would call me to this assembly. I was called by name to say what does the Jew bring to America—by a lady from Philadelphia. Miss Repplier, not long ago, in an article in her inimitable fashion, called things by their name, and sometimes miscalled them, spoke of "the Jew in America who has received from us so much and has given us so little." This comment was called down by something that I had said about certain things in American life that did not come up to the American standard. "The Jew who has given so little." Tonight I am the Jew—you are the Americans. Let us look over these things.

What do we bring you besides our poverty and our rags? Men, women, and children—the stuff that nations are built of. What sort of men and women? I shall not seek to tire you with a list of shining names of Jewish notables. If you want to know who's who among the Jews, I refer you to your biographical dictionary. You are as familiar as I am with the name of Jews who shine in the professions, who have done notable service to the state, in politics, in diplomacy, and where you will. . . .

You know as well as I what numbers of Jewish youth are always taking high ranks, high honors in the schools, colleges and universities. You know

General Federation of Women's Clubs, *Thirteenth Biennial Convention* (New York, 1916).

as well as I do in what numbers our people crowd your lecture halls and your civic centers, in all those places where the spiritual wine of life may be added to our daily bread. These are things that you know. I don't want you to be thinking of any list of Jewish notables.

A very characteristic thing of Jewish life is the democracy of virtue that you find in every Jewish community. We Jews have never depended for our salvation on the supreme constellations of any chosen ones. . . . Our shining ones were to us always examples by means of which the whole community was to be disciplined to what was Jewish virtue.

Take a group of Jews anywhere, and you will have the essence of their Jewishness, though there be not present one single shining luminary. The average Jew presents the average of whatsoever there is of Jewish virtue, talent or capacity.

What is this peculiar Jewish genius? If I must sum it up in a word, I will say that the Jewish genius is a love for living out the things that they believe. What do we believe? We Jews believe that the world is a world of law. Law is another name for our God, and the quest after the law, the formulation of it, has always permeated our schools, and the incorporation of the laws of life, as our scholars noted it down, has been the chief business of the Jewish masses. No wonder that when we come to America, a nation founded as was our ancient nation, a nation founded on law and principle, on an ideal— no wonder that we so quickly find ourselves at home, that presently we fall into the regulation habit of speaking of America as our own country, until Miss Repplier reproves us, and then we do it no more. I used formerly when speaking of American sins, tribulations, etc., I used to speak of them as "ours"; no more—your sins. I have been corrected.

Why then, now that we have come here, to this nation builded on the same principle as was our nation, no wonder that we so quickly seize on the fundamentals. We make no virtue of the fact—it is the Jewishness in us—that has been our peculiar characteristics, our habit. We need no one from outside of our ranks to remind us of the goodly things we have found and taken from your hands. We have been as eloquent as any that has spoken in appreciation of what we have found here, of liberty, justice, and a square deal. We give thanks. We have rendered thanks, we Jews, some of you are witnesses. We know the value of the gifts that we have found here.

Who shall know the flavor of bread if not they that have gone hungry, and we, who have been for centuries without the bread of justice, we know the full flavor of American justice, liberty, and equality.

To formulate and again formulate, and criticise the law,—what do our Rabbis in the Ghetto besides the study of law? To them used to come our lawyers, to our Rabbis, not to find the way how to get around the law, but to be sure that we were walking straight in the path indicated by the law. So to-day in America we are busy in the same fashion.

The Jewish virtues, such as they are, are widespread throughout the Jewish masses. Here in New York City is congregated the largest Jewish community in the whole world, and what is true of the Jews of New York, is true of the Jews of America, and the Jews of the world. If I speak of the characteristics of Jewish life on the East side, one of the great characteristics is its restlessness in physical form, due to the oppression of city life, and the greater restlessness, due to the unquenchable, turbulent quest for the truth, and more truth. You know that the East side of New York is a very spawning ground for debate, and debating clubs. There are more boys and girls in debating clubs than in boys' basket ball teams, or baseball teams. I believe in boys playing baseball, but I also believe in that peculiar enthusiasm of our Jewish people for studying the American law, just as they used to study their own law, to see whether any of the American principles find incorporation in American institutions and habits. We are the critics. We are never satisfied with things as they are. Go out and hear the boys and girls. They like to go to school and learn the names of liberty, and equality and justice, and after school they gather in their debating circles and discuss what might be the meaning of these names, and what is their application to life. That is the reason there is so much stirring, rebellion, and protest that comes out of the East side.

In the great labor movement, it is the effort of the people to arrive at a program of economic justice that shall parallel the political justice. Consider for a moment the present condition of the garment-making trade. That is a Jewish trade. Ages ago when the lords of the nations, among whom we lived, were preventing us from engaging in other occupations, they thrust into the hands of our people the needle, and the needle was our tool, why through the needle we have still thought to give expression to the Jewish genius in our life.

This immense clothing industry—a Jewish industry primarily—is today in a better condition as regards unionization, is further on the road to economic justice than any other great industry that you could name. Mind you, the sweatshop we found here when we came here. We took it just as it was, but the barring of the sweatshop and the organization of the clothing industry in such fashion that it is further in advance, more nearly on a basis that affords just treatment to all concerned—that has been the contribution of our tailor men and tailor women. We have done this thing. . . . The Protocol[1] is a piece of machinery for bringing about justice in this great industry. We have invented that thing, we Jews. We are putting it in operation, we are fighting for its perpetuation. Whatsoever good comes from it, we have done it. . . .

Consider us, if you will, in the most barbarous sense, but I point to this as our great contribution, we are always protesting, and if you want to know the value of that contribution, I remind you that the formulae of the rights of men, which was a criticism of things as they used to be, and a formularizing of things as they ought to be, was at least as efficient as all the armies of the continent put together in the revolutionary war. The Spirit of '76 is the spirit of criticism. We Jews in America are busy at our ancient business of pulling down false gods.

---

1. **The Protocol:** A labor–management agreement recognizing union rights and providing for improved working conditions in the garment industry.—*Eds.*

10

CLOSING THE DOORS

For a half century after the Civil War the United States maintained a relatively unrestrictive policy toward immigration from Europe. Yet the coming of so many millions of immigrants, particularly so many who were neither Protestant nor northern Europeans, caused growing alarm among "old-stock" Americans, who associated the newcomers with saloons, political corruption, and other "ills" of urban society. Labor leaders feared such floods of uncontrollable cheap labor; upper-class spokesmen were concerned about the possible "mongrelization" of the country.

The first broad effort to restrict immigration was the Literacy Test of 1917, which actually had little effect because most immigrants could in fact read and write. In 1921, Congress limited immigration from any country to 3 percent of that country's proportion of the American population as of 1910. By 1924 the public favored even more restrictive measures. The sweeping National Origins Act, excerpted below, brought the tradition of unrestricted entry by Europeans to a definitive close. Only people from the Western Hemisphere could come freely now. (A separate Oriental Exclusion Act later banned Asians altogether.) The national-origins standard, though modified, persisted until 1965, when the emphasis shifted from national origin to refugees, relatives, and occupational skills.

Questions to Consider. The Immigration Act of 1924 shows how American society rated the different nationalities at that time. According to the quotas listed in the act, for example, a Czech was worth thirty Chinese, a Swiss equaled twenty Syrians, and an Irishman ten Italians. Is this a fair interpretation of the act? Not even at this peak of feverish nationalism did the U.S. government discriminate arbitrarily between nationalities or allot immigration space on a random basis. With the notable exception of Asians, national quotas were figured on a percentage basis: limiting Armenians also meant limiting Austrians. Most of the Western Hemisphere, moreover, was exempt from the act. Nevertheless, by basing quotas on the 1890 rather than the 1910 census, the act did embody clear racial preferences. Why, then, was such care taken to employ percentages rather than absolute numbers?

★═══★═══★

Immigration Act of 1924

It will be remembered that the quota limit act of May 1921, provided that the number of aliens of any nationality admissible to the United States in any fiscal year should be limited to 3 per cent of the number of persons of such nationality who were resident in the United States according to the census of 1910, it being also provided that not more than 20 per cent of any annual quota could be admitted in any one month. Under the act of 1924 the number of each nationality who may be admitted annually is limited to 2 per cent of the population of such nationality resident in the United States according to the census of 1890, and not more than 10 per cent of any annual quota may be admitted in any month except in cases where such quota is less than 300 for the entire year.

Under the act of May, 1921, the quota area was limited to Europe, the Near East, Africa, and Australasia. The countries of North and South America, with adjacent islands, and countries immigration from which was otherwise regulated, such as China, Japan, and countries within the Asiatic barred zone, were not within the scope of the quota law. Under the new act, however, immigration from the entire world, with the exception of the Dominion of Canada, Newfoundland, the Republic of Mexico, the Republic of Cuba, the Republic of Haiti, the Dominican Republic, the Canal Zone, and independent countries of Central and South America, is subject to quota limitations. The various quotas established under the new law are shown in the . . . proclamation of the President, issued on the last day of the present fiscal year: . . .

Country or Area of Birth	Quota 1924–1925
Afghanistan	100
Albania	100
Andorra	100
Arabian peninsula	100
Armenia	124
Australia, including Papua, Tasmania, and all islands appertaining to Australia	121
Austria	785
Belgium	512
Bhutan	100
Bulgaria	100
Cameroon (proposed British mandate)	100
Cameroon (French mandate)	100
China	100
Czechoslovakia	3,073
Danzig, Free City of	228
Denmark	2,789
Egypt	100

Annual Report of the Commissioner-General of Immigration (Government Printing Office, Washington, D.C., 1924).

Estonia	124
Ethiopia (Abyssinia)	100
Finland	170
France	3,954
Germany	51,227
Great Britain and Northern Ireland	34,007
Greece	100
Hungary	473
Iceland	100
India	100
Iraq (Mesopotamia)	100
Irish Free State	28,567
Italy, including Rhodes, Dodekanesia, and Castellorizzo	3,845
Japan	100
Latvia	142
Liberia	100
Liechtenstein	100
Lithuania	344
Luxemburg	100
Monaco	100
Morocco (French and Spanish Zones and Tangier)	100
Muscat (Oman)	100
Nauru (Proposed British mandate)	100
Nepal	100
Netherlands	1,648
New Zealand (including appertaining islands)	100
Norway	6,453
New Guinea, and other Pacific Islands under proposed Australian mandate	100
Palestine (with Trans-Jordan, proposed British mandate)	100
Persia	100
Poland	5,982
Portugal	503
Ruanda and Urundi (Belgium mandate)	100
Rumania	603
Russia, European and Asiatic	2,248
Samoa, Western (proposed mandate of New Zealand)	100
San Marino	100
Siam	100
South Africa, Union of	100
South West Africa (proposed mandate of Union of South Africa)	100
Spain	131
Sweden	9,561
Switzerland	2,081
Syria and The Lebanon (French mandate)	100
Tanganyika (proposed British mandate)	100
Togoland (proposed British mandate)	100
Togoland (French mandate)	100
Turkey	100
Yap and other Pacific islands (under Japanese mandate)	100
Yugoslavia	671

A Bessemer steel converter, heart of Andrew Carnegie's steel empire, with the machinery dwarfing the human steelworkers, about 1890. (Hagley Museum & Library)

CHAPTER THREE

Industry, Expansion, and Reform

11

PRODUCTION AND WEALTH

During the late nineteenth century the United States experienced re-markable industrial development. In 1860 it was largely a nation of farms, villages, small businesses, and small-scale manufacturing estab-lishments; by 1900 it had become a nation of cities, machines, facto-ries, offices, shops, and powerful business combinations. Between 1860 and 1900, railroad trackage increased, annual production of coal rose steadily, iron and steel production soared, oil refining flourished, and development of electric power proceeded apace. "There has never been in the history of civilization," observed economist Edward Atkin-son in 1891, "a period, or a place, or a section of the earth in which science and invention have worked such progress or have created such opportunity for material welfare as in these United States in the period which has elapsed since the end of the Civil War." By the end of the century, America's industrial production exceeded that of Great Britain and Germany combined, and the United States was exporting huge quantities of farm and factory goods to all parts of the world. The country had become one of the richest and most powerful nations in history.

More than any other single element, steel permitted and laid the foundation for industrialization. The process of steel production pow-ered industrial development, because it was from steel that railroad tracks and cars, bridges and girders, machines and farm equipment, el-evators, ships, and automobiles were all manufactured. One key to ris-ing steel production was the adaptation of the so-called Bessemer process to American conditions. The emergence of mass steel manu-facture by this method involved a dynamic interplay between foreign and domestic production ideas, patent law, firm capitalization and competition, creative marketing, and, perhaps most important, con-stant technical improvement on the factory floor.

At the other end of the production scale was Andrew Carnegie, the "King of Steel." Carnegie liked to boast of the accomplishments of effi-cient business organization in the American steel industry, as he did in the excerpt below from *Triumphant Democracy* (1886), a best seller.

"Two pounds of ironstone mined upon Lake Superior and transported nine hundred miles to Pittsburgh; one pound and a half of coal mined and manufactured into coke, and transported to Pittsburgh; one-half pound of lime, mined and transported to Pittsburgh; a small amount of manganese ore mined in Virginia and brought to Pittsburgh—and these four pounds of materials manufactured into one pound of steel, for which the consumer pays one cent."

Carnegie preached what he called a "gospel of wealth." His gospel emphasized individual initiative, private property, competition, and the accumulation of wealth in the hands of those with superior ability and energy. But in the last quarter of the nineteenth century, less than 1 percent of the population controlled more than 50 percent of the nation's wealth, the highest concentration in U.S. history up to that time, and the benefits of spectacular industrial growth were hardly shared equitably. The nation had been built on the assumption that all men were created equal, and most Americans took for granted that in a republican society property and power would be widely distributed. Yet the disparity between the very rich and the very poor had grown extreme.

Thoughtful observers, troubled by the concentration of wealth and power in the hands of so few, raised their voices in protest. Andrew Carnegie was unusual in that, on the one hand, he defended the absolute right of the entrepreneur to accumulate wealth and also the Social Darwinist notion of "survival of the fittest." But at the same time, like some of the radicals of his era, Carnegie argued that the rich should dispense their wealth in ways that would benefit society. The "man who dies rich," he asserted, "dies disgraced."

Andrew Carnegie, the son of a handloom weaver, was born in Scotland in 1835. With his family, he moved to Allegheny, Pennsylvania, at the age of twelve and got a job in a textile mill at $1.20 a week. During this period he studied telegraphy, a skill that landed him a position as the personal secretary and telegrapher of a leading raiload executive. Carnegie was himself a railroad executive for a time, and then amassed a fortune selling bonds, dealing in oil, and building bridges. In 1873 he concentrated his efforts on steel and gradually built his Carnegie Steel Company into a massive industrial giant. In 1901 he sold the firm to J. P. Morgan, who made it the core of the world's first billion-dollar company, the United States Steel Corporation. Over the next two decades Carnegie gave away some $350 million for libraries and other public works. He died in Lenox, Massachusetts, in 1919.

Questions to Consider. The excerpt from *Triumphant Democracy* is typical of the many articles and books Andrew Carnegie wrote celebrating the American system. Why did Carnegie think life "has become vastly better worth living" than it had been a century before?

What particular aspects of American life did he single out for special mention? In what ways did he think life in the United States was better than life in Europe? Was he writing mainly about the life of the average or of the well-to-do American? How did he relate America's economic achievements to democracy?

★═══★═══★

Triumphant Democracy (1886)

ANDREW CARNEGIE

A community of toilers with an undeveloped continent before them, and destitute of the refinements and elegancies of life—such was the picture presented by the Republic sixty years ago. Contrasted with that of today, we might almost conclude that we were upon another planet and subject to different primary conditions. The development of an unequaled transportation system brings the products of one section to the doors of another, the tropical fruits of Florida and California to Maine, and the ice of New England to the Gulf States. Altogether life has become vastly better worth living than it was a century ago.

Among the rural communities, the change in the conditions is mainly seen in the presence of labor-saving devices, lessening the work in house and field. Mowing and reaping machines, horse rakes, steam plows and threshers, render man's part easy and increase his productive power. Railroads and highways connect him with the rest of the world, and he is no longer isolated or dependent upon his petty village. Markets for his produce are easy of access, and transportation swift and cheap. If the roads throughout the country are yet poor compared with those of Europe, the need of good roads has been rendered less imperative by the omnipresent railroad. It is the superiority of the iron highway in America which has diverted attention from the country roads. It is a matter of congratulation, however, that this subject is at last attracting attention. Nothing would contribute so much to the happiness of life in the country as such perfect roads as those of Scotland. It is a difficult problem, but its solution will well repay any amount of expenditure necessary. [British historian Thomas] Macaulay's test of the civilization of a people— the condition of their roads—must be interpreted, in this age of steam, to include railroads. Communication between great cities is now cheaper and more comfortable than in any other country. Upon the principal railway lines, the cars—luxurious drawing-rooms by day, and sleeping chambers by night—are ventilated by air, warmed and filtered in winter, and cooled in

Andrew Carnegie, *Triumphant Democracy* (Scribner's, New York, 1886), 164–183.

Andrew Carnegie. Carnegie was the country's biggest industrialist in the late 1800s, with a fortune estimated to be a half-billion dollars. He was also industry's most articulate spokesman, writing books and articles that were widely read. Carnegie exemplified two cherished American ideals: self-help in the accumulation of wealth and stewardship in the disposal of it. He endowed hundreds of public libraries and donated to a wide range of charities. (Library of Congress)

summer. Passenger steamers upon the lakes and rivers are of gigantic size, and models of elegance.

It is in the cities that the change from colonial conditions is greatest. Most of these—indeed all, excepting those upon the Atlantic coast—have been in great measure the result of design instead of being allowed, like Topsy, to "just grow." In these modern days cities are laid out under definite, far-seeing plans; consequently the modern city presents symmetry of form unknown in mediaeval ages. The difference is seen by contrasting the crooked cowpaths of old Boston with the symmetrical, broad streets of Washington or Denver. These are provided with parks at intervals for breathing spaces; amply supplied with pure water, in some cases at enormous expense; the most modern ideas are embodied in their sanitary arrangements; they are well lighted, well policed, and the fire departments are very efficient. In these modern cities an extensive fire is rare. The lessening danger of this risk is indicated by the steady fall in the rate of fire insurance.

The variety and quality of the food of the people of America excels that found elsewhere, and is a constant surprise to Europeans visiting the States. The Americans are the best-fed people on the globe. Their dress is now of the richest character—far beyond that of any other people, compared class for class. The comforts of the average American home compare favorably with those of other lands, while the residences of the wealthy classes are unequaled. The first-class American residence of today in all its appointments excites the envy of the foreigner. One touch of the electric button calls a messenger; two bring a telegraph boy; three summon a policeman; four give the alarm of fire. Telephones are used to an extent undreamt of in Europe, the stables and other out-buildings being connected with the mansion; and the houses of friends are joined by the talking wire almost as often as houses of business. Speaking tubes connect the drawing-room with the kitchen; and the dinner is brought up "piping hot" by a lift. Hot air and steam pipes are carried all over the house; and by the turning of a tap the temperature of any room is regulated to suit the convenience of the occupant. A passenger lift is common. The electric light is an additional home comfort. Indeed, there is no palace or great mansion in Europe with half the conveniences and scientific appliances which characterize the best American mansions. New York Central Park is no unworthy rival of Hyde Park and the Bois de Boulogne in its display of fine equipages; and in winter the hundreds of graceful sleighs dashing along the drives form a picture. The opera-houses, theatres, and public halls of the country excel in magnificence those of other lands, if we except the latter constructions in Paris and Vienna, with which the New York, Philadelphia, and Chicago opera-houses rank. The commercial exchanges, and the imposing structures of the life insurance companies, newspaper buildings, hotels, and many edifices built by wealthy firms, not only in New York but in the cities of the West, never fail to excite the Europeans' surprise. The postal system is equal in every respect to that of Europe. Mails are taken up by express trains, sorted on board, and dropped at all important points without stopping. Letters are delivered several times a day in every considerable town, and a ten-cent special delivery stamp insures delivery at once by special messenger in the large cities. The uniform rate of postage for all distances, often exceeding three thousand miles, is only two cents . . . per ounce.

In short, the conditions of life in American cities may be said to have approximated those of Europe during the sixty years of which we are speaking.

Year by year, as the population advances, the general standard of comfort in the smaller Western cities rises to that of the East. Herbert Spencer [an English philosopher] was astonished beyond measure at what he saw in American cities. "Such books as I had looked into," said he, "had given me no adequate idea of the immense developments of material civilization which I have found everywhere. The extent, wealth, and magnificence of your cities, and especially the splendors of New York, have altogether astonished me. Though I have not visited the wonder of the West, Chicago, yet some of your minor modern places, such as Cleveland, have sufficiently amazed me by the marvelous results of one generation's activity. Occasionally, when I have been in places of some ten thousand inhabitants, where the telephone is in general use, I have felt somewhat ashamed of our own unenterprising towns, many of which, of fifty thousand inhabitants and more, make no use of it."

Such is the Democracy; such its conditions of life. In the presence of such a picture can it be maintained that the rule of the people is subversive of government and religion? Where have monarchical institutions developed a community so delightful in itself, so intelligent, so free from crime or pauperism—a community in which the greatest good of the greatest number is so fully attained, and one so well calculated to foster the growth of self-respecting men—which is the end civilization seeks?

> "For ere man made us citizens
> God made us men."

The republican is necessarily self-respecting, for the laws of his country begin by making him a man indeed, the equal of other men. The man who most respects himself will always be found the man who most respects the rights and feelings of others.

The rural democracy of America could be as soon induced to sanction the confiscation of the property of its richer neighbors, or to vote for any violent or discreditable measure, as it could be led to surrender the President for a king. Equal laws and privileges develop all the best and noblest characteristics, and these always lead in the direction of the Golden Rule. These honest, pure, contented, industrious, patriotic people really do consider what they would have others do to them. They ask themselves what is fair and right. Nor is there elsewhere in the world so conservative a body of men; but then it is the equality of the citizen—just and equal laws—republicanism, they are resolved to conserve. To conserve these they are at all times ready to fight and, if need be, to die; for, to men who have once tasted the elixir of political equality, life under unequal conditions could possess no charm.

To every man is committed in some degree, as a sacred trust, the manhood of man. This he may not himself infringe or permit to be infringed by others. Hereditary dignities, political inequalities, do infringe the right of man, and hence are not to be tolerated. The true democrat must live the peer of his fellows, or die struggling to become so.

The American citizen has no further need to struggle, being in possession of equality under the laws in every particular. He has not travelled far in the path of genuine Democracy who would not scorn to enjoy a privilege which was not the common birthright of all his fellows.

12

LABOR'S VISION

The decades following the Civil War brought an enormous expansion of activity in railroads, coal, steel, and other basic industries. This rapid rise in the development of America's natural resources was accompanied by a sharp rise in the country's per capita wealth and income and, in the long run, a higher standard of living for most people. But it resulted in other things as well: greater wealth and power for "capitalists," as the new leaders of industry were called; a deterioration in conditions for many workers; and a society repeatedly torn by class conflict.

The Noble Order of the Knights of Labor, formed as a secret workingmen's lodge in 1869, represented an early response to these trends. Secrecy seemed essential at first because of the hostility of employers toward labor unions. Not until 1881 did the Knights of Labor abandon secrecy and announce its objectives to the world. Its slogan was "An injury to one is the concern of all." The Knights took pride in their admission of all workers—regardless of race, sex, or level of skill—and in their moderate, public-spirited vision of a cooperative economic order. These factors, together with their support of successful railroad strikes, swelled the Knights of Labor membership rolls to nearly 800,000 by 1886. After that, however, a wave of antiradicalism, combined with internal problems and the loss of several bitter industrial struggles, sent membership plummeting. By 1900 the organization was gone. It was replaced by two other labor organizations: the American Federation of Labor (AFL), founded in 1886, which organized skilled labor and struck over wages and working conditions, and the Industrial Workers of the World (IWW), founded in 1905, which appealed to the unskilled and stood for industrial reorganization. The AFL, which opposed most of the Knights principles, endured; the IWW, which shared many of them, did not.

The American Federation of Labor was a combination of national craft unions with an initial membership of about 140,000. It was the result of craft disagreement with the Knights of Labor partly over tactics and partly over leadership. The unions that constituted the AFL were central players in a nationwide campaign in support of an eight-hour workday. Centered in Chicago but spreading rapidly to other cities, the campaign (whose major statement appears below) culminated in a series of mass strikes and demonstrations on May 1, 1886. The campaign failed in its efforts to impose a uniform eight-hour day throughout American industry. It succeeded, however, in making a shortened workday one of the cardinal ongoing demands of union organizers and negotiators. When major breakthroughs in union representation and influence came during the 1930s and 1940s, eight hours—"nine to five" with an hour for lunch—became in fact the standard workday everywhere.

Samuel Gompers was the president of the AFL in 1886 and a key figure in the Eight-Hour Association. Gompers was a London-born cigar maker who emigrated to New York City with his parents at age thirteen. At first a strong socialist, he became a leader of the Cigar Makers' Union in the 1870s, moving it away from social and political reform and toward "pure and simple unionism" based on demands for higher wages, benefits, and security. Gompers was president of the AFL every year but one from 1886 to 1924. During this time, he built an organization that was both powerful and conservative—one that was hostile to radicalism, party alignments, and the admission of the unskilled. He died in San Antonio, Texas, in 1924.

Questions to Consider. In this May Day speech, what impression of American workers was Gompers eager to convey? What arguments did he use to try to make this point? What different arguments did he use to support the demand for an eight-hour workday? Which of these do you find most persuasive? Which do you find most surprising? What was Gompers's purpose in mentioning foreign countries, from England to China, so frequently in this speech? Gompers did not mention governmental action. How, then, did he hope to achieve a standard eight-hour day? May Day (May 1) became Labor Day across the entire industrializing world except for the United States, where in 1894 Congress, following the lead of certain New York trade unions, declared the first Monday in September as Labor Day, a legal holiday. Why might the U.S. government have picked a different day from the rest of the world?

★━━★━━★

What Does the Working Man Want? (1890)

SAMUEL GOMPERS

My friends, we have met here today to celebrate the idea that has prompted thousands of working-people of Louisville and New Albany to parade the

Labor Tribune, April 1890.

streets. . . ; that prompts the toilers of Chicago to turn out by their fifty or hundred thousand of men; that prompts the vast army of wage-workers in New York to demonstrate their enthusiasm and appreciation of the importance of this idea; that prompts the toilers of England, Ireland, Germany, France, Italy, Spain, and Austria to defy the manifestos of the autocrats of the world and say that on May the first, 1890, the wage-workers of the world will lay down their tools in sympathy with the wage-workers of America, to establish a principle of limitations of hours of labor to eight hours for sleep, eight hours for work, and eight hours for what we will.

It has been charged time and again that were we to have more hours of leisure we would merely devote it to debauchery, to the cultivation of vicious habits—in other words, that we would get drunk. I desire to say this in answer to that charge: As a rule, there are two classes in society who get drunk. One is the class who has no work to do in consequence of too much money; the other class, who also has no work to do, because it can't get any, and gets drunk on its face. I maintain that that class in our social life that exhibits the greatest degree of sobriety is that class who are able, by a fair number of hours of day's work to earn fair wages—not overworked. . . .

. . . They tell us that the eight-hour movement can not be enforced, for the reason that it must check industrial and commercial progress. I say that the history of this country, in its industrial and commercial relations, shows the reverse. I say that is the plane on which this question ought to be discussed—that is the social question. As long as they make this question an economic one, I am willing to discuss it with them. I would retrace every step I have taken to advance this movement did it mean industrial and commercial stagnation. But it does not mean that. It means greater prosperity; it means a greater degree of progress for the whole people; it means more advancement and intelligence, and a nobler race of people. . . .

They say they can't afford it. Is that true? Let us see for one moment. If a reduction in the hours of labor causes industrial and commercial ruination, it would naturally follow increased hours of labor would increase the prosperity, commercial and industrial. If that were true, England and America ought to be at the tail end, and China at the head of civilization.

Is it not a fact that we find laborers in England and the United States, where the hours are eight, nine and ten hours a day—do we not find that the employers and laborers are more successful? Don't we find them selling articles cheaper? We do not need to trust the modern moralist to tell us those things. In all industries where the hours of labor are long, there you will find the least development of the power of invention. Where the hours of labor are long, men are cheap, and where men are cheap there is no necessity for invention. How can you expect a man to work ten or twelve or fourteen hours at his calling and then devote any time to the invention of a machine or discovery of a new principle or force? If he be so fortunate as to be able to read a paper he will fall asleep before he has read through the second or third line.

Why, when you reduce the hours of labor, say an hour a day, just think what it means. Suppose men who work ten hours a day had the time lessened to nine, or men who work nine hours a day have it reduced to eight hours; what does it mean? It means millions of golden hours and opportunities for thought. Some men might say you will go to sleep. Well, some men might sleep sixteen hours a day; the ordinary man might try that, but he would soon find he could not do it long. He would have to do something. He would probably go to the theater one night, to a concert another night, but he could not do that every night. He would probably become interested in some study and the hours that have been taken from manual labor are devoted to mental labor, and the mental labor of one hour will produce for him more wealth than the physical labor of a dozen hours.

I maintain that this is a true proposition—that men under the short-hour system not only have opportunity to improve themselves, but to make a greater degree of prosperity for their employers. Why, my friends, how is it in China, how is it in Spain, how is it in India and Russia, how is it in Italy? Cast your eye throughout the universe and observe the industry that forces nature to yield up its fruits to man's necessities, and you will find that where the hours of labor are the shortest the progress of invention in machinery and the prosperity of the people are the greatest. It is the greatest impediment to progress to hire men cheaply. Wherever men are cheap, there you find the least degree of progress. It has only been under the great influence of our great republic, where our people have exhibited their great senses, that we can move forward, upward and onward, and are watched with interest in our movements of progress and reform. . . .

The man who works the long hours has no necessities except the barest to keep body and soul together, so he can work. He goes to sleep and dreams of work; he rises in the morning to go to work; he takes his frugal lunch to work; he comes home again to throw himself down on a miserable apology for a bed so that he can get that little rest that he may be able to go to work again. He is nothing but a veritable machine. He lives to work instead of working to live. . . .

My friends, you will find that it has been ascertained that there is more than a million of our brothers and sisters—able-bodied men and women—on the streets, and on the highways and byways of our country willing to work but who cannot find it. You know that it is the theory of our government that we can work or cease to work at will. It is only a theory. You know that it is only a theory and not a fact. It is true that we can cease to work when we want to, but I deny that we can work when we will, so long as there are a million idle men and women tramping the streets of our cities, searching for work. The theory that we can work or cease to work when we will is a delusion and a snare. It is a lie.

What we want to consider is, first, to make our employment more secure, and, secondly, to make wages more permanent, and, thirdly, to give these poor people a chance to work. The laborer has been regarded as a mere producing machine . . . but back of labor is the soul of man and honesty of purpose and aspiration. Now you can not, as the political economists and college professors, say that labor is a commodity to be bought and sold. I say we are American citizens with the heritage of all the great men who have stood before us; men who have sacrificed all in the cause except honor. . . . I say the labor movement is a fixed fact. It has grown out of the necessities of the people, and, although some may desire to see it fail, still the labor movement will be found to have a strong lodgment in the hearts of the people, and we will go on until success has been achieved!

13

THE LURE OF THE EAST

The United States went to war with Spain over Cuba in 1898. But the U.S. victory in the brief war brought acquisitions in the Pacific (the Philippines and Guam) as well as in the Caribbean (Puerto Rico); at this time the United States also got control of the Hawaiian Islands and Wake Island. In part these acquisitions represented the resumption of a long tradition of westward territorial expansion that had been abandoned since the purchase of Alaska in 1867. In part they represented America's desire for "great power" status at a time when the European nations were winning colonies in Asia and Africa. But powerful economic forces were at work, too, as they had been in the formulation of the recent Open Door policy on access to Chinese markets or, for that matter, in President James Monroe's assertion of his famous Doctrine in 1823.

At the beginning of the war, President William McKinley was unsure himself whether or not the United States should take over the Philippines, and if it did, whether its forces would take only Manila, or the whole island of Luzon, or the entire archipelago. Not until December 1898 did the president finally announce that the United States would pursue a policy of "benevolent assimilation" toward the whole territory. This decision gave rise to a small but vocal anti-imperialist movement at home and, more important, a strong Filipino resistance struggle against the American occupation.

At this point, however, forceful advocates of imperialism rose to defend the president in the most vigorous terms. Of these none was more forceful or more important than Senator Albert J. Beveridge. His Senate speech of January 1900 in support of a (successful) resolution urging colonial status for the Philippines, excerpted below, provided the broadest possible grounds for the president's policy. With the fight thus in hand at home, McKinley turned to winning the fight abroad. Having made his decision, moreover, he stuck doggedly with it. In fact, the Americans overcame the insurgents only after another year's hard fighting and the death of more than a hundred thousand Filipinos.

President McKinley's ally and fellow Ohioan, Albert Beveridge, was only thirty-seven at the time of his imperialist speech of 1900, but he was already known as a proponent of military strength and Anglo-Saxon supremacy. This speech further enhanced his standing in Republican circles. Beveridge left the Senate in 1912 to devote himself to writing. In 1919, eight years before his death in Indiana, his *Life of John Marshall* was awarded the Pulitzer Prize for historical biography.

Questions to Consider. Beveridge's speech makes enormous claims for the strategic importance of the Philippines. On what grounds did Beveridge make these claims? Has history borne out Beveridge's predictions about the Pacific Ocean and world commerce? Did Beveridge think acquiring the Philippines would increase or reduce the chances of war? How did he seem to view the Declaration of Independence and the Constitution? Was Beveridge's main concern economics or race?

★══★══★

America's Destiny (1900)

ALBERT BEVERIDGE

Mr. President, the times call for candor. The Philippines are ours forever, "territory belonging to the United States," as the Constitution calls them. And just beyond the Philippines are China's illimitable markets. We will not retreat from either. We will not repudiate our duty in the archipelago. We will not abandon our opportunity in the Orient. We will not renounce our part in the mission of our race, trustee, under God, of the civilization of the world. And we will move forward to our work, not howling out regrets like slaves whipped to their burdens, but with gratitude for a task worthy of our strength, and thanksgiving to Almighty God that He has marked us as His chosen people, henceforth to lead in the regeneration of the world.

This island empire is the last land left in all the oceans. If it should prove a mistake to abandon it, the blunder once made would be irretrievable. If it proves a mistake to hold it, the error can be corrected when we will. Every other progressive nation stands ready to relieve us.

But to hold it will be no mistake. Our largest trade henceforth must be with Asia. The Pacific is our ocean. More and more Europe will manufacture the most it needs, secure from its colonies the most it consumes. Where shall we turn for consumers of our surplus? Geography answers the question. China is our natural customer. She is nearer to us than to England, Germany, or Russia, the commercial powers of the present and the future. They have moved nearer to China by securing permanent bases on her borders. The Philippines give us a base at the door of all the East.

Congressional Record, 56th Congress, 1st session, 704–712.

Lines of navigation from our ports to the Orient and Australia; from the Isthmian Canal to Asia; from all Oriental ports to Australia, converge at and separate from the Philippines. They are a self-supporting, dividend-paying fleet, permanently anchored at a spot selected by the strategy of Providence, commanding the Pacific. And the Pacific is the ocean of the commerce of the future. Most future wars will be conflicts for commerce. The power that rules the Pacific, therefore, is the power that rules the world. And, with the Philippines, that power is and will forever be the American Republic. . . .

Nothing is so natural as trade with one's neighbors. The Philippines make us the nearest neighbors of all the East. Nothing is more natural than to trade with those you know. This is the philosophy of all advertising. The Philippines bring us permanently face to face with the most sought-for customers of the world. National prestige, national propinquity, these and commercial activity are the elements of commercial success. The Philippines give the first; the character of the American people supply the last. It is a providential conjunction of all the elements of trade, of duty, and of power. If we are willing to go to war rather than let England have a few feet of frozen Alaska, which affords no market and commands none, what should we not do rather than let England, Germany, Russia, or Japan have all the Philippines? And no man on the spot can fail to see that this would be their fate if we retired. . . .

Here, then, Senators, is the situation. Two years ago there was no land in all the world which we could occupy for any purpose. Our commerce was daily turning toward the Orient, and geography and trade developments made necessary our commercial empire over the Pacific. And in that ocean we had no commercial, naval, or military base. Today we have one of the three great ocean possessions of the globe, located at the most commanding commercial, naval, and military points in the eastern seas, within hail of India, shoulder to shoulder with China, richer in its own resources than any equal body of land on the entire globe, and peopled by a race which civilization demands shall be improved. Shall we abandon it? That man little knows the common people of the Republic, little understands the instincts of our race, who thinks we will not hold it fast and hold it forever, administering just government by simplest methods. We may trick up devices to shift our burden and lessen our opportunity; they will avail us nothing but delay. We may tangle conditions by applying academic arrangements of self-government to a crude situation; their failure will drive us to our duty in the end. . . .

But, Senators, it would be better to abandon this combined garden and Gibraltar of the Pacific, and count our blood and treasure already spent a profitable loss, than to apply any academic arrangement of self-government to these children. They are not capable of self-government. How could they be? They are not of a self-governing race. They are Orientals, Malays, instructed by Spaniards in the latter's worst estate.

They know nothing of practical government except as they have witnessed the weak, corrupt, cruel, and capricious rule of Spain. What magic will anyone employ to dissolve in their minds and characters those impressions of governors and governed which three centuries of misrule have created? What alchemy will change the oriental quality of their blood and set the self-governing currents of the American pouring through their Malay veins? How shall they, in the twinkling of an eye, be exalted to the heights of self-governing peoples which required a thousand years for us to reach, Anglo-Saxon though we are . . . ?

The Declaration of Independence does not forbid us to do our part in the regeneration of the world. If it did, the Declaration would be wrong, just as the Articles of Confederation, drafted by the very same men who signed the Declaration, was found to be wrong. The Declaration has no application to the present situation. It was written by self-governing men for self-governing men. . . .

Senators in opposition are stopped from denying our constitutional power to govern the Philippines as circumstances may demand, for such power is admitted in the case of Florida, Louisiana, Alaska. How, then, is it denied in the Philippines? Is there a geographical interpretation to the Constitution? Do degrees of longitude fix constitutional limitations? Does a thousand miles of ocean diminish constitutional power more than a thousand miles of land . . . ?

No; the oceans are not limitations of the power which the Constitution expressly gives Congress to govern all territory the nation may acquire. The Constitution declares that "Congress shall have power to dispose of and make all needful rules and regulations respecting the territory belonging to the United States." . . .

Mr. President, this question is deeper than any question of party politics; deeper than any question of the isolated policy of our country even; deeper even than any question of constitutional power. It is elemental. It is racial. God has not been preparing the English-speaking and Teutonic peoples for a thousand years for nothing but vain and idle self-contemplation and self-admiration. No! He has made us the master organizers of the world to establish system where chaos reigns. He has given us the spirit of progress to overwhelm the forces of reaction throughout the earth. He has made us adepts in government that we may administer government among savage and senile peoples. Were it not for such a force as this the world would relapse into barbarism and night. And of all our race He has marked the American people as His chosen nation to finally lead in the regeneration of the world. This is the divine mission of America, and it holds for us all the profit, all the glory, all the happiness possible to man. We are trustees of the world's progress, guardians of its righteous peace. The judgment of the Master is upon us: "Ye have been faithful over a few things; I will make you ruler over many things."

What shall history say of us? Shall it say that we renounced that holy trust, left the savage to his base condition, the wilderness to the reign of waste, deserted duty, abandoned glory, forgot our sordid profit even, because we feared our strength and read the charter of our powers with the doubter's eye and the quibbler's mind? Shall it say that, called by events to captain and command the proudest, ablest, purest race of history in history's noblest work, we declined that great commission? Our fathers would not have had it so. No! They founded no paralytic government, incapable of the simplest acts of administration. They planted no sluggard people, passive while the world's work calls them. They established no reactionary nation. They unfurled no retreating flag. . . .

Mr. President and Senators, adopt the resolution offered, that peace may quickly come and that we may begin our saving, regenerating, and uplifting work. . . . Reject it, and the world, history, and the American people will know where to forever fix the awful responsibility for the consequences that will surely follow such failure to do our manifest duty. . . .

14

THE WOMAN MOVEMENT

Abigail Adams and other isolated voices urged voting rights for women at the time of the American Revolution, to no avail. In 1848 women convened at Seneca Falls, New York, to demand legal and political rights, including the vote, and they kept up their demand during the postwar debate on the enfranchisement of the freedmen. In 1869 two organizations emerged, the National Woman Suffrage Association, which fought for federal voting rights via a Constitutional amendment, and the American Woman Suffrage Association, which sought victories in the states. A woman suffrage amendment was introduced in the Senate in 1878 but gained little backing and was seldom debated. By the 1890s nineteen states allowed women to vote on school issues; three allowed them to vote on tax and bond issues; Wyoming, Colorado, Utah, and Idaho allowed full political rights.

In 1890, fearing (correctly) that the movement was about to stall in the face of the typical male view that "equal suffrage is a repudiation of manhood," the two main suffrage organizations combined in the National American Woman Suffrage Association, which focused its efforts on the most promising states and on Congress. Raising the level of argument and agitation as best they could, suffrage leaders met annually to resolve, write, speak, and strategize. Several more states now gave women the vote, including the key battlegrounds of Illinois and New York. Pressure thus built in Congress to pass a suffrage amendment.

World War I proved the turning point. President Woodrow Wilson, an opponent of woman suffrage, wanted women's organizations to support the war. Most of them did so and even served in the government—but only if he promised to support a suffrage amendment. Wilson told the Senate in 1918 that the vote for women was "vital to the winning of the war." In 1919 Congress passed the Nineteenth Amendment. Ratification came the next year. After a century of struggle, women had the vote.

Born in Wisconsin in 1859, Carrie Chapman Catt, whose presidential address to the Woman Suffrage Association in 1902 is reprinted below, worked her way through Iowa State Agricultural College, read law, was a high-school principal, and in 1883 became one of the country's first female school superintendents. Twice widowed, in the

1880s Catt became an organizer for women's suffrage in Iowa, and in 1900 succeeded the great suffragist, Susan B. Anthony, as president of the National American Woman Suffrage Association. In 1915 she led a drive to make New York the first eastern state to give the vote to women. She then helped lead the campaign that finally resulted in the Nineteenth Amendment that gave the vote to women everywhere in the country. Increasingly committed to the struggle for world peace, Catt was a staunch supporter of the League of Nations and later the United Nations. When she died in New York in 1947, she was widely recognized as one of the outstanding women of her time.

Questions to Consider. Why did Catt in this address argue that women faced twice the obstacles to popular voting that ordinary men had faced previously? Did it strengthen or weaken her argument for suffrage to mention specific instances of sex prejudice, as she did in paragraph four? Was she right to describe such prejudice as "outside the domain of reason"? What did Catt mean by the "New Woman"? Were the opponents of women's suffrage all male? Catt's last paragraph argues that the liberty from male domination that women had finally achieved in their homes should now logically be extended to freedom from male domination in politics. Was Catt right that all women as of 1902 had achieved domestic independence? If so, do you find this reasoning persuasive?

★══★══★

Address to the Woman Suffrage Association (1902)

CARRIE CHAPMAN CATT

The question of woman suffrage is a very simple one. The plea is dignified, calm and logical. Yet, great as is the victory over conservatism which is represented in the accomplishment of man suffrage, infinitely greater will be the attainment of woman suffrage. Man suffrage exists through the surrender of many a stronghold of ancient thought, deemed impregnable, yet these obstacles were the veriest Don Quixote windmills compared with the opposition which has stood arrayed against woman suffrage.

Woman suffrage must meet precisely the same objections which have been urged against man suffrage, but in addition, it must combat sex-prejudice,

Ida Husted Harper, ed., *The History of Woman Suffrage* (National American Woman Suffrage Association, New York, 1922), V: 29–30.

the oldest, the most unreasoning, the most stubborn of all human idiosyn-
cracies. What *is* prejudice? An opinion, which is not based upon reason;
a judgment, without having heard the argument; a feeling, without being
able to trace from whence it came. And sex-prejudice is a pre-judgment
against the rights, liberties and opportunities of women. A belief, without
proof, in the incapacity of women to do that which they have never done.
Sex-prejudice has been the chief hindrance in the rapid advance of the
woman's rights movement to its present status, and it is still a stupendous
obstacle to be overcome.

In the United States, at least, we need no longer argue woman's intellectual, moral and physical qualification for the ballot with the intelligent. The
Reason of the best of our citizens has long been convinced. The justice of the
argument has been admitted, but sex-prejudice is far from conquered.

When a great church official exclaims petulantly, that if women are no
more modest in their demands men may be obliged to take to drowning female infants again; when a renowned United States Senator declares no human being can find an answer to the arguments for woman suffrage, but
with all the force of his position and influence he will oppose it; when a popular woman novelist speaks of the advocates of the movement as the "shriek-
ing sisterhood"; when a prominent politician says "to argue against woman
suffrage is to repudiate the Declaration of Independence," yet he hopes it
may never come, the question flies entirely outside the domain of reason,
and retreats within the realm of sex-prejudice, where neither logic nor common sense can dislodge it. . . .

Four chief causes led to the subjection of women, each the logical deduc-
tion from the theory that men were the units of the race—obedience, ignorance, the denial of personal liberty, and the denial of right to property and
wages. These forces united in cultivating a spirit of egotism and tyranny in
men and weak dependence in women. . . . In fastening these disabilities upon
women, the world acted logically when reasoning from the premise that man
is the race and woman his dependent. The perpetual tutelage and subjection
robbed women of all freedom of thought and action, and all incentive for
growth, and they logically became the inane weaklings the world would
have them, and their condition strengthened the universal belief in their incapacity. This world taught woman nothing skillful and then said her work
was valueless. It permitted her no opinions and said she did not know how
to think. It forbade her to speak in public, and said the sex had no orators.
It denied her the schools, and said the sex had no genius. It robbed her of
every vestige of responsibility, and then called her weak. It taught her that
every pleasure must come as a favor from men, and when to gain it she
decked herself in paint and fine feathers, as she had been taught to do, it
called her vain. . . .

When at last the New Woman came, bearing the torch of truth, and with
calm dignity asked a share in the world's education, opportunities and duties, it is no wonder these untrained weaklings should have shrunk away in

horror. . . . Nor was it any wonder that man should arise to defend the woman of the past, whom he had learned to love and cherish. Her very weakness and dependence were dear to him and he loved to think of her as the tender clinging vine, while he was the strong and sturdy oak. He had worshiped her ideal through the age of chivalry as though she were a goddess, but he had governed her as though she were an idiot. Without the slightest comprehension of the inconsistency of his position, he believed this relation to be in accordance with God's command. . . .

The whole aim of the woman movement has been to destroy the idea that obedience is necessary to women; to train women to such self-respect that they would not grant obedience and to train men to such comprehension of equity they would not exact it. . . . As John Stuart Mill said in speaking of the conditions which preceded the enfranchisement of men: "The noble has been gradually going down on the social ladder and the commoner has been gradually going up. Every half century has brought them nearer to each other"; so we may say, for the past hundred years, man as the dominant power in the world has been going down the ladder and woman has been climbing up. Every decade has brought them nearer together. The opposition to the enfranchisement of women is the last defense of the old theory that obedience is necessary for women, because man alone is the creator of the race.

The whole effort of the woman movement has been to destroy obedience of woman in the home. That end has been very generally attained, and the average civilized woman enjoys the right of individual liberty in the home of her father, her husband, and her son. The individual woman no longer obeys the individual man. She enjoys self-government in the home and in society. The question now is, shall all women as a body obey all men as a body? Shall the woman who enjoys the right of self-government in every other department of life be permitted the right of self-government in the State? It is no more right for all men to govern all women than it was for one man to govern one woman. It is no more right for men to govern women than it was for one man to govern other men. . . .

15

THE BIG STICK

Although the Monroe Doctrine of 1823 had proclaimed a special interest in Latin American affairs, it was neither militaristic nor especially interventionist in spirit. But the Spanish-American War signaled a new military and economic aggressiveness in Washington and a new determination to assert the country's ambitions. It was probably inevitable, therefore, that President Theodore Roosevelt should modify the Monroe Doctrine to provide a rationale for direct intervention by armed force on behalf of "progress" and "responsible government." A hero of the U.S. Army's recent Cuban campaign against Spain and an admirer of Admiral George Dewey, Roosevelt, who had succeeded the slain William McKinley as president, urged a policy of expanding the country's military might. Advising the United States to "speak softly and carry a big stick," Roosevelt believed the United States should act as the policeman of Central America and the Caribbean. Between Roosevelt's and Coolidge's administrations the United States sent warships and soldiers to several Caribbean countries, usually to protect U.S. investments, and in some cases left them there for decades.

Theodore Roosevelt, who inaugurated this era of gunboat diplomacy, was born to well-to-do parents in New York City in 1858. After college he juggled politics, writing, and ranching and hunting, until McKinley appointed him assistant secretary of the navy in 1897. He resigned in 1898 to lead a cavalry unit called the Rough Riders in Cuba, but returned to win the governorship of New York in 1899 and 1900. He moved on to the vice presidency in 1901, and in that same year to the presidency when McKinley was killed. Over the next ten years Roosevelt promised a "square deal" and a "new nationalism," both embodying his notions of social and military progress. In 1912 he bolted the Republican Party to head a Progressive ticket that lost to Woodrow Wilson, a Democrat, whose internationalism Roosevelt relentlessly castigated until his death in 1919.

Questions to Consider. The Monroe Doctrine had asserted the right of the United States to prevent foreign intervention in the affairs of the Western Hemisphere. Did Roosevelt's "corollary" seem to be concerned mainly with external threats or with internal ones? According to the corollary, under what circumstances would the United States feel justified in interfering in Caribbean and Central American countries? Do you find Roosevelt's insistence on a U.S. right to intervene in this area to insure "reasonable efficiency and decency in social and political matters" valid and persuasive? Why did he describe unilateral U.S. intervention as the exercise of an "international police power"? Roosevelt argued that the interests of the United States and the Caribbean and Central American countries were in fact identical. Do you find this argument persuasive?

★═══★═══★

Monroe Doctrine Corollary (1904)

THEODORE ROOSEVELT

It is not true that the United States feels any land hunger or entertains any projects as regards the other nations of the Western Hemisphere save such as are for their welfare. All that this country desires is to see the neighboring countries stable, orderly, and prosperous. Any country whose people conduct themselves well can count upon our hearty friendship. If a nation shows that it knows how to act with reasonable efficiency and decency in social and political matters, if it keeps order and pays its obligations, it need fear no interference from the United States. Chronic wrongdoing, or an impotence which results in a general loosening of the ties of civilized society, may in America, as elsewhere, ultimately require intervention by some civilized nation, and in the Western Hemisphere the adherence of the United States to the Monroe Doctrine may lead the United States, however reluctantly, in flagrant cases of such wrongdoing or impotence, to the exercise of an international police power. If every country washed by the Caribbean Sea would show the progress in stable and just civilization which with the aid of the Platt amendment Cuba has shown since our troops left the island, and which so many of the republics in both Americas are constantly and brilliantly showing, all question of interference by this Nation with their affairs would be at an end. Our interests and those of our southern neighbors are in reality identical. They have great natural riches, and if within their borders the reign of law and justice obtains, prosperity is sure to come to them. While they thus obey the primary laws of civilized society they may rest assured that they will be treated by us in a spirit of cordial and helpful sympathy. We would interfere with them only in the last resort, and then only if it became evident

James D. Richardson, ed., *A Compilation of the Messages and Papers of the Presidents* (Government Printing Office, Washington, D.C., 1897–1907), XVI: 7371–7377.

that their inability or unwillingness to do justice at home and abroad had violated the rights of the United States or had invited foreign aggression to the detriment of the entire body of American nations. It is a mere truism to say that every nation, whether in America or anywhere else, which desires to maintain its freedom, its independence, must ultimately realize that the right of such independence can not be separated from the responsibility of making good use of it.

In asserting the Monroe Doctrine, in taking such steps as we have taken in regard to Cuba, Venezuela, and Panama, and in endeavoring to circumscribe the theater of war in the Far East, and to secure the open door in China, we have acted in our own interest as well as in the interest of humanity at large. There are, however, cases in which, while our own interests are not greatly involved, strong appeal is made to our sympathies. . . . In extreme cases action may be justifiable and proper. What form the action shall take must depend upon the circumstances of the case; that is, upon the degree of the atrocity and upon our power to remedy it.

16

INDUSTRIAL BLIGHT

Industrialization brought, among other things, the factory system: big machines in large buildings where thousands of workers did specialized tasks under strict supervision. The factory system vastly increased America's output of such products as glass, machinery, newspapers, soap, cigarettes, beef, and beer. Factories thus provided innumerable new goods and millions of new jobs for Americans. But factories also reduced workers' control over their place of work, made the conditions of labor more dangerous, and played no small part in destroying the dignity of that labor. The first part of the following excerpt from Upton Sinclair's novel *The Jungle* offers a glimpse into the factory system as it operated in a Chicago meatpacking plant around 1905.

Industrialization produced not only big factories but also big cities, particularly in the Northeast and Midwest. Sinclair therefore took pains to show the role of industry and new production techniques in creating urban transportation and other services. The second part of the excerpt suggests a few of the links between industrial growth and Chicago's leaders—the so-called gray wolves who controlled the city's government and businesses. Here again, Sinclair indicates the high toll in human life exacted by unrestrained development.

The Jungle caused a sensation when it was first published. The pages describing conditions in Chicago's meatpacking plants aroused horror, disgust, and fury, and sales of meat dropped precipitously. "I aimed at the public's heart," said Sinclair ruefully, "and hit it in the stomach." President Theodore Roosevelt ordered a congressional investigation of meatpacking plants in the nation, and Congress subsequently passed the Meat Inspection Act. But Sinclair, a socialist, did not seek to inspire reform legislation. He was concerned mainly with dramatizing the misery of workers under the capitalist mode of production and with winning recruits to socialism.

Upton Sinclair was born in Baltimore, Maryland, in 1878. After attending college in New York City, he began to write essays and fiction, experiencing his first real success with the publication of *The Jungle* in 1906. Dozens of novels on similar subjects—the coal and oil industries, newspapers, the liquor business, the persecution of radicals, the threat of dictatorship—poured from his pen in the following years, though none had the immediate impact of *The Jungle*. Sinclair's style, with its emphasis on the details of everyday life, resembles the realism of other writers of the time. But he also wrote as a "muckraker" (as Theodore Roosevelt called journalists who wrote exposés), trying to alert readers to the deceit and corruption then prevalent in American life. Unlike most muckrakers, however, Sinclair was politically active, running in California in the 1920s as a socialist candidate for the U.S. Congress. In 1934 he won the Democratic nomination for governor with the slogan "End Poverty in California"(EPIC), but he lost the election. During World War II he was a warm supporter of President Franklin D. Roosevelt and wrote novels about the war, one of which won a Pulitzer Prize. Not long before Sinclair's death in 1968 in Bound Brook, New Jersey, President Lyndon Johnson invited him to the White House to be present at the signing of the Wholesome Meat Act.

Questions to Consider. *The Jungle* has been regarded as propaganda, not literature, and has been placed second only to Harriet Beecher Stowe's *Uncle Tom's Cabin* in its effectiveness as a propagandistic novel. Why do you think the novel caused demands for reform rather than converts to socialism? What seems more shocking in the passages from the novel reprinted below, the life of immigrant workers in Chicago in the early twentieth century or the filthy conditions under which meat was prepared for America's dining tables? What did Sinclair reveal about the organization of the work force in Chicago's meat-packing plants? Sinclair centered his story on a Lithuanian worker named Jurgis Rudkus and his wife, Ona. In what ways did he make Jurgis's plight seem typical of urban workers of his time? Why did Jurgis deny that he had ever worked in Chicago before? What did Sinclair reveal about the attitude of employers toward labor unions at that time?

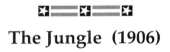

The Jungle (1906)

UPTON SINCLAIR

There was another interesting set of statistics that a person might have gathered in Packingtown—those of the various afflictions of the workers. When Jurgis had first inspected the packing plants with Szedvilas, he had marveled while he listened to the tale of all the things that were made out of the carcasses

Upton Sinclair, *The Jungle* (Doubleday, Page and Co., New York, 1906), 116–117, 265–269.

A meatpacking house. Trimmers wielding razor-sharp knives in a Chicago packing house in 1892, more than a decade before the publication of *The Jungle*. (Chicago Historical Society)

of animals and of all the lesser industries that were maintained there; now he found that each one of these lesser industries was a separate little inferno, in its way as horrible as the killing-beds, the source and fountain of them all. The workers in each of them had their own peculiar diseases. And the wandering visitor might be skeptical about all the swindles, but he could not be skeptical about these, for the worker bore the evidence of them about on his own person—generally he had only to hold out his hand.

There were the men in the pickle rooms, for instance, where old Antanas had gotten his death; scarce a one of these had not some spot of horror on his person. Let a man so much as scrape his finger pushing a truck in the pickle rooms, and he might have a sore that would put him out of the world; all the joints in his fingers might be eaten by the acid, one by one. Of the butchers and floormen, the beef boners and trimmers, and all those who used knives, you could scarcely find a person who had the use of his thumb; time and time again the base of it had been slashed, till it was a mere lump of flesh against which the man pressed the knife to hold it. The hands of these men would be criss-crossed with cuts, until you could no longer pretend to count them or to trace them. They would have no nails—they had worn them off pulling hides; their knuckles were swollen so that their fingers spread out like a fan. There were men who worked in the cooking rooms, in the midst of steam and sickening odors, by artificial light; in these rooms the germs of tuberculosis might live for two years, but the supply was renewed every hour. There were the beef luggers, who carried two-hundred-pound quarters into the refrigerator cars, a fearful kind of work, that began at four o'clock in the morning, and that wore out the most powerful man in a few years. There were those who worked in the chilling rooms, and whose special disease was rheumatism; the time limit that a man could work in the chilling rooms was said to be five years. There were the wool pluckers, whose hands went to pieces even sooner than the hands of the pickle men; for the pelts of the sheep had to be painted with acid to loosen the wool, and then the pluckers had to pull out this wool with their bare hands, till the acid had eaten their fingers off. There were those who made the tins for the canned meat, and their hands, too, were a maze of cuts, and each cut represented a chance for blood poisoning. Some worked at the stamping machines, and it was very seldom that one could work long there at the pace that was set, and not give out and forget himself, and have a part of his hand chopped off. There were the "hoisters," as they were called, whose task it was to press the lever which lifted the dead cattle off the floor. They ran along upon a rafter, peering down through the damp and the steam, and as old Durham's architects had not built the killing room for the convenience of the hoisters, at every few feet they would have to stoop under a beam, say four feet above the one they ran on, which got them into the habit of stooping, so that in a few years they would be walking like chimpanzees. Worst of any, however, were the fertilizer men, and those who served in the cooking rooms. These people could not be shown to the visitor—for the odor of a fertilizer man would scare any ordinary visitor at a hundred yards, and as for the other men, who worked in tank rooms full of steam and in some of which there were open vats near the level of the floor, their peculiar trouble was that they fell into the vats; and when they were fished out, there was never enough of them left to be worth exhibiting—sometimes they would be overlooked for days, till all but the bones of them had gone out to the world as Durham's Pure Leaf Lard! . . .

Early in the fall Jurgis set out for Chicago again. All the joy went out of tramping as soon as a man could not keep warm in the hay; and, like many thousands of others, he deluded himself with the hope that by coming early he could avoid the rush. He brought fifteen dollars with him, hidden away in one of his shoes, a sum which had been saved from the saloon keepers, not so much by his conscience, as by the fear which filled him at the thought of being out of work in the city in the wintertime.

He traveled upon the railroad with several other men, hiding in freight cars at night, and liable to be thrown off at any time, regardless of the speed of the train. When he reached the city he left the rest, for he had money and they did not, and he meant to save himself in this fight. He would bring to it all the skill that practice had brought him, and he would stand, whoever fell.

On fair nights he would sleep in the park or on a truck or an empty barrel or box, and when it was rainy or cold he would stow himself upon a shelf in a ten-cent lodging-house, or pay three cents for the privileges of a "squatter" in a tenement hallway. He would eat at free lunches, five cents a meal, and never a cent more—so he might keep alive for two months and more, and in that time he would surely find a job. He would have to bid farewell to his summer cleanliness, of course, for he would come out of the first night's lodging with his clothes alive with vermin. There was no place in the city where he could wash even his face, unless he went down to the lake front— and there it would soon be all ice.

First he went to the steel mill and the harvester works, and found that his places there had been filled long ago. He was careful to keep away from the stockyards—he was a single man now, he told himself, and he meant to stay one, to have his wages for his own when he got a job. He began the long, weary round of factories and warehouses, tramping all day, from one end of the city to the other, finding everywhere from ten to a hundred men ahead of him. He watched the newspapers, too—but no longer was he to be taken in by the smooth-spoken agents. He had been told of all those tricks while "on the road."

In the end it was through a newspaper that he got a job, after nearly a month of seeking. It was a call for a hundred laborers, and though he thought it was a "fake," he went because the place was near by. He found a line of men a block long, but as a wagon chanced to come out of an alley and break the line, he saw his chance and sprang to seize a place. Men threatened him and tried to throw him out, but he cursed and made a disturbance to attract a policeman, upon which they subsided, knowing that if the latter interfered it would be to "fire" them all.

An hour or two later he entered a room and confronted a big Irishman behind a desk.

"Ever worked in Chicago before?" the man inquired; and whether it was a good angel that put it into Jurgis's mind, or an intuition of his sharpened wits, he was moved to answer, "no, sir."

"Where do you come from?"

"Kansas City, sir."

"Any references?"

"No sir. I'm just an unskilled man, I've got good arms."

"I want men for hard work—it's all underground, digging tunnels for telephones. Maybe it won't suit you."

"I'm willing, sir—anything for me. What's the pay?"

"Fifteen cents an hour."

"I'm willing, sir."

"All right; go back there and give your name."

So within half an hour he was at work, far underneath the streets of the city. The tunnel was a peculiar one for telephone wires; it was about eight feet high, and with a level floor nearly as wide. It had innumerable branches—

a perfect spider-web beneath the city; Jurgis walked over half a mile with his gang to the place where they were to work. Stranger yet, the tunnel was lighted by electricity, and upon it was laid a double-tracked, narrow gauge railroad!

But Jurgis was not there to ask questions, and he did not give the matter a thought. It was nearly a year afterward that he finally learned the meaning of this whole affair. The City Council had passed a quiet and innocent little bill allowing a company to construct telephone conduits under the city streets; and upon the strength of this, a great corporation had proceeded to tunnel all Chicago with a system of railway freight subways. In the city there was a combination of employers, representing hundreds of millions of capital, and formed for the purpose of crushing the labor unions. The chief union which troubled it was the teamsters'; and when these freight tunnels were completed, connecting all the big factories and stores with the railroad depots, they would have the teamsters' union by the throat. Now and then there were rumors and murmurs in the Board of Aldermen, and once there was a committee to investigate—but each time another small fortune was paid over, and the rumors died away; until at last the city woke up with a start to find the work completed. There was a tremendous scandal, of course; it was found that the city records had been falsified and other crimes committed, and some of Chicago's big capitalists got into jail—figuratively speaking. The aldermen declared that they had had no idea of it all, in spite of the fact that the main entrance to the work had been in the rear of the saloon of one of them. . . .

In a work thus carried out, not much thought was given to the welfare of the laborers. On an average, the tunneling cost a life a day and several manglings; it was seldom, however, that more than a dozen or two men heard of any one accident. The work was all done by the new boring-machinery, with as little blasting as possible; but there would be falling rocks and crushed supports and premature explosions—and in addition all the dangers of railroading. So it was that one night, as Jurgis was on his way out with his gang, an engine and a loaded car dashed round one of the innumerable right-angle branches and struck him upon the shoulder, hurling him against the concrete wall and knocking him senseless.

When he opened his eyes again it was to the clanging of the bell of an ambulance. He was lying in it, covered by a blanket, and it was heading its way slowly through the holiday-shopping crowds. They took him to the county hospital, where a young surgeon set his arm, then he was washed and laid upon a bed in a ward with a score or two more of maimed and mangled men.

17

CITY DANGERS, CITY LIGHTS

Progressivism was a powerful force in turn-of-the-century America. Progressives believed in efficiency, so they fought to reform the civil service and to make government as effective and accountable as private business. They believed that capital, labor, and government should work together, so they urged the mediation of labor conflicts and the regulation of giant corporations. Believing in citizen participation, Progressives pioneered women's suffrage, the secret ballot, and the removal from office of corrupt officials by popular vote. Concerned with the suffering poor, Progressives promoted charity work, better public schools, university extension service, and better housing. They thought saloons and liquor caused trouble, so they struggled for prohibition. Most Progressives were educated, middle-class, native-born Protestants who felt uneasy around corporate greed and slum violence; they could be both self-righteous and narrow-minded. But they cared about the country. They were confident they could change things and tried energetically to do just that. As President Theodore Roosevelt once cried on their behalf, "We stand at Armageddon and do battle for the Lord."

Settlement houses were quintessential Progressive institutions. Established throughout urban America between 1880 and 1920, settlement houses—largely the handiwork of women reformers—arose to serve the vast swarm of newcomers to the country's great cities. These new "settlers" were European immigrants for the most part, but they also included recent arrivals, black and white, from the rural South. The settlement houses provided meeting halls. The staffs sponsored lectures, encouraged political participation and sometimes union activity, taught English classes, agitated for tighter health codes, and held citizenship and naturalization classes. These early social workers paid special attention to the problems of poor women and inevitably, therefore, to the problems of immigrant families.

Urban youth were a particular concern of the settlements. Settlement workers labored ceaselessly for child labor laws, more playgrounds, better schools. They worked to heal the generation gap between immigrant parents clinging to older ways and children rejecting everything old and old-fashioned, including the parents. The social workers tried to explain the new land to these children and to give them a smattering of self-improvement and urban survival skills. The following excerpt was written by Jane Addams, founder of Chicago's Hull House and in 1909 probably the country's most illustrious woman—almost certainly its most famous reformer. She did settlement work to benefit local Chicagoans. She then used local Chicagoans as case studies to demonstrate how badly the industrial system was damaging urban youth and how the system might be counteracted. This approach understandably brought great credit to the settlement houses and also great prestige to the reformers. Eventually their influence spread from neighborhood to city to state to, at last, nation.

Jane Addams was born in 1860 into a small-town middle-class Illinois family. After her graduation from college in 1881, Addams visited Europe, where she became inspired by a pioneer English settlement house that worked with the London poor. By 1889 she had founded a similar house in a ramshackle Chicago mansion. Addams attracted numerous bright, dedicated young women to work with her, including Florence Kelley, later an Illinois factory inspector, and Mary Kenny, a labor organizer. Together the three made Hull House famous. Addams's writings and speeches helped spread its reputation. *The Spirit of Youth and the City Streets* alone sold twenty thousand copies, and Addams's autobiography far more. She received the Nobel Peace Prize in 1931, four years before her death.

Questions to Consider. Why did Addams see the theater as a serious urban problem, and how did she propose to combat it? Does her distinction between baseball and theater seem valid? How did she account for the popularity of saloons among youth? What would she offer as a substitute? What role did factory labor play in the lives of the urban youth described by Addams? How did factory labor affect their behavior? Did she propose fundamental changes? Do her alternatives seem realistic? Would the problems of the theater, the saloon, and the factory have affected small-town youth, too?

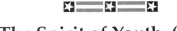

The Spirit of Youth (1909)

JANE ADDAMS

This spring a group of young girls accustomed to the life of a five-cent theater, reluctantly refused an invitation to go to the country for a day's outing

Jane Addams, *The Spirit of Youth and the City Streets* (The Macmillan Company, New York, 1909).

Jane Addams. Addams never used the words "adolescent" or "teenager." She thought the first too dry and academic; the second, slang. But it was this age group that most concerned her, as indeed it worried other adults of that period, who often wanted to pound delinquency out of the young by finger-wagging, confinement, and force. "Saint Jane" hoped to bury the bad tendencies of young people by giving their good ones a fighting chance. (Brown Brothers)

because the return on a late train would compel them to miss one evening's performance. They found it impossible to tear themselves away not only from the excitements of the theater itself but from the gaiety of the crowd of young men and girls invariably gathered outside discussing the sensational posters.

A steady English shopkeeper lately complained that unless he provided his four daughters with the money for the five-cent theaters every evening they would steal it from his till, and he feared that they might be driven to procure it in even more illicit ways. Because his entire family life had been thus disrupted he gloomily asserted that "this cheap show had ruined his 'ome and was the curse of America." This father was able to formulate the anxiety of many immigrant parents who are absolutely bewildered by the keen absorption of their children in the cheap theater. This anxiety is not, indeed, without foundation. An eminent alienist[1] of Chicago states that he has had a number of patients among neurotic children whose emotional natures have been so over-wrought by the crude appeal to which they had been so constantly subjected in the theaters, that they have become victims of hallucination and mental disorder. . . .

This testimony of a physician that the conditions are actually pathological, may at last induce us to bestir ourselves in regard to procuring a more wholesome form of public recreation. Many efforts in social amelioration have been undertaken only after such exposures; in the meantime, while the occasional child is driven distraught, a hundred children permanently injure their eyes watching the moving films, and hundreds more seriously model their conduct upon the standards set before them on this mimic stage.

Three boys, aged nine, eleven, and thirteen years, who had recently seen depicted the adventures of frontier life including the holding up of a stage coach and the lassoing of the driver, spent weeks planning to lasso, murder, and rob a neighborhood milkman, who started on his route at four o'clock in the morning. They made their headquarters in a barn and saved enough money to buy a revolver, adopting as their watchword the phrase "Dead Men Tell no Tales." . . . Fortunately for him, as the lariat was thrown the horse shied, and, although the shot was appropriately fired, the milkman's life was saved. Such a direct influence of the theater is by no means rare, even among older boys. Thirteen young lads were brought into the Municipal Court in Chicago during the first week that "Raffles, the Amateur Cracksman" was upon the stage, each one with an outfit of burglar's tools in his possession, and each one shamefacedly admitting that the gentlemanly burglar in the play had suggested to him a career of similar adventure.

In so far as the illusions of the theater succeed in giving youth the rest and recreation which comes from following a more primitive code of morality, it has a close relation to the function performed by public games. It is, of course, less valuable because the sense of participation is largely confined to the emotions and the imagination, and does not involve the entire nature. . . .

Well considered public games easily carried out in a park or athletic field, might both fill the mind with the imaginative material constantly supplied by the theater, and also afford the activity which the cramped muscles of the town dweller so sorely need. Even the unquestioned ability which the theater possesses to bring men together into a common mood and to afford

1. **Alienist:** psychiatrist.—*Eds.*

them a mutual topic of conversation, is better accomplished with the one national game which we already possess, and might be infinitely extended through the organization of other public games.

The theater even now by no means competes with the baseball league games which are attended by thousands of men and boys who, during the entire summer, discuss the respective standing of each nine and the relative merits of every player. During the noon hour all the employees of a city factory gather in the nearest vacant lot to cheer their own home team in its practice for the next game with the nine of a neighboring manufacturing establishment and on a Saturday afternoon the entire male population of the city betakes itself to the baseball field; the ordinary means of transportation are supplemented by gay stage-coaches and huge automobiles, noisy with blowing horns and decked with gay pennants. The enormous crowd of cheering men and boys are talkative, good-natured, full of the holiday spirit, and absolutely released from the grind of life. They are lifted out of their individual affairs and so fused together that a man cannot tell whether it is his own shout or another's that fills his ears; whether it is his own coat or another's that he is wildly waving to celebrate a victory. He does not call the stranger who sits next to him his "brother" but he unconsciously embraces him in an overwhelming outburst of kindly feeling when the favorite player makes a home run. Does not this contain a suggestion of the undoubted power of public recreation to bring together all classes of a community in the modern city unhappily so full of devices for keeping men apart? . . .

We are only beginning to understand what might be done through the festival, the street procession, the band of marching musicians, orchestral music in public squares or parks, with the magic power they all possess to formulate the sense of companionship and solidarity. . . .

As it is possible to establish a connection between the lack of public reaction and the vicious excitements and trivial amusements which become their substitutes, so it may be illuminating to trace the connection between the monotony and dullness of factory work and the petty immoralities which are often the youth's protest against them.

There are many city neighborhoods in which practically every young person who has attained the age of fourteen years enters a factory. When the work itself offers nothing of interest, and when no public provision is made for recreation, the situation becomes almost insupportable to the youth whose ancestors have been rough-working and hard-playing peasants.

In such neighborhoods the joy of youth is well nigh extinguished; and in that long procession of factory workers, each morning and evening, the young walk almost as wearily and listlessly as the old. Young people working in modern factories situated in cities still dominated by the ideals of Puritanism face a combination which tends almost irresistibly to overwhelm the spirit of youth. When the Puritan repression of pleasure was in the ascendant in America the people it dealt with lived on farms and villages where, although youthful pleasures might be frowned upon and crushed out, the young people still had a chance to find self-expression in their work. Plowing the field and spinning the flax could be carried on with a certain joyousness and vigor which the organization of modern industry too often precludes. Present industry based upon the inventions of the nineteenth century has little connection with the old patterns in which men have worked for generations. The modern factory calls for an expenditure of nervous energy almost more than it demands muscular effort, or at least machinery so far performs the work of the massive muscles, that greater stress is laid upon fine and exact movements necessarily involving nervous strain. But these movements are exactly of the type to which the muscles of a growing boy least readily respond, quite as the admonition to be accurate and faithful is that which appeals the least to his big primitive emotions. . . .

In vast regions of the city which are completely dominated by the factory, it is as if the development of industry had outrun all the educational and social arrangements.

The revolt of youth against uniformity and the necessity of following careful directions laid down by some one else, many times results in such nervous irritability that the youth, in spite of all sorts of prudential reasons, "throws up his job," if only to get outside the factory walls into the freer street, just as the narrowness of the school inclosure induces many a boy to jump the fence.

When the boy is on the street, however, and is "standing around on the corner" with the gang to which he mysteriously attaches himself, he finds the difficulties of direct untrammeled action almost as great there as they were in the factory, but for an entirely different set of reasons. The necessity so strongly felt in the factory for an outlet to his sudden and furious bursts of energy, his overmastering desire to prove that he could do things "without being bossed all the time," finds little chance for expression, for he discovers that in whatever really active pursuit he tries to engage, he is promptly suppressed by the police. . . .

The unjustifiable lack of educational supervision during the first years of factory work makes it quite impossible for the modern educator to offer any real assistance to young people during that trying transitional period between school and industry. The young people themselves who fail to conform can do little but rebel against the entire situation.

There are many touching stories by which this might be illustrated. One of them comes from a large steel mill of a boy of fifteen whose business it was to throw a lever when a small tank became filled with molten metal. During the few moments when the tank was filling it was his foolish custom to catch the reflection of the metal upon a piece of looking-glass, and to throw the bit of light into the eyes of his fellow workmen. Although an exasperated foreman had twice dispossessed him of his mirror, with a third fragment he was one day flicking the gloom of the shop when the neglected tank overflowed, almost instantly burning off both his legs. Boys working in the stock yards, during their moments of wrestling and rough play, often slash each other painfully with the short knives which they use in their work, but in spite of this the play impulse is too irrepressible to be denied. . . .

The discovery of the labor power of youth was to our age like the discovery of a new natural resource, although it was merely incidental to the invention of modern machinery and the consequent subdivision of labor. In utilizing it thus ruthlessly we are not only in danger of quenching the divine fire of youth, but we are imperiling industry itself when we venture to ignore these very sources of beauty, of variety and of suggestion.

18

THE WAR FOR DEMOCRACY

Woodrow Wilson won the presidency in 1912 on behalf of a "new freedom," a program involving lower tariffs, banking reform, antitrust legislation, and, in foreign policy, the repudiation of Theodore Roosevelt's gunboat diplomacy. Even after sending troops to various Caribbean countries and to Mexico, Wilson claimed that his main concern was to promote peace and democracy in the world. When World War I erupted in Europe, Wilson saw the war as the result of imperialistic rivalries ("a war with which we have nothing to do") and urged, despite personal sympathy with Great Britain, that the United States stay neutral so as to influence the peace negotiations. Wilson won reelection in 1916 largely on a promise to keep the country out of war. But a combination of pro-British propaganda in American newspapers and German submarine attacks on American ships proved formidable, and in April 1917, Wilson finally requested a declaration of war in the following address to Congress. The sweeping, visionary arguments of this remarkable speech shaped not only America's expectations about the war itself but also attitudes about the proper U.S. role in international affairs for years to come.

Born in 1856 in Virginia, Woodrow Wilson grew up in the South; his father was a Presbyterian minister. He attended Princeton and Johns Hopkins, where he earned a doctorate, and began to write and teach in the field of constitutional government and politics. He gained national stature while president of Princeton from 1902 until 1910; he became the Democratic governor of New Jersey in 1911 and, two years later, president of the United States. Wilson's main objective at the peace conference after World War I was to create a League of Nations to help keep the peace. In 1919 during an intensive speechmaking campaign to arouse public support for the League, Wilson suffered a debilitating stroke. He died in Washington, D.C., in 1924.

Questions to Consider. Note, in reading the following message, that although Woodrow Wilson believed in the unique and superior character of American institutions, he was willing to enter into alliances with European powers. What were the four principal grounds on

which Wilson was willing to reverse the American diplomatic tradition? Which of these did he seem to take most seriously? Were there
other American interests that he might have stressed but did not? What
reasons might Wilson have had for stressing so strongly America's attachment to Germany's people as opposed to its government? Might
Wilson's arguments and rhetoric have served to prolong rather than to
shorten the war?

★━━★━━★

Address to Congress (1917)

WOODROW WILSON

I have called the Congress into extraordinary session because there are serious, very serious choices of policy to be made, and made immediately, which
it was neither right nor constitutionally permissible that I should assume the
responsibility of making.

On the third of February last I officially laid before you the extraordinary
announcement of the Imperial German Government that on and after the
first day of February it was its purpose to put aside all restraints of law or of
humanity and use its submarines to sink every vessel that sought to approach either the ports of Great Britain and Ireland or the western coasts of
Europe or any of the ports controlled by the enemies of Germany within the
Mediterranean. . . .

I was for a little while unable to believe that such things would in fact be
done by any government that had hitherto subscribed to the humane practices of civilized nations. International law had its origin in the attempt to set
up some law which would be respected and observed upon the seas, where
no nation had right of dominion and where lay the free highways of the
world. . . . This minimum of right the German Government has swept aside
under the plea of retaliation and necessity and because it had no weapons
which it could use at sea except these which it is impossible to employ as it is
employing them without throwing to the winds all scruples of humanity or
of respect for all understandings that were supposed to underlie the intercourse of the world. I am not now thinking of the loss of property involved,
immense and serious as that is, but only of the wanton and wholesale destruction of the lives of noncombatants, men, women, and children, engaged
in pursuits which have always, even in the darkest periods of modern history, been deemed innocent and legitimate. Property can be paid for; the lives
of peaceful and innocent people cannot be. The present German submarine
warfare against commerce is a warfare against mankind.

The New York Times, April 3, 1917.

It is a war against all nations. American ships have been sunk, American lives taken, in ways which it has stirred us very deeply to learn of, but the ships and people of other neutral and friendly nations have been sunk and overwhelmed in the waters in the way. There has been no discrimination. The challenge is to all mankind. Each nation must decide for itself how it will meet it. The choice we make for ourselves must be made with a moderation of counsel and a temperateness of judgement befitting our character and our motives as a nation. We must put excited feeling away. Our motive will not be revenge or the victorious assertion of the physical might of the nation, but only the vindication of right, of human right, of which we are only a single champion. . . .

With a profound sense of the solemn and even tragical character of the step I am taking and of the grave responsibilities which it involves, but in un-hesitating obedience to what I deem my constitutional duty, I advise that the Congress declare the recent course of the Imperial German Government to be in fact nothing less than war against the government and people of the United States; that it formally accept the status of belligerent which has thus been thrust upon it; and that it take immediate steps not only to put the coun-try in a more thorough state of defense but also to exert all its power and em-ploy all its resources to bring the Government of the German Empire to terms and end the war. . . .

We have no quarrel with the German people. We have no feeling towards them but one of sympathy and friendship. It was not upon their impulse that their government acted in entering this war. It was not with their previous knowledge or approval. It was a war determined upon as wars used to be de-termined upon in the old, unhappy days when peoples were nowhere con-sulted by their rulers and wars were provoked and waged in the interest of dynasties or of little groups of ambitious men who were accustomed to use their fellow men as pawns and tools. . . .

We are accepting this challenge of hostile purpose because we know that in such a Government, following such methods, we can never have a friend; and that in the presence of its organized power, always lying in wait to ac-complish we know not what purpose, there can be no assured security for the democratic Governments of the world. We are now about to accept gauge of battle with this natural foe to liberty and shall, if necessary, spend the whole force of the nation to check and nullify its pretensions and its power. We are glad, now that we see the facts with no veil of false pretense about them, to fight thus for the ultimate peace of the world and for the liberation of its peoples, the German peoples included: for the rights of nations great and small and the privilege of men everywhere to choose their way of life and of obedience. The world must be made safe for democracy. Its peace must be planted upon the tested foundations of political liberty. We have no selfish ends to serve. We desire no conquest, no dominion. We seek no indemnities for ourselves, no material compensation for the sacrifices we shall freely make. We are but one of the champions of the rights of mankind.

We shall be satisfied when those rights have been made as secure as the faith and the freedom of nations can make them. . . .

It will be all the easier for us to conduct ourselves as belligerents in a high spirit of right and fairness because we act without animus, not in enmity towards a people or with the desire to bring any injury or disadvantage upon them, but only in armed opposition to an irresponsible government which has thrown aside all considerations of humanity and of right and is running amuck. We are, let me say again, the sincere friends of the German people, and shall desire nothing so much as the early reestablishment of intimate relations of mutual advantage between us,—however hard it may be for them, for the time being, to believe that this is spoken from our hearts. We have borne with their present Government through all these bitter months because of that friendship,—exercising a patience and forbearance which would otherwise have been impossible. We shall, happily, still have an opportunity to prove that friendship in our daily attitude and actions towards the millions of men and women of German birth and native sympathy who live amongst us and share our life, and we shall be proud to prove it towards all who are in fact loyal to their neighbors and to the Government in the hour of test. They are, most of them, as true and loyal Americans as if they had never known any other fealty of allegiance. They will be prompt to stand with us in rebuking and restraining the few who may be of a different mind and purpose. If there should be disloyalty, it will be dealt with with a firm hand of stern repression; but, if it lifts its head at all, it will lift it only here and there and without countenance except from a lawless and malignant few.

It is a distressing and oppressive duty, Gentlemen of the Congress, which I have performed in thus addressing you. There are, it may be, many months of fiery trial and sacrifice ahead of us. It is a fearful thing to lead this great peaceful people into war, into the most terrible and disastrous of all wars, civilization itself seeming to be in the balance. But the right is more precious than peace, and we shall fight for the things which we have always carried nearest our hearts,—for democracy, for the right of those who submit to authority to have a voice in their own Governments, for the rights and liberties of small nations, for a universal dominion of right by such a concert of free peoples as shall bring peace and safety to all nations and make the world itself at last free. To such a task we can dedicate our lives and our fortunes, everything that we have, with the pride of those who know that the day has come when America is privileged to spend her blood and her might for the principles that gave her birth and happiness and the peace which she has treasured. God helping her, she can do no other.

19

The Diplomacy of Isolation

Many Americans found great glory in World War I. After all, the dough-boys, as the American infantrymen were called, had turned the tide against Germany, and John ("Black Jack") Pershing, commander of the U.S. forces, emerged from the conflict a national hero. But the human price had been stiff: 100,000 Americans dead and 200,000 wounded. American casualties in World War I were low compared with European casualties (almost 2 million Germans and 1 million British died) or with U.S. losses in the Civil War (600,000) or in World War II (400,000). But the American losses were hardly insignificant, particularly since the country was in the war for only eighteen months and mobilized only about 4 million men. Much of the dying occurred in the appalling conditions of the Argonne Forest, where years of trenching and shelling had created a veritable wasteland of death.

Justifying such remarkable carnage would have taken remarkable results—something similar to the new international order that Woodrow Wilson had promised. But the physically weakened president was not able to deliver on this. So the skepticism that had attended U.S. entry into the war persisted, engendering a somber, even cynical mood beneath the boisterous patriotic surface. Extended into the 1930s, this mood would make it difficult for the country to strengthen itself for the looming conflict with the Axis powers. Some historians argue that it actually played a role in the unraveling of European collective security measures, since the absence of an American commitment made Great Britain reluctant to ally itself formally with France, thereby weakening the common front against a resurgent Germany.

A major reason for the failure of the Senate to ratify the Treaty of Versailles, and therefore U.S. membership in the League of Nations, was the opposition of Republican Senator Henry Cabot Lodge of Massachusetts, the chairman of the Senate Foreign Relations Committee. Wealthy, elderly, conservative, and nationalistic, Lodge opposed virtually every reform of the era, including women's suffrage, the direct election of senators, prohibition, and compulsory international arbitration. A "strong navy" man who had endorsed the imperialist policies of William McKinley and Teddy Roosevelt, he was vituperatively critical of Wilson for not entering the war on the side of England right away, and once threw (and landed) a punch at a young American of Swiss-German descent who came to his office to agitate for peace; Lodge's staff then jumped the hapless man and beat him badly. When the war ended Lodge urged harsh peace terms. When Wilson submitted the treaty for Senate confirmation, Lodge's committee reported it out with so many amendments to safeguard U.S. sovereignty that Wilson urged even Senate Democrats to oppose it, thus dooming the measure, and with it the hopes of Wilsonian internationalists. Lodge's victory in the struggle over ratification increased his popularity, which he used to defeat a proposal by President Warren G. Harding to have the United States join the World Court. Lodge remained a senator until his death in Boston in 1924, but his influence endured, as may be seen in the charter of the United Nations, founded in 1945, which gave the Great Powers veto authority over measures they disapproved.

Questions to Consider.   On what main grounds did Lodge rest his arguments for opposing the Treaty of Versailles as submitted? What two groups did Lodge characterize as the chief "internationalists" of his time? Was this a fair way to deal with the Wilsonians? What was Lodge's attitude toward Europe? Did he want the United States to become part of a broader transatlantic community? What role did Lodge wish to see America play in world affairs? Do you find his arguments for American distinctiveness and exceptionalism compelling? Would they carry the day in the early twentieth-first century as they did in 1919?

★══★══★

Speech to the Senate (1919)

HENRY CABOT LODGE

I am anxious as any human being can be to have the United States render every possible service to the civilization and peace of mankind, but I am certain we can do it best by not putting ourselves in leading strings or subjecting our policies and our sovereignty to other nations. The independence of the United States is not only more precious to ourselves but to the world than any single possession.

Look at the United States today. We have made mistakes in the past. We have had shortcomings. We shall make mistakes in the future and fall short of our own best hopes. But nonetheless is there any country today on the face of the earth which can compare with this in ordered liberty, in peace, and in the largest freedom? I feel that I can say this without being accused of undue boastfulness, for it is the simple fact, and in making this treaty and taking on these obligations all that we do is in a spirit of unselfishness and in a desire for the good of mankind. But it is well to remember that we are dealing with nations every one of which has a direct individual interest to serve, and there is grave danger in an unshared idealism.

Contrast the United States with any country on the face of the earth today and ask yourself whether the situation of the United States is not the best to be found. I will go as far as anyone in world service, but the first step to world service is the maintenance of the United States. You may call me selfish if you will, conservative or reactionary, or use any other harsh adjective you see fit to apply, but an American I was born, an American I have remained all my life. I can never be anything else but an American, and I must think of the United States first, and when I think of the United States first in an arrangement like this I am thinking of what is best for the world, for if the United States fails, the best hopes of mankind fail with it. I have never had but one allegiance—I cannot divide it now. I have loved but one flag and I cannot share that devotion and give affection to the mongrel banner invented for a league.

Internationalism, illustrated by the Bolshevik and by the men to whom all countries are alike provided they can make money out of them, is to me repulsive. National I must remain, and in that way I like all other Americans can render the amplest service to the world. The United States is the world's best hope, but if you fetter her in the interests and quarrels of other nations, if you tangle her in the intrigues of Europe, you will destroy her power for good and endanger her very existence. Leave her to march freely through the centuries to come as in the years that have gone. Strong, generous, and confident, she has nobly served mankind. Beware how you trifle with your marvelous inheritance, this great land of ordered liberty, for if we stumble and fall freedom and civilization everywhere will go down in ruin.

We are told that we shall "break the heart of the world" if we do not take this league just as it stands. I fear that the hearts of the vast majority of mankind would beat on strongly and steadily and without any quickening if the league were to perish altogether. If it should be effectively and beneficently changed the people who would lie awake in sorrow for a single night could be easily gathered in one not very large room but those who would draw a long breath of relief would reach to millions.

We hear much of visions and I trust we shall continue to have visions and dream dreams of a fairer future for the race. But visions are one thing and visionaries are another, and the mechanical appliances of the rhetorician designed to give a picture of a present which does not exist and of a future which no man can predict are as unreal and shortlived as the steam or canvas clouds, the angels suspended on wires and the artificial lights of the stage. They pass with the moment of effect and are shabby and tawdry in the daylight. Let us at least be real. Washington's entire honesty of mind and his fearless look into the face of all facts are qualities which can never go out of fashion and which we should all do well to imitate.

Ideals have been thrust upon us as an argument for the league until the healthy mind which rejects cant revolts from them. Are ideals confined to this deformed experiment upon a noble purpose, tainted, as it is, with bargains and tied to a peace treaty which might have been disposed of long ago to the great benefit of the world if it had not been compelled to carry this rider on its back? . . . No doubt many excellent and patriotic people see a coming fulfillment of nobler ideals in the words "league for peace." We all respect and share these aspirations and desires, but some of us see no hope, but rather defeat, for them in this murky covenant. For we, too, have our ideals, even if we differ from those who have tried to establish a monopoly of idealism. Our first ideal is our country, and we see her in the future, as in the past, giving service to all her people and to the world. Our ideal of the future is that she should continue to render that service of her own free will. She has great problems of her own to solve, very grim and perilous problems, and a right solution, if we can attain to it, would largely benefit mankind. We would have our country strong to resist a peril from the West, as she has flung back the German menace from the East. We would not have our politics distracted and embittered by the dissensions of other lands. We would not have our country's vigor exhausted or her moral force abated, by everlasting meddling and muddling in every quarrel, great and small, which afflicts the world. Our ideal is to make her ever stronger and better and finer, because in that way alone, as we believe, can she be of the greatest service to the world's peace and to the welfare of mankind.

20

THE BUSINESS OF AMERICA

Beginning in 1922 the United States experienced an era of tremendous economic expansion and unprecedented prosperity. The country's industrial output more than doubled, per capita income increased by one-third, and there was almost no inflation. The use of labor-saving devices such as refrigerators, vacuum cleaners, and washing machines became widespread, and millions of Americans purchased automobiles on readily available credit. The United States had become a "consumer culture."

Nevertheless, production levels were so high that consumers were unable to buy all the products that industry produced, and new markets had to be created. It was in this climate that the advertising industry came of age. Among the most successful "ad men" of the era was Bruce Barton, chairman of the board of the New York advertising agency Batten, Barton, Durstine & Osborne, and author of an immensely popular book, part of which is reproduced below. In *The Man Nobody Knows,* Barton portrayed Jesus Christ as a salesman—not an ordinary salesman, but the world's greatest salesman—and exhorted readers to profit by his example. The story of the carpenter from Nazareth, Barton added, is "the story of the founder of modern business." Or as a contemporary observed: "The sanest religion is business. Any relationship that forces a man to follow the Golden Rule rightfully belongs amid the ceremonials of the church. A great business enterprise includes and presupposes this relationship."

Business leaders turned not only to religion for inspiration, but also to sports. This era, after all, was the heyday of Ford, Kodak, Armour, General Electric, and U.S. Steel. The Hoover man and his fellow salesmen were cogs in large industrial enterprises with many functions and many layers of labor. Dale Carnegie taught people to sell themselves as well as their product, to "win friends," to "get along," and to appreciate teamwork. Corporations were in fact giant collectivities: huge teams working toward the common goal of corporate profit. Who better, then, to instruct and inspire them than the head of a winning sports team?

The 1920s were the first golden age of big-time sports. Athletes such as Babe Ruth, Red Grange, Bill Tilden, and Jack Dempsey captivated the throngs with their exploits on the diamond, the gridiron, the court, and the canvas. College football shared this big-time sporting scene. Fans, alumni, and students packed the oval stadiums week after week all across the country, and in a sizable arena with major rivals—Army and Navy, Harvard and Yale, Notre Dame and almost anyone—crowds could reach nearly a hundred thousand people. Understandably, college football coaches became celebrities in their own right, much sought after for charity events or after-dinner speeches. Walter Camp of Yale football was as big a draw as John McGraw of New York baseball. Sports, like relgion, thus came to resemble business—and vice versa.

Born in Tennessee in 1886, Bruce Barton grew up in Illinois, attended Amherst College in Massachusetts, and worked in publishing in Chicago and New York. In 1918 Barton organized an advertising agency. Within a decade Batten, Barton, Durstine & Osborn (BBDO) had become a giant of the advertising industry and one of the most famous names in American business. Barton remained president or chairman of the board of BBDO until 1961. He also authored numerous popular books and articles, won election to Congress from Tennessee as a Republican, and vigorously opposed virtually all of Franklin Roosevelt's New Deal. He died in New York City in 1967.

Knute Rockne was a Norwegian by birth who emigrated in 1893 to the United States, where he obtained what all good Catholic boys longed for—an education at Notre Dame and a spot on its football team. From 1918, when Rockne became head coach at Notre Dame, to 1931, when he died in a plane crash, the "Fighting Irish" compiled an astounding 105 wins and 12 losses. After 1928 he also gave sales talks like the one excerpted below given for the Studebaker Automobile Corporation. A famous Rockne line—"Win one for the Gipper!"—was later immortalized in a movie about his career. The part of George Gipp was played by a young actor named Ronald Reagan.

Questions to Consider. Do you think Bruce Barton was right that the key to the success of Jesus lay in his techniques of persuasion? Why did he emphasize the need for religion and the church to reach out to the marketplace? What means did he recommend? Would businesses other than advertising benefit from what Barton saw as Jesus's four rules for successful communication? Some Christians criticized Barton for seeing Jesus as essentially a marketing genius. Do you think their criticism was valid?

In Knute Rockne's talk, was he teaching technique, as Barton did, or instilling values? Which values did he stress? Why would those values have been of special importance to Studebaker and other big mass-consumption companies? Would Rockne have given this talk to Studebaker's factory workers or only its sales force? Would playing college football actually resemble working for a corporation? Would another sport—baseball, say, or tennis—have worked as well, or was football, with its ball-carrying backfield and its self-sacrificing offensive line, particularly appropriate?

★──★──★

The Man Nobody Knows (1925)

BRUCE BARTON

Jesus was, as we say, many-sided, and every man sees the side of His nature which appeals most to himself. . . .

I propose in this chapter to consider some words and deeds of Jesus which persuaded and still persuade men of the wisdom and justice in His teaching. . . .

Let us begin by asking why He could command public attention and why, in contrast, His churches have not done so well. The answer is twofold. His mission was to teach men. But before even He could teach, He must get men to listen. He was never trite; He had no single method. The Gospels show clearly that no one could predict what He would say or do; His actions and words were always new, arresting, challenging and meaningful to the men among whom He lived. . . .

These are Jesus' works, done in Jesus' name. If He lived again now, He would be known by His service, not merely by His sermons. One thing is certain: He would not neglect the market place. Few of His sermons were delivered in synagogues. For the most part He was in the crowded places—the Temple court, the city squares, the centers where goods were bought and sold. I emphasized this fact once to a group of preachers.

"You mean that we ought to do street preaching!" one of them exclaimed. . . .

No. Few ideas gain currency unless they may be presented simultaneously to hundreds of thousands. Magazines, newspapers, and radio networks are now the street in Capernaum. Here our goods are sold; here voices are raised to win our loyalty to ideas, to causes—to faiths. That the voice of Jesus should be still in our market place is an omission which He could soon find a way to correct. . . .

Benjamin Franklin in his autobiography tells the process which he went through in acquiring an effective style. He would read a passage from some great master of English, then lay the book aside and attempt to reproduce the thought in his own words. Comparing his version with the original, he discovered wherein he had obscured the thought or wasted words or failed to drive straight to the point. Every man who wishes to know a little more of

Jesus should study the parables in the same fashion, schooling himself in their language and learning the elements of their power.

1. First of all they are marvelously condensed. . . .

Jesus had no introductions. A single sentence grips attention; three or four more tell the story; one or two more and both the thought and its application are clear. And this is true of ideas that reformed the moral structure of the world! When He wanted a new disciple, He said simply "Follow me." . . .

Two men spoke on the battleground of Gettysburg nearly a century ago. The first delivered an oration of more than two hours in length; not one person in ten who reads this page can even recall his name; certainly not one in a thousand can quote a single sentence from his masterly effort. The second speaker uttered two hundred and fifty words, and those words, Lincoln's Gettysburg Address, are a part of the mental endowment of almost every American. . . .

Jesus hated prosy dullness. He praised the Centurion who was anxious not to waste His time; the only prayer which He publicly commended was uttered by a poor publican who merely cried out, "God, be merciful to me a sinner." A seven-word prayer, and Jesus called it a good one. A sixty-six word prayer, He said, contained all that men needed to say or God to hear. What would be His verdict on most of our prayers and our speeches and our writing?

2. His language was marvelously simple—a second great essential. There is hardly a sentence in His teaching which a child cannot understand. His illustrations were all drawn from the commonest experiences of life: "a sower went forth to sow"; "a certain man had two sons"; "a man built his house on the sands"; "the kingdom of heaven is like a grain of mustard seed." . . .

Jesus used few qualifying words and no long ones. We referred a minute ago to those three literary masterpieces. The Lord's Prayer, The Twenty-third Psalm, The Gettysburg Address. Recall their phraseology:

> *Our Father which art in Heaven, hallowed be thy name*
> *The Lord is my shepherd; I shall not want*
> *Four score and seven years ago*

Not a single three-syllable word; hardly any two-syllable words. All the greatest things in human life are one-syllable things—love, joy, hope, home, child, wife, trust, faith, God—and the great pieces of writing, generally speaking, use the small word in place of the large if meaning permits.

3. Sincerity illuminates strongly every word, every sentence He uttered; sincerity is the third essential. Many wealthy men have purchased newspapers with the idea of advancing their personal fortunes or bringing about some political action in which they have a private interest. Such newspapers almost invariably fail. No matter how much money is spent on them, no matter how zealously the secret of their ownership is guarded, readers eventually become conscious that something is wrong. They come to feel that the voice of the editor is not his own.

It was the way Jesus looked at men, and the life He led among them, that gave His words transforming power. What He was and what He said were one and the same thing. Nobody could stand at His side for even a minute without being persuaded that here was a man who loved people and considered even the humblest of them worthy of the best He had to give. There is no presupposition more deadening to a writer than the idea that he can "write down" to his readers. . . .

Persuasion depends on respect for the listeners, and in Jesus great respect coupled with great love.

4. Finally Jesus knew that any idea may have to be repeated. . . .

It has been said that "reputation is repetition." No important truth can be impressed on the minds of any large number of people by being said only once. The thoughts which Jesus had to give the world were revolutionary, but they were few in number. "God is your father," He said, "caring more for the welfare of every one of you than any human father can possibly care for his children. His Kingdom is happiness! His rule is love." This is what He had to teach, and He knew the necessity of driving it home from every possible angle. So in one of His stories God is the Shepherd searching the wilds for one wandering sheep; in another the Father welcoming home a prodigal boy; in another a King who forgives his debtors large amounts and expects them to be forgiving in turn—many stories but the same big Idea. . . .

Whoever feels an impulse to make his own life count in the grand process of human betterment can have no surer guide for his activities than Jesus. Let him learn the lesson of the parables: that in teaching people you first capture their interest; that your service rather than your sermons must be your claim on their attention; that what you say must be simple and brief and above all *sincere.*

★══★══★

A Sales Promotion Address (1928)

KNUTE ROCKNE

I don't know anything about selling automobiles; I never sold one in my life; but perhaps a few remarks here on the psychology that is necessary for success in a football organization might not be out of place because it seems to me that the same psychology that makes for success in a football organization will make for success in any organization, and particularly in a selling organization.

Now in the fall when we make our first call for the team, about three

McCready Huston, *Salesman from the Sidelines: Being the Business Career of Knute K. Rockne* (New York: Ray Long and Richard R. Smith, 1932), 26–33. Reprinted by permission of Anne Huston Barron, Executor, Estate of McCready Huston, and Mary Jeanne Rockne Kochendorfer.

hundred and fifty lads assemble in a large room in the library; and it is my idea to talk to them on the correct psychology before I take them out on the field. I talk to them on ambition and I tell them that most of what I read about ambition is bunk. There is not plenty of room at the top. There is very little room at the top. There is room at the top only for the few who have the ability and the imagination and the daring and the personality and the energy that make them stand out from among their fellow men. But there is success for any man in his own job if he does it as well as it can be done. As far as I am able to observe the greatest satisfaction I can get on this earth is to do the particular job I am doing as well as it can be done; and I think that holds good for every one. There may be other things that are easier, but they generally leave a headache or a heartache the day after.

I tell the lads there are five types I do not want. And I say the first type I have in mind is the swelled head. The man who was a success a year ago and who is content to rest on his laurels, who wants to play on his reputation. Dry rot sets in and he ceases to make an effort. To that kind of boy there will come quite a shock because the chances are there will be someone playing in his place.

The second type is the chronic complainer. They crab at everyone but themselves. And I say no organization can afford to have that type of man among them because complaining is infectious. And I say the complainer is in for quite a shock, too, because as soon as I can find out who the complainers are, why some evening when they come out for practice there will be no suits in their lockers.

And third is the quitter. The quitter is the fellow who wishes he could play but who is not willing to pay the price; and I tell the boys if one of that type is here he might just as well quit now and not wear out the equipment.

I don't want boys to dissipate physically or emotionally. I tell them that I have no brief against playing pool long hours in the afternoon, dancing half the night, or learning to drive an automobile with one hand; but I tell them we have no time for it. If we are going to compete with organizations who do not do that sort of thing and who are saving all their energy for the contest, I say do not dissipate any energy emotionally. By that I mean they should not give way to emotions such as jealousy, hatred or anything of that sort. I say that this sort of thing destroys any organization; and then I tell them that we should look upon one another in a friendly way. Look for the good in one another and be inspired by the fine qualities in those around us and forget about their faults. I tell them that the chances are that I will notice their faults and won't stutter when I mention them to the particular individual who has them. . . .

In two weeks I call them together again and tell them that there are certain among them who have great potentialities but that they haven't shown any improvement. There are certain among them that I do not want unless they change.

The first is the chap who alibis, one who justifies his own failure, and I tell them that a boy who does this had better watch out or he will get into a second class, that of feeling sorry for himself, in which case the bony part of his spine turns into a soft substance known as soap and he is absolutely worthless.

The second class of lad—I generally have very few of them—is the slicker, the mucker, who tries to get by by playing unfair football. I tell that type of boy that we cannot afford to have him on the team for he will bring discredit on the school and on our organization. I also impress on him that slugging and unfairness do not pay either in a game or in life after leaving school.

Then, third, there is the boy who lacks courage, who is afraid. What is courage? Courage means to be afraid to do something and still going ahead and doing it. If a man has character, the right kind of energy, mental ability, he will learn that fear is something to overcome and not to run away from.

And before the first game of the year I talk to them along the same lines on ambition. I say ambition, the right kind of ambition, means that you must have the ability to co-operate with the men around you, men working with you; and it is my observation that ability to co-operate is more essential than individual technique. In this day and age no individual stands alone; he must be able to co-operate in every sense of the word; and that is not a very easy thing to do. . . .

Now I want to impress the necessity of co-operation on the minds of you distributors, dealers, and sellers of automobiles and trucks. Unless you understand the problems of production, engineering, bookkeeping, service advertising and all departments that go to make up your organization, your organization cannot succeed. The failure of any one of them may cause you to fail.

Later on after a game or two, and particularly after a game where I have seen the lads give up, I talk to them further some noon on ambition. I tell them that there can be no ambition without perseverance. By perseverance I mean the ability to stick in there and keep giving the best of one's self. The ability to keep in there and keep trying when the going is tough and you are behind and everything seems hopeless. There can be no success, no reward, unless every man has the ability to stay in there until the last whistle blows. . . .

That applies to you automobile men out there on the firing line. You men are facing keen competition this year, perhaps facing more opposition than you ever faced in your lives, but I say that is the sort of thing you should thrill to—any kind of challenge. Any kind of organization ought to thrill to it. I think your organization, the Studebaker organization, has demonstrated that you can go better when the going is tough, so I say to you that this year you should thrill to this challenge.

The "White Angel Breadline" in San Francisco, 1933. (Copyright the Dorothea Lange Collection, Oakland Museum of California, City of Oakland. Gift of Paul S. Taylor)

CHAPTER FOUR

Crisis and Hope

21

AMERICAN EARTHQUAKE

American industrialization meant not only surging production but also periodic business "busts"—in the 1870s, the 1890s, 1907, and 1919–21. In each of these cases, prices, profits, and employment all plunged and remained low until the economy's basic strength pushed them again to higher levels. But no previous bust matched the Great Depression, which descended on the nation in the early 1930s. From 1929, when Herbert Hoover became the third consecutive Republican president since World War I, until 1933, when Franklin D. Roosevelt, a Democrat, succeeded him, the economy all but collapsed. Stocks and bonds lost three-fourths of their value, bank failures increased from five hundred to four thousand a year, farm income fell by half, and unemployment rose from 4 percent to almost 25 percent.

It was this last figure that most stunned and terrified ordinary Americans. There had been unemployment before, but never so much or for so long. And this joblessness was not limited to minorities or factory workers, as so often had been the case. The ranks of the destitute now included hundreds of thousands of white-collar workers, small businesspeople, and sharecroppers. Most disturbing of all, millions of women were now jobless and impoverished; many were homeless, with nowhere to turn. The country found it disquieting in the extreme.

People were aware of the massive human suffering of the Great Depression both because it was so widespread and because it was reported with such immediacy and attention to stark detail. Great fiction appeared, from Jack Conroy's *The Disinherited* at the beginning of the period to *The Grapes of Wrath*, John Steinbeck's epic of displaced Okies, at its end. Gripping photography and murals and innovative drama and poetry, glittering with unprecedented concreteness of detail, all depicted facets of the American ordeal. Journalism followed a similar path. Meridel LeSueur's article on Minnesota women, excerpted below, appeared in *New Masses*, a lively, irreverent Communist party literary journal that attracted and published much excellent social writing. In this case, the editors—staunch Stalinists—praised LeSueur's writing but also reproached her for defeatism and lack of "true revolutionary spirit."

Meridel LeSueur was born in 1900 in Iowa. Her grandfather was a Protestant fundamentalist temperance zealot; her father helped found the Industrial Workers of the World. After high school LeSueur attended the American Academy of Dramatic Art and worked in Hollywood as an actress and stuntwoman in the 1920s. During the 1930s she lived with her two children in Minneapolis while writing what a critic called "luminous short stories" as well as articles on farmers and the unemployed, especially women. Hailed in the 1930s as a major writer, she was blacklisted during the 1940s as a Communist sympathizer and lived by writing children's books and women's articles under a pseudonym. One of the first writers to examine the lives of poor women, her literary career revived during the 1970s with the emergence of feminism. Between 1971 and 1985 twelve of her books, new and old, appeared.

Questions to Consider. Who were the poor women LeSueur described in "Women on the Breadlines"? What did they have in common besides their poverty? Were they equally poor? Were their aspirations the same? How did their gender affect their condition and behavior during the Great Depression? How did they relate to one another, to authority figures, and to men? In later years conservatives would attack LeSueur for her radicalism. Can the reasons for these attacks be seen in this article? When Stalinists of the 1930s attacked her for being too negative and defeatist, were the attacks justified?

★━━★━━★

Women on the Breadlines (1932)

MERIDEL LESUEUR

I am sitting in the city free employment bureau. It's the woman's section. We have been sitting here now for four hours. We sit here every day, waiting for a job. There are no jobs. Most of us have had no breakfast. Some have had scant rations for over a year. Hunger makes a human being lapse into a state of lethargy, especially city hunger. Is there any place else in the world where a human being is supposed to go hungry amidst plenty without an outcry, without protest, where only the boldest steal or kill for bread, and the timid crawl the streets, hunger like the beak of a terrible bird at the vitals?

We sit looking at the floor. No one dares think of the coming winter. There are only a few more days of summer. Everyone is anxious to get work to lay

New Masses (January 1932), 5–7.

"Migrant Mother," a Dorothea Lange portrait of Florence Thompson, age 32, a Cherokee from Oklahoma in a California migrant labor camp. One of the foremost photographers of her time, Lange captured the pathos of the 1930s on film as brilliantly as Meridel LeSueur captured it in prose. (Library of Congress)

up something for that long siege of bitter cold. But there is no work. Sitting in the room we all know it. That is why we don't talk much. We look at the floor dreading to see that knowledge in each other's eyes. There is a kind of humiliation in it. We look away from each other. We look at the floor. It's too terrible to see this animal terror in each other's eyes.

So we sit hour after hour, day after day, waiting for a job to come in. There are many women for a single job. A thin sharp woman sits inside the wire cage looking at a book. For four hours we have watched her looking at that book. She has a hard little eye. In the small bare room there are half a dozen women sitting on the benches waiting. Many come and go. Our faces are all familiar to each other, for we wait here everyday.

This is a domestic employment bureau. Most of the women who come here are middle-aged, some have families, some have raised their families and are now alone, some have men who are out of work. Hard times and the man leaves to hunt for work. He doesn't find it. He drifts on. The woman probably doesn't hear from him for a long time. She expects it. She isn't surprised. She struggles alone to feed the many mouths. Sometimes she gets help from the charities. If she's clever she can get herself a good living from the charities, if she's naturally a lick-spittle, naturally a little docile and cunning. If she's proud then she starves silently, leaving her children to find work, coming home after a day's searching to wrestle with her house, her children.

Some such story is written on the faces of all these women. There are young girls too, fresh from the country. Some are made brazen too soon by the city. There is a great exodus of girls from the farms into the city now. Thousands of farms have been vacated completely in Minnesota. The girls are trying to get work. The prettier ones can get jobs in the stores when there are any, or waiting on table, but these jobs are only for the attractive and the adroit; the others, the real peasants, have a more difficult time. . . .

A young girl who went around with Ellen [a poor, attractive young woman] tells about seeing her last evening back of a cafe downtown outside the kitchen door, kicking, showing her legs so that the cook came out and gave her some food and some men gathered in the alley and threw small coin on the ground for a look at her legs. And the girl says enviously that Ellen had a swell breakfast and treated her to one too, that cost two dollars.

A scrub woman whose hips are bent forward from stooping with hands gnarled like water soaked branches clicks her tongue in disgust. No one saves their money, she says, a little money and these foolish young things buy a hat, a dollar for breakfast, a bright scarf. And they do. If you've ever been without money, or food, something very strange happens when you get a bit of money, a kind of madness. You don't care. You can't remember that you had no money before, that the money will be gone. You can remember nothing but that there is the money for which you have been suffering. Now here it is. A lust takes hold of you. You see food in the windows. In imagina-tion you eat hugely; you taste a thousand meals. You look in windows. Colours are brighter; you buy something to dress up in. An excitement takes hold of you. You know it is suicide but you can't help it. You must have food, dainty, splendid food and a bright hat so once again you feel blithe, rid of that ratty gnawing shame.

"I guess she'll go on the street now," a thin woman says faintly and no one takes the trouble to comment further. Like every commodity now the body is difficult to sell and the girls say you're lucky if you get fifty cents. . . .

It's one of the great mysteries of the city where women go when they are out of work and hungry. There are not many women in the bread line. There are no flop houses for women as there are for men, where a bed can be had for a quarter or less. You don't see women lying on the floor at the mission in the free flops. They obviously don't sleep in the jungle or under newspapers in the park. There is no law I suppose against their being in these places but the fact is they rarely are.

Yet there must be as many women out of jobs in cities and suffering extreme poverty as there are men. What happens to them? Where do they go? Try to get into the Y.W. without any money or looking down at heel. Charities take care of very few and only those that are called "deserving." The lone girl is under suspicion by the virgin women who dispense charity.

I've lived in cities for many months broke, without help, too timid to get in bread lines. I've known many women to live like this until they simply faint on the street from privations, without saying a word to anyone. A woman will shut herself up in a room until it is taken away from her, and eat a cracker a day and be as quiet as a mouse so there are no social statistics concerning her. . . .

Sometimes a girl facing the night without shelter will approach a man for lodging. A woman always asks a man for help. Rarely another woman. I have known girls to sleep in men's rooms for the night, on a pallet without molestation, and given breakfast in the morning. . . .

Mrs. Gray, sitting across from me is a living spokesman for the futility of labour. She is a warning. Her hands are scarred with labour. Her body is a great puckered scar. She has given birth to six children, buried three, supported them all alive and dead, bearing them, burying them, feeding them. Bred in hunger they have been spare, susceptible to disease. For seven years she tried to save her boy's arm from amputation, diseased from tuberculosis of the bone. It is almost too suffocating to think of that long close horror of years of child bearing, child feeding, rearing, with the bare suffering of providing a meal and shelter.

Now she is fifty. Her children, economically insecure, are drifters. She never hears of them. She doesn't know if they are alive. She doesn't know if she is alive. Such subtleties of suffering are not for her. For her the brutality of hunger and cold, the bare bone of life. That is enough. These will occupy a life. Not until these are done away with can those subtle feelings that make a human being be indulged.

She is lucky to have five dollars ahead of her. That is her security. She has a tumour that she will die of. She is thin as a worn dime with her tumour sticking out of her side. She is brittle and bitter. Her face is not the face of a human being. She has borne more than it is possible for a human being to bear. She is reduced to the least possible denominator of human feelings.

It is terrible to see her little bloodshot eyes like a beaten hound's, fearful in terror.

We cannot meet her eyes. When she looks at any of us we look away. She is like a woman drowning and we turn away. . . .

The young ones know though. I don't want to marry. I don't want any children. So they all say. No children. No marriage. They arm themselves alone, keep up alone. The man is helpless now. He cannot provide. If he propagates he cannot take care of his young. The means are not in his hands. So they live alone. Get what fun they can. The life risk is too horrible now. Defeat is too clearly written on it.

It is appalling to think that these women sitting so listless in the room may work as hard as it is possible for a human being to work, may labour night and day, like Mrs. Gray wash street cars from midnight to dawn and offices in the early evening, scrubbing for fourteen and fifteen hours a day, sleeping only five hours or so, doing this their whole lives, and never earn one day of security, having always before them the pit of the future. The endless labour, the bending back, the water soaked hands, earning never more than a week's wages, never having in their hands more life than that.

22

THE POLITICS OF UPHEAVAL

There are cycles in American presidential politics. Of the first nine presidential elections, for instance, Jefferson's Democratic Republicans won seven, the Federalists two. The Democrats also won six of the next nine elections. Then a new cycle began in which the Republicans won seven of nine elections from 1860 to 1892 (versus just two for the once-mighty Democrats) and also won seven of the next nine, with their only setbacks coming at the hands of Woodrow Wilson in 1912 and 1916. At this point, the cataclysm of the Great Depression and the charisma of Franklin D. Roosevelt returned the Democrats to dominance. They won, often by landslide margins, every election from 1932 to 1964, except for two losses to Dwight Eisenhower in the 1950s. Since then, however, they have reverted to their post–Civil War form, enabling the Nixon-Reagan-Bush-Bush GOP to post a six-to-three score through 2000.

Given the magnitude of the Great Depression and Franklin D. Roosevelt's role in triggering so massive a political realignment, his inaugural address in 1933 might appear moderate. It calls for confidence, honest labor, the protection of agriculture and land, organized relief, and a bit of economic planning. Only Roosevelt's castigation of the "money changers" and his plea for executive authority to meet the crisis seemed to prefigure the sweeping liberalism that many observers instinctively associate with the Roosevelt years. Nevertheless, the address was charged with emotion and a sense of mission. Its moderation reflected both the confusion of the times, when few people understood the nation's problems and still fewer had solutions, and the personal conservatism of the speaker, who was ultimately American capitalism's savior as well as its reformer.

Franklin Delano Roosevelt, a distant cousin of Theodore Roosevelt, was born in 1882 to a wealthy New York family. He attended exclusive schools and colleges and practiced law in New York City. He married his cousin Eleanor in 1905, entered Democratic politics—serving in the state senate from 1910 to 1913—and became assistant secretary of the navy in 1913. After running (and losing) as the Democrats' vice-presidential candidate in 1920, he contracted polio, which left him permanently crippled. Remaining active in politics, he served as governor of New York from 1928 to 1932, when he defeated Hoover for the presidency. During the 1932 campaign Roosevelt criticized Hoover for excessive government spending and an unbalanced budget. Nevertheless, after entering the White House, Roosevelt also was obliged to adopt a spending policy to help those who were starving, put people to work, and revive the economy. His New Deal stressed economic recovery as well as relief and reform. Roosevelt's programs, backed by the great Democratic majorities that he forged, mitigated many of the effects of the Great Depression, though the slump never actually ended until the advent of World War II. Roosevelt achieved reelection in 1936, 1940, and 1944, a record unequaled then and unconstitutional since 1951. He died in office in Warm Springs, Georgia, in 1945.

Questions to Consider. Why, in his first inaugural address, did Roosevelt place great emphasis on candor, honesty, and truth? Did he display these qualities himself in discussing the crisis? In what ways did he try to reassure the American people? What reasons did he give for the Great Depression? What values did he think were important for sustaining the nation in a time of trouble? What solutions did he propose for meeting the economic crisis? How did he regard his authority to act under the Constitution? How would you have reacted to his address if you had been an unemployed worker, a hard-pressed farmer, or a middle-class citizen who had lost a home through foreclosure?

★━━★━━★

First Inaugural Address (1933)

FRANKLIN D. ROOSEVELT

This is a day of national consecration, and I am certain that my fellow-Americans expect that on my induction into the Presidency I will address them with a candor and a decision which the present situation of our nation impels. This is pre-eminently the time to speak the truth, the whole truth, frankly and boldly. Nor need we shrink from honestly facing conditions in our country today. This great nation will endure as it has endured, will revive and will prosper.

So first of all let me assert my firm belief that the only thing we have to fear is fear itself—nameless, unreasoning, unjustified terror which paralyzes needed efforts to convert retreat into advance. In every dark hour of our

The New York Times, March 5, 1933.

national life a leadership of frankness and vigor has met with that under-standing and support of the people themselves which is essential to victory. I am convinced that you will again give that support to leadership in these critical days.

In such a spirit on my part and on yours we face our common difficulties. They concern, thank God, only material things. Values have shrunken to fan-tastic levels; taxes have risen; our ability to pay has fallen; government of all kinds is faced by serious curtailment of income; the means of exchange are frozen in the currents of trade; the withered leaves of industrial enterprise lie on every side; farmers find no markets for their produce; the savings of many years in thousands of families are gone.

More important, a host of unemployed citizens face the grim problem of existence, and an equally great number toil with little return. Only a foolish optimist can deny the dark realities of the moment.

Yet our distress comes from no failure of substance. We are stricken by no plague of locusts. Compared with the perils which our forefathers conquered because they believed and were not afraid, we have still much to be thankful for. Nature still offers her bounty and human efforts have multiplied it. Plenty is at our doorstep, but a generous use of it languishes in the very sight of the supply. Primarily, this is because the rulers of the exchange of mankind's goods have failed through their own stubbornness and their own incompetence, have admitted their failure and abdicated. Practices of the un-scrupulous money changers stand indicted in the court of public opinion, re-jected by the hearts and minds of men.

True, they have tried, but their efforts have been cast in the pattern of an outworn tradition. Faced by failure of credit, they have proposed only the lending of more money. Stripped of the lure of profit by which to induce our people to follow their false leadership, they have resorted to exhortations, pleading tearfully for restored confidence. They know only the rules of a generation of self-seekers. They have no vision, and when there is no vision the people perish.

The money changers have fled from their high seats in the temple of our civilization. We may now restore that temple to the ancient truths. The meas-ure of the restoration lies in the extent to which we apply social values more noble than mere monetary profit.

Happiness lies not in the mere possession of money; it lies in the joy of achievement, in the thrill of creative effort. The joy and moral stimulation of work no longer must be forgotten in the mad chase of evanescent profits. These dark days will be worth all they cost us if they teach us that our true destiny is not to be ministered unto but to minister to ourselves and to our fellow-men.

Recognition of the falsity of material wealth as the standard of success goes hand in hand with the abandonment of the false belief that public office and high political position are to be valued only by the standards of pride of place and personal profit; and there must be an end to a conduct in banking and in business which too often has given to a sacred trust the likeness of callous and selfish wrongdoing. Small wonder that confidence languishes, for it thrives only on honesty, on honor, on the sacredness of obligations, on faithful protection, on unselfish performance. Without them it cannot live.

Restoration calls, however, not for changes in ethics alone. This nation asks for action, and action now.

Our greatest primary task is to put people to work. This is no unsolvable problem if we face it wisely and courageously. It can be accomplished in part by direct recruiting by the Government itself, treating the task as we would treat the emergency of war, but at the same time, through this employment, accomplishing greatly needed projects to stimulate and reorganize the use of our natural resources.

Hand in hand with this, we must frankly recognize the overbalance of population in our industrial centers and, by engaging on a national scale in the redistribution, endeavor to provide a better use of the land for those best fitted for the land. The task can be helped by definite efforts to raise the values of agricultural products and with this the power to purchase the output of our cities. It can be helped by preventing realistically the tragedy of the growing loss, through foreclosure, of our small homes and our farms. It can be helped by insistence that the Federal, State and local governments act forthwith on the demand that their cost be drastically reduced. It can be helped by the unifying of relief activities which today are often scattered, uneconomical and unequal. It can be helped by national planning for a supervision of all forms of transportation and of communications and other utilities which have a definitely public character. There are many ways in which it can be helped, but it can never be helped merely by talking about it. We must act, and act quickly. . . .

This I propose to offer, pledging that the larger purposes will bind upon us all as a sacred obligation with a unity of duty hitherto evoked only in the time of armed strife.

With this pledge taken, I assume unhesitatingly the leadership of this great army of our people, dedicated to a disciplined attack upon our common problems.

Action in this image and to this end is feasible under the form of government which we have inherited from our ancestors. Our Constitution is so simple and practical that it is possible always to meet extraordinary needs by changes in emphasis and arrangement without loss of essential form. That is why our constitutional system has proved itself the most superbly enduring political mechanism the modern world has produced. It has met every stress of vast expansion of territory, of foreign wars, of bitter internal strife, of world relations.

It is to be hoped that the normal balance of executive and legislative authority may be wholly adequate to meet the unprecedented task before us.

But it may be that an unprecedented demand and need for undelayed action may call for temporary departure from that normal balance of public procedure.

I am prepared under my constitutional duty to recommend the measures that a stricken nation in the midst of a stricken world may require. These measures, or such other measures as the Congress may build out of its experience and wisdom, I shall seek, within my constitutional authority, to bring to speedy adoption.

But in the event that the Congress shall fail to take one of these two courses, and in the event that the national emergency is still critical, I shall not evade the clear course of duty that will then confront me. I shall ask the Congress for the one remaining instrument to meet the crisis—broad Executive power to wage a war against the emergency as great as the power that would be given me if we were in fact invaded by a foreign foe.

For the trust reposed in me I will return the courage and the devotion that befit the time. I can do no less. . . .

23

NEED AND AFFLICTION

The New Deal was a grab bag of efforts to cope with the ravages of the Great Depression. "It is common sense to take a method and try it," said Franklin Roosevelt. "If it fails, admit it frankly and try another. But above all, try something." Gradually, however, administration officials began to categorize New Deal measures in terms of their objectives: relief (emergency public works and aid to the poor); recovery (business price supports and low-interest loans); and reform (business regulation, progressive taxation, public housing, and electric power).

No legislation of the first Roosevelt administration was more significant than the Social Security Act of 1935, which provided for old-age pensions, unemployment compensation, and aid to the blind, crippled, and other dependents. Drafted by a committee chaired by Secretary of Labor Frances Perkins, adopted in part to appease radical critics such as Senator Huey Long of Louisiana, the social security program actually represented a fusion of all three New Deal goals. It expanded the relief effort, spurred recovery a bit by giving consumers more purchasing power, and laid the groundwork for a new system of economic security. Early benefits were modest and coverage limited. Even so, the measure embodied the unprecedented and far-reaching idea that society should provide, as a Democratic congressman put it, "security of the individual from birth to death." With the Social Security Act, the "welfare state" in a real sense began.

Frances Perkins was born in Boston in 1882. A college graduate and one-time schoolteacher and church worker, Perkins took advanced degrees in economics and worked from 1911 to 1933 in various New York agencies related to consumer protection and industrial safety. As one of Roosevelt's first and most important cabinet appointees, she became the first woman cabinet member in American history. A strong advocate and defender of innovative welfare and labor measures, Perkins was surrounded by controversy throughout her twelve-year tenure. Despite this, or perhaps because of it, she became one of the president's most trusted lieutenants. She died in New York City in 1965.

Questions to Consider. In legislation the "devil" is in the details, and in a complex measure like the Social Security Act there is much revealing detail. For example, to what extent might the act's attention to crippled children, vocational rehabilitation, public health work, and the blind have reflected the experience of President Roosevelt himself? What provisions of the act revealed the administration's desire to reassure congressmen that the social security system, a federal program, would respect the prerogatives of the states? Go through the provisions of the act to determine the different dollar amounts devoted to various parts of the program. What does this indicate about the government's priorities? Do the provisions for payments to retirees strike you as lavish?

The act targeted mothers and children as well as retirees and the handicapped. What particular group of mothers and children were considered most at risk and in need of help? How do you explain the fact that domestic workers and farm laborers, although added twenty years later, were excluded from retirement benefits in this original act? A "regressive" tax system takes a higher percentage of revenue from those at the bottom than at the top of the income ladder. Was the social security funding system "regressive" in this sense? Later laws capped the amount of wages to be taxed. Did this change make the system regressive?

★══★══★

The Social Security Act (1935)

FRANCES PERKINS

Title I—Grants to States for Old-Age Assistance

Appropriation

SECTION 1. For the purpose of enabling each State to furnish financial assistance, as far as practicable under the conditions in such State, to aged needy individuals, there is hereby authorized to be appropriated for the fiscal year ending June 30, 1936, the sum of $49,750,000, and there is hereby authorized to be appropriated for each fiscal year thereafter a sum sufficient to carry out the purposes of this title. The sums made available under this section shall be used for making payments to States which have submitted, and had approved by the Social Security Board established by Title VII, State plans for old-age assistance. . . .

U.S. Statutes at Large 49: 620ff.

Title II—Federal Old-Age Benefits

Old-Age Reserve Account

SECTION 201. (a) There is hereby created an account in the Treasury of the United States to be known as the "Old-Age Reserve Account." . . .

Old-Age Benefit Payments

SEC. 202. (a) Every qualified individual shall be entitled to receive, with respect to the period beginning on the date he attains the age of sixty-five, or on January 1, 1942, whichever is the later, and ending on the date of his death, an old-age benefit (payable as nearly as practicable in equal monthly installments) as follows:

(1) If the total wages determined by the Board to have been paid to him, with respect to employment after December 31, 1936, and before he attained the age of sixty-five, were not more than $3,000, the old-age benefit shall be at a monthly rate of one-half of 1 per centum of such total wages;

(2) If such total wages were more than $3,000, the old-age benefit shall be at a monthly rate equal to the sum of the following:

(A) One-half of 1 per centum of $3,000; plus

(B) One-twelfth of 1 per centum of the amount by which such total wages exceeded $3,000 and did not exceed $45,000; plus

(C) One-twenty-fourth of 1 per centum of the amount by which such total wages exceeded $45,000.

(b) In no case shall the monthly rate computed under subsection (a) exceed $85. . . .

Title III—Grants to States for Unemployment Compensation Administration

Appropriation

SECTION 301. For the purpose of assisting the States in the administration of their unemployment compensation laws, there is hereby authorized to be appropriated, for the fiscal year ending June 30, 1936, the sum of $4,000,000, and for each fiscal year thereafter the sum of $49,000,000, to be used as hereinafter provided. . . .

(b) The term "employment" means any service, of whatever nature, performed within the United States by an employee for his employer, except—

(1) Agricultural labor;

(2) Domestic service in a private home;

(3) Casual labor not in the course of the the employer's trade or business;

(4) Service performed as an officer or member of the crew of a vessel documented under the laws of the United States or of any foreign country;

(5) Service performed in the employ of the United States Government or of an instrumentality of the United States;

(6) Service performed in the employ of a State, a political subdivision thereof, or an instrumentality of one or more States or political subdivisions. . . .

Title IV—Grants to States for Aid to Dependent Children

Appropriation

Section 401. For the purpose of enabling each State to furnish financial assistance, as far as practicable under the conditions in such State, to needy dependent children, there is hereby authorized to be appropriated for the fiscal year ending June 30, 1936, the sum of $24,750,000, and there is hereby authorized to be appropriated for each fiscal year thereafter a sum sufficient to carry out the purposes of this title. The sums made available under this section shall be used for making payments to States which have submitted, and had approved by the Board, State plans for aid to dependent children. . . .

Definitions

Sec. 406. When used in this title—

(a) The term "dependent child" means a child under the age of sixteen who has been deprived of parental support or care by reason of the death, continued absence from the home, or physical or mental incapacity of a parent, and who is living with his father, mother, grandfather, grandmother, brother, sister, stepfather, stepmother, stepbrother, stepsister, uncle, or aunt, in a place of residence maintained by one or more of such relatives as his or their own home. . . .

Title V—Grants to States for Maternal and Child Welfare

Part 1—Maternal and Child Health Services

Appropriation

Section 501. For the purpose of enabling each State to extend and improve, as far as practicable under the conditions in such State, services for promoting the health of mothers and children, especially in rural areas and in areas suffering from severe economic distress, there is hereby authorized to be appropriated for each fiscal year, beginning with the fiscal year ending June 30, 1936, the sum of $3,800,000. The sums made available under this section shall be used for making payments to States which have submitted, and had approved by the Chief of the Children's Bureau, State plans for such services. . . .

Part 2—Services for Crippled Children

Appropriation

SEC. 511. For the purpose of enabling each State to extend and improve (especially in rural areas and in areas suffering from severe economic distress), as far as practicable under the conditions in such State, services for locating crippled children, and for providing medical, surgical, corrective, and other services and care, and facilities for diagnosis, hospitalization, and aftercare, for children who are crippled or who are suffering from conditions which lead to crippling, there is hereby authorized to be appropriated for each fiscal year, beginning with the fiscal year ending June 30, 1936, the sum of $2,850,000. The sums made available under this section shall be used for making payments to States which have submitted, and had approved by the Chief of the Children's Bureau, State plans for such services. . . .

Part 4—Vocational Rehabilitation

SEC. 531. (a) In order to enable the United States to cooperate with the States and Hawaii in extending and strengthening their programs of vocational rehabilitation of the physically disabled, and to continue to carry out the provisions and purposes of the Act entitled "An Act to provide for the promotion of vocational rehabilitation of persons disabled in industry or otherwise and their return to civil employment," approved June 2, 1920, . . . there is hereby authorized to be appropriated for the fiscal years ending June 30, 1936, and June 30, 1937, the sum of $841,000 for each such fiscal year in addition to the amount of the existing authorization, and for each fiscal year thereafter the sum of $1,938,000.

Title VI—Public Health Work

Appropriation

SECTION 601. For the purpose of assisting States, counties, health districts, and other political subdivisions of the States in establishing and maintaining adequate public-health services, including the training of personnel for State and local health work, there is hereby authorized to be appropriated for each fiscal year, beginning with the fiscal year ending June 30, 1936, the sum of $8,000,000 to be used as hereinafter provided. . . .

Title VII—Social Security Board

Establishment

SECTION 701. There is hereby established a Social Security Board to be composed of three members to be appointed by the President, by and with the advice and consent of the Senate. During his term of membership on the Board, no member shall engage in any other business, vocation, or employment. Not more than two of the members of the Board shall be members of the same political party. Each member shall receive a salary at the rate of $10,000 a year and shall hold office for a term of six years. . . .

Duties of Social Security Board

SEC. 702. The Board shall perform the duties imposed upon it by this Act and shall also have the duty of studying and making recommendations as to the most effective methods of providing economic security through social insurance, and as to legislation and matters of administrative policy concerning old-age pensions, unemployment compensation, accident compensation, and related subjects. . . .

Title VIII—Taxes With Respect to Employment

Income Tax on Employees

SECTION 801. In addition to other taxes, there shall be levied, collected, and paid upon the income of every individual a tax equal to the following percentages of the wages (as defined in section 811) received by him after December 31, 1936, with respect to employment (as defined in section 811) after such date:

(1) With respect to employment during the calendar years 1937, 1938, and 1939, the rate shall be 1 per centum . . . [and rise to 3 per centum in 1948].

Deduction of Tax from Wages

SEC. 802. (a) The tax imposed by section 801 shall be collected by the employer of the taxpayer, by deducting the amount of the tax from the wages as and when paid. . . .

Excise Tax on Employers

SEC. 804. In addition to other taxes, every employer shall pay an excise tax, with respect to having individuals in his employ, equal to the following percentages of the wages (as defined in section 811) paid by him after December 31, 1936, with respect to employment (as defined in section 811) after such date:

(1) With respect to employment during the calendar years 1937, 1938, and 1939, the rate shall be 1 per centum . . . [and 3 per centum by 1948].

Title IX—Tax on Employers of Eight or More

Imposition of Tax

SECTION 901. On and after January 1, 1936, every employer shall pay for each calendar year an excise tax, with respect to having individuals in his employ, equal to the following percentages of the total wages payable by him with respect to employment during such calendar year:

(1) With respect to employment during the calendar 1936 the rate shall be 1 per centum. . . .

(3) With respect to employment after December 31, 1937, the rate shall be 3 per centum. . . .

Certification of State Laws

SEC. 903. (a) The Social Security Board shall approve any State law submitted to it, within thirty days of such submission, which it finds provides that— . . .

(5) Compensation shall not be denied in such State to any otherwise eligible individual for refusing to accept new work under any of the following conditions: (A) If the position offered is vacant due directly to a strike, lockout, or other labor dispute; (B) if the wages, hours, or other conditions of the work offered are substantially less favorable to the individual than those prevailing for similar work in the locality; (C) if as a condition of being employed the individual would be required to join a company union or to resign from or refrain from joining any bona fide labor organization.

Title X—Grants to States for Aid to the Blind

Appropriation

SECTION 1001. For the purpose of enabling each State to furnish financial assistance, as far as practicable under the conditions in such State, to needy individuals who are blind, there is hereby authorized to be appropriated for the fiscal year ending June 30, 1936, the sum of $3,000,000, and there is hereby authorized to be appropriated for each fiscal year thereafter a sum sufficient to carry out the purposes of this title. The sums made available under this section shall be used for making payments to States which have submitted, and had approved by the Social Security Board, State plans for aid to the blind. . . .

24

ORGANIZING THE MASSES

Economic conditions in the 1930s had a tremendous impact on American labor. The Great Depression wreaked havoc with the lives of working people. By 1932, New York had a million jobless and Chicago another 600,000; 50 percent of Cleveland's workforce was unemployed, as was 60 percent of Akron's and 80 percent of Toledo's. Even those who still had jobs saw their wages and hours decline dramatically, and things did not greatly improve as the decade wore on.

The New Deal gave labor unions an opportunity to replenish their membership, which had plummeted to half of its World War I strength. The chief piece of legislation was the Labor Relations Act of 1935, which established a national board to keep employers from interfering with labor organizers or union members and to supervise union elections. Leaders of several large unions bolted the conservative American Federation of Labor (AFL) to form the Committee for Industrial Organization, which soon became the Congress of Industrial Organizations (CIO). The AFL emphasized craft unions (which were made up of workers in a given trade); the CIO insisted that industrial unions (which included all industrial workers, skilled and unskilled, in an industry) were essential in the mass-production industries in which labor previously had been unorganized. In 1936 and 1937 the CIO, led by John L. Lewis, president of the United Mine Workers, mounted successful, though bloody, organizing campaigns to establish unions in the steel, rubber, electrical, automobile, and other basic industries. The AFL soon responded with organizing drives of its own. Total union membership tripled by 1940.

Whatever the setting or the union, individual labor organizers bore the brunt of the struggle, urging workers to join unions, providing advice and shoe leather for organizing drives and job actions—all in the face of being fired, arrested, fined, jailed, or, on occasion, shot. Understandably, they used every tactic they thought would help, including one-on-one talks, group rallies, picket lines, leaflets, posters—and songs, which became an enormous part of the whole 1930s labor movement. The four reprinted below were all sung to traditional religious or folk melodies with limited range and a rocking rhythm for good group singing, usually to banjo or guitar accompaniment. One of them contains references to the mining conflicts of Harlan County, Kentucky; another, to the Michigan auto plant drive. Generally, the references were generic to the movement as a whole, making them applicable to any situation.

Questions to Consider. On the evidence of the songs, what were the goals of the great union drives of the Great Depression? Why did the organizers set them to traditional Protestant hymns or folk tunes? Why do you think group singing of this kind was an important tool for the organizers? Who, according to the songs, were the enemies of the workers? Two of the songs arose from conflicts in the country's coal mining regions, others from industrial settings. Can you detect any difference in the mining songs as opposed to the others? To what extent did the songs assume a certain level of intimidation and violence between workers and owners? To what extent did they seem to reinforce the idea of irreconcilable differences between workers and owners? To what extent did they indicate concern for middle-class public opinion? Would these songs, which were in fact helpful in labor organizing in the 1930s, be helpful today? If not, why not?

★═══★═══★

Four Union Songs (1930s)

1. Which Side Are You On?

Come all of you good workers,
Good news to you I'll tell
Of how the good old union
Has come in here to dwell.

My daddy was a miner
And I'm a miner's son,
And I'll stick with the union
Till ev'ry battle's won.

CHORUS: Tell me, which side are you on?
        Which side are you on?
        Which side are you on?
        Which side are you on?

They say in Harlan County
There are no neutrals there;
You'll either be a union man
Or a thug for J. H. Blair.

Oh, workers, can you stand it?
Oh, tell me how you can.
Will you be a lousy scab
Or will you be a man?

Don't scab for the bosses,
Don't listen to their lies.
Us poor folks haven't got a chance
Unless we organize.

2. Roll the Union On

CHORUS: We're gonna roll, we're gonna roll,
        We're gonna roll the union on!
        We're gonna roll, we're gonna roll,
        We're gonna roll the union on!

If the boss is in the way we're gonna roll right over him,
We're gonna roll right over him, we're gonna roll right over him.
If the boss is in the way we're gonna roll right over him;
We're gonna roll the union on!

If the scab is in the way we're gonna roll right over him,
We're gonna roll right over him, we're gonna roll right over him.
If the scab is in the way we're gonna roll right over him;
We're gonna roll the union on!

If the sheriff's in the way we're gonna roll right over him,
We're gonna roll right over him, we're gonna roll right over him.
If the sheriff's in the way we're gonna roll right over him;
We're gonna roll the union on!

3. We Shall Not Be Moved

The union is behind us; we shall not be moved.
The union is behind us; we shall not be moved.
Just like a tree standing by the water,
We shall not be moved.

CHORUS: We shall not be, we shall not be moved.
        We shall not be, we shall not be moved.
        Just like a tree standing by the water,
        We shall not be moved.

We're fighting for our freedom; we shall not be moved.
We're fighting for our freedom; we shall not be moved.
Just like a tree standing by the water,
We shall not be moved.

We're fighting for our children; we shall not be moved.
We're fighting for our children; we shall not be moved.
Just like a tree standing by the water,
We shall not be moved.

We'll build a mighty union; we shall not be moved.
We'll build a mighty union; we shall not be moved.
Just like a tree standing by the water,
We shall not be moved.

4. Sit Down!

When they tie a can
To a union man,
Sit down! Sit down!
When they give'm the sack,
They'll take him back,
Sit down! Sit down!

CHORUS: Sit down, just take a seat,
Sit down, and rest your feet,
Sit down, you've got 'em beat,
Sit down! Sit down!

When they smile and say,
"No raise in pay,"
Sit down! Sit down!
When you want the boss
To come across,
Sit down! Sit down!

When the speed-up comes,
Just twiddle your thumbs,
Sit down! Sit down!
When you want 'em to know
They'd better go slow,
"Sit down! Sit down!

When the boss won't talk,
Don't take a walk,
Sit down! Sit down!
When the boss sees that,
He'll want a chat;
Sit down! Sit down!

25

THE RIGHTS OF LABOR

Until the late 1930s the federal judiciary was largely unsympathetic to the American trade union movement. Between 1880 and 1930 judges issued 4,300 injunctions against workers attempting to strike for better wages, hours, and working conditions. In many cases federal or National Guard troops enforced the injunctions at gunpoint, leading to a practice that union leaders called "Gatling gun injunctions." The courts also prohibited "secondary boycotts" that tried to pressure employers to settle strikes or face organized consumer retaliation.

The Great Depression witnessed a shift in the political climate as the reputation and standing of both corporations and the Republican party declined, and the Supreme Court shifted accordingly. In 1935, for example, the Court struck down the National Industrial Recovery Act (NIRA), a key piece of New Deal legislation, as an infringement on states' rights and the right of contract. But in 1937 it upheld not only the constitutionality of the National Labor Relations Act, which Congress had passed in 1935 to enhance the organizing efforts of labor, but specific rulings of the National Labor Relations Board, the federal agency established by the 1935 act.

National Labor Relations Board v. *Jones & Laughlin Steel* (excerpted below) has been called the Magna Carta and even the Emancipation Proclamation of the American labor movement because it seemed to guarantee the union organizing rights that generations of workers had sought. It was in practice nothing of the kind, since its protections and guarantees were gradually whittled down by more conservative Court decisions and acts of Congress, beginning in the 1940s. But it was important at the time. Moreover, by construing "interstate commerce" in a very broad way, the decision gave Congress unprecedented authority to regulate the American economy, a view that has largely endured. In this sense, *NLRB* v. *Jones & Laughlin* marked perhaps the most dramatic about-face in the history of the Supreme Court.

Charles Evans Hughes, the author of the 1937 decision, was born in 1862 in upstate New York. He attended Brown University, practiced law in New York City, and won fame for exposing abusive insurance company practices. A lifelong Republican, he had served two terms as governor when President William Howard Taft appointed him to the Supreme Court in 1910. In 1916 Hughes resigned from the Court in order to run for president against Woodrow Wilson. Defeated, he returned to the law until 1921, when he became Warren G. Harding's secretary of state. In 1930 Herbert Hoover appointed him chief justice of the Supreme Court, where he was moderately supportive of civil liberties, civil rights, and (despite voting in 1935 to strike down the NIRA) expansive federal economic powers, as in his *NLRB* v. *Jones & Laughlin* opinion. Hughes resigned from the Court for the last time in 1941. He died in Massachusetts in 1948.

Questions to Consider. What led Charles Evans Hughes to devote more space to a description of the operations of the Jones & Laughlin Steel Corporation than to any other part of his opinion? Hughes argued here that workers needed the right to form labor unions because an individual worker, dependent on his daily wage to survive, had no power to bargain with a big business except collectively with other workers. Was this a reasonable argument given the conditions of the American economy in the 1930s? Do you find it still persuasive today? Hughes defended his position in defense of union organizing rights in part by arguing (next to last paragraph below) that collective bargaining agreements would promote industrial peace. Some constitutional lawyers have detected a fundamental contradiction between support for union rights and the goal of industrial peace. Are they right? If this is a contradiction, is it an important one?

★═══★═══★

National Labor Relations Board v. Jones & Laughlin Steel (1937)

CHARLES EVANS HUGHES

In a proceeding under the National Labor Relations Act of 1935, the National Labor Relations Board found that the petitioner, Jones & Laughlin Steel Corporation, had violated the Act by engaging in unfair labor practices affecting commerce. . . .

The National Labor Relations Board . . . ordered the corporation to cease and desist from such discrimination and coercion, to offer reinstatement to ten of the employees named, to make good their losses in pay, and to post for thirty days notices that the corporation would not discharge or discriminate against members, or those desiring to become members, of the labor union. . . .

NLRB v. *Jones & Laughlin Steel,* 301 U.S. 1 (1937).

The facts as to the nature and scope of the business of the Jones & Laughlin Steel Corporation have been found by the Labor Board and, so far as they are essential to the determination of this controversy, they are not in dispute. The Labor Board has found: The corporation is organized under the laws of Pennsylvania and has its principal office at Pittsburgh. It is engaged in the business of manufacturing iron and steel in plants situated in Pittsburgh and nearby Aliquippa, Pennsylvania. It manufactures and distributes a widely diversified line of steel and pig iron, being the fourth largest producer of steel in the United States. With its subsidiaries—nineteen in number—it is a completely integrated enterprise, owning and operating ore, coal and limestone properties, lake and river transportation facilities and terminal railroads located at its manufacturing plants. It owns or controls mines in Michigan and Minnesota. It operates four ore steamships on the Great Lakes, used in the transportation of ore to its factories. It owns coal mines in Pennsylvania. It operates towboats and steam barges used in carrying coal to its factories. It owns limestone properties in various places in Pennsylvania and West Virginia. It owns the Monongahela connecting railroad which connects the plants of the Pittsburgh works and forms an interconnection with the Pennsylvania, New York Central and Baltimore and Ohio Railroad systems. It owns the Aliquippa and Southern Railroad Company which connects the Aliquippa works with the Pittsburgh and Lake Erie, part of the New York Central system. Much of its product is shipped to its warehouses in Chicago, Detroit, Cincinnati and Memphis,—to the last two places by means of its own barges and transportation equipment. In Long Island City, New York, and in New Orleans it operates structural steel fabricating shops in connection with the warehousing of semi-finished materials sent from its works. Through one of its wholly-owned subsidiaries it owns, leases and operates stores, warehouses and yards for the distribution of equipment and supplies for drilling and operating oil and gas mills and for pipe lines, refineries and pumping stations. It has sales offices in twenty cities in the United States and a wholly-owned subsidiary which is devoted exclusively to distributing its product in Canada. Approximately 75 per cent of its product is shipped out of Pennsylvania.

Summarizing these operations, the Labor Board concluded that the works in Pittsburgh and Aliquippa "might be likened to the heart of a self-contained, highly integrated body. They draw in the raw materials from Michigan, Minnesota, West Virginia, Pennsylvania in part through arteries and by means controlled by the respondent; they transform the materials and then pump them out to all parts of the nation through the vast mechanism which the respondent has elaborated."

To carry on the activities of the entire steel industry, 33,000 men mine ore, 44,000 men mine coal, 4,000 men quarry limestone, 16,000 men manufacture coke, 343,000 men manufacture steel, and 83,000 men transport its product. Respondent has about 10,000 employees in its Aliquippa plant, which is located in a community of about 30,000 persons.

Practically all the factual evidence in the case, except that which dealt with the nature of respondent's business, concerned its relations with the employees in the Aliquippa plant whose discharge was the subject of the complaint. These employees were active leaders in the labor union. . . .

The right of employees to self-organization and to select representatives of their own choosing for collective bargaining or other mutual protection without restraint or coercion by their employer . . . is a fundamental right. Employees have as clear a right to organize and select their representatives for lawful purposes as the respondent has to organize its business and select its own officers and agents. Discrimination and coercion to prevent the free exercise of the right of employees to self-organization and representation is a proper subject for condemnation by competent legislative authority. Long ago we stated the reason for labor organizations. We said that they were organized out of the necessities of the situation; that a single employee was helpless in dealing with an employer; that he was dependent ordinarily on his daily wage for the maintenance of himself and family; that if the employer refused to pay him the wages that he thought fair, he was nevertheless unable to leave the employ and resist arbitrary and unfair treatment; that union was essential to give laborers opportunity to deal on an equality with their employer. . . . Fully recognizing the legality of collective action on the part of employees in order to safeguard their proper interests, we said that Congress was not required to ignore this right but could safeguard it. Congress could seek to make appropriate collective action of employees an instrument of peace rather than of strife. We said that such collective action would be a mockery if representation were made futile by interference with freedom of choice. . . .

Experience has abundantly demonstrated that the recognition of the right of employees to self-organization and to have representatives of their own choosing for the purpose of collective bargaining is often an essential condition of industrial peace. Refusal to confer and negotiate has been one of the most prolific causes of strife. This is such an outstanding fact in the history of labor disturbances that it is a proper subject of judicial notice and requires no citation of instances. But with respect to the appropriateness of the recognition of self-organization and representation in the promotion of peace, the question is not essentially different in the case of employees in industries of such a character that interstate commerce is put in jeopardy from the case of employees of transportation companies. And of what avail is it to protect the facility of transportation, if interstate commerce is throttled with respect to the commodities to be transported!

Our conclusion is that the order of the Board was within its competency and that the Act is valid as here applied.

26

War Aims

Circumstances change, said Franklin D. Roosevelt, and so did he as president, from (in other words) "Mr. New Deal" facing the dangers of the Great Depression in the 1930s to "Mr. Win-the-War" facing the dangers of the Axis Powers in the 1940s. Historians have sometimes seen the coming of war as a discontinuity in his administration.

But the break was not so sharp as it might have been. One thread providing continuity was that Roosevelt was never disinterested in world affairs, even during the most urgent days of the Depression. As the Nazi threat to France and England and the Japanese threat to China grew in the late 1930s, so did Roosevelt's determination to help—if he could do so without declaring war. Another thread was that Roosevelt perceived the looming conflict partly in ideological terms—as a struggle, with the forces of authoritarianism and social reaction pitted against the forces of democracy and social progress. To some extent, Roosevelt's view of the conflict resembled Woodrow Wilson's goal in World War I of making the world "safe for democracy." It also followed logically from the nature of the enemy, which most people regarded as nothing but a coalition of racist, militaristic tyrants. Opposing such an enemy meant, by extension, opposing what the enemy stood for.

In his "Four Freedoms" address, delivered to Congress and broadcast to the public in January 1941—prior to America's formal entry into the war—Roosevelt went beyond Woodrow Wilson in his statement of war goals. In this speech, as in others he delivered over the next four years, the president made it clear that he considered this war to be not just about freedom of speech, press, and religion, as his predecessors might have it. This was also a war about freedom from want, the philosophy underlying many of the New Deal programs. And it was about freedom from fear, a sentiment that had filled his first inaugural address eight years before. At least in this 1941 statement, "Mr. Win-the-War" continued to be "Mr. New Deal."

Questions to Consider. Isolationist, antiwar feelings were still very strong in the country in early 1941. How did Roosevelt try at the beginning of his speech to neutralize antiwar sentiment? At what point in the address did he introduce what might be considered progressive political ideas of the kind that characterized the New Deal? According to Roosevelt, what were the foundations of "a healthy and strong democracy"? Would all Americans have agreed with his list of democratic "foundations"? Why did the president demand individual sacrifice and warn people not to try to get rich from his programs? Of the "four freedoms" Roosevelt eventually enumerated, which do you think would have been most popular in the 1940s?

★═══★═══★

The Four Freedoms (1941)

FRANKLIN D. ROOSEVELT

I address you, the Members of the Seventy-seventh Congress, at a moment unprecedented in the history of the Union. I use the word "unprecedented," because at no previous time has American security been as seriously threatened from without as it is today. . . .

Every realist knows that the democratic way of life is at this moment being directly assailed in every part of the world—assailed either by arms, or by secret spreading of poisonous propaganda by those who seek to destroy unity and promote discord in nations still at peace.

During sixteen months this assault has blotted out the whole pattern of democratic life in an appalling number of independent nations, great and small. The assailants are still on the march, threatening other nations, great and small.

Therefore, as your President, performing my constitutional duty to "give to the Congress information on the state of the Union," I find it necessary to report that the future and the safety of our country and of our democracy are overwhelmingly involved in events far beyond our borders.

Armed defense of democratic existence is now being gallantly waged in four continents. If that defense fails, all the population and all the resources of Europe, Asia, Africa, and Australasia will be dominated by the conquerors. The total of those populations and their resources greatly exceeds the sum total of the population and resources of the whole of the Western Hemisphere—many times over. . . .

No realistic American can expect from a dictator's peace international generosity, or return of true independence, or world disarmament, or freedom of expression, or freedom of religion—or even good business.

The New York Times, January 7, 1941.

Such a peace would bring no security for us or for our neighbors. Those who would give up essential liberty to purchase a little temporary safety deserve neither liberty nor safety. . . .

There is much loose talk of our immunity from immediate and direct invasion from across the seas. Obviously, as long as the British Navy retains its power, no such danger exists. Even if there were no British Navy, it is not probable that any enemy would be stupid enough to attack us by landing troops in the United States from across thousands of miles of ocean, until it had acquired strategic bases from which to operate.

But we learn much from the lessons of the past years in Europe—particularly the lesson of Norway, whose essential seaports were captured by treachery and surprise built up over a series of years. . . .

As long as the aggressor nations maintain the offensive, they, not we, will choose the time and the place and the method of their attack. . . .

Let us say to the democracies, "We Americans are vitally concerned in your defense of freedom. We are putting forth our energies, our resources, and our organizing powers to give you the strength to regain and maintain a free world. We shall send you, in ever-increasing numbers, ships, planes, tanks, guns. This is our purpose and our pledge."

In fulfillment of this purpose we will not be intimidated by the threats of dictators that they will regard as a breach of international law and as an act of war our aid to the democracies which dare to resist their aggression. Such aid is not an act of war, even if a dictator should unilaterally proclaim it so to be.

When the dictators are ready to make war upon us, they will not wait for an act of war on our part. They did not wait for Norway or Belgium or The Netherlands to commit an act of war.

Their only interest is in a new one-way international law, which lacks mutuality in its observance and, therefore, becomes an instrument of oppression. . . .

As men do not live by bread alone, they do not fight by armaments alone. Those who man our defenses, and those behind them who build our defenses, must have the stamina and courage which come from an unshakable belief in the manner of life which they are defending. The mighty action which we are calling for cannot be based on a disregard of all things worth fighting for.

There is nothing mysterious about the foundations of a healthy and strong democracy. The basic things expected by our people of their political and economic systems are simple.

They are:

Equality of opportunity for youth and for others.
Jobs for those who can work.
Security for those who need it.
The ending of special privilege for the few.
The preservation of civil liberties for all.
The enjoyment of the fruits of scientific progress in a wider and constantly rising standard of living.

These are the simple and basic things that must never be lost sight of in the turmoil and unbelievable complexity of our modern world. The inner and abiding strength of our economic and political systems is dependent upon the degree to which they fulfill these expectations. . . .

I have called for personal sacrifice. I am assured of the willingness of almost all Americans to respond to that call.

A part of the sacrifice means the payment of more money in taxes. . . .

No person should try, or be allowed to get rich out of this program. . . .

In the future days, which we seek to make secure, we look forward to a world founded upon four essential human freedoms.

The first is freedom of speech and expression, everywhere in the world.

The second is freedom of every person to worship God in his own way, everywhere in the world.

The third is freedom from want, which, translated into world terms, means economic understandings which will secure to every nation a healthy peacetime life for its inhabitants, everywhere in the world.

The fourth is freedom from fear—which, translated into world terms, means a worldwide reduction of armaments to such a point and in such a thorough fashion that no nation will be in a position to commit an act of physical aggression against any neighbor—anywhere in the world.

That is no vision of a distant millennium. It is a definite basis for a kind of world attainable in our own time and not the so-called new order of tyranny which the dictators seek to impose. That kind of world is the very antithesis of the kind created with the crash of a bomb.

To that new order we oppose the greater conception—the moral order. A good society is able to face schemes of world domination and foreign revolutions alike without fear.

Since the beginning of our American history we have been engaged in change—in a perpetual peaceful revolution—a revolution which goes on steadily, quietly adjusting itself to changing conditions—without the concentration camp or the quicklime in the ditch. The world order which we seek is the cooperation of free countries, working together in a friendly, civilized society.

This Nation has placed its destiny in the hands and heads and hearts of its millions of free men and women; and its faith in freedom under the guidance of God. Freedom means the supremacy of human rights everywhere. Our support goes to those who struggle to gain those rights or keep them. Our strength is in our unity of purpose.

To that high concept there can be no end save victory.

27

SHATTERING THE AXIS

Franklin D. Roosevelt was in the White House not only through most of America's bitterest economic collapse but through its biggest, costliest, and at that time longest war. A brutal slog from 1941 to 1945 that drew over twelve million Americans into military duty on four continents and five oceans and tens of millions more into vital war industries, World War II was in many ways the defining event in modern world history. As head of state and commander in chief of a major combatant nation, Roosevelt found his communications and political skills challenged as they had not been even during the Great Depression. He therefore understandably turned to the most important of the era's mass media, one that he had long used to good effect: radio.

Politicians had broadcast speeches over radio as early as the 1920s, and many more began to as mass-production techniques steadily lowered the price of radio sets. By 1930 most households with electricity owned a radio or had access to a neighbor's for important announcements. Radio brought the human voice, and therefore the human being, into people's living rooms for family listening in a way that newspapers, consumed individually, or movies, consumed outside the home, did not. But for a long time politicians thought of radio microphones the way they thought of meeting-hall microphones, as electronic megaphones to shout into. It was not until the 1930s that people realized that the radio wasn't a megaphone—but an ear, into which you could speak in a neighborly, conversational way, like someone visiting far-flung families around their fireside.

Franklin Roosevelt proved a radio master. During the 1930s he gave a dozen so-called fireside chats—informal-sounding talks about what he was doing and hoped to do to address the challenges of the Depression. He gave even more during the war years. The excerpts below are from his fireside chat of July 28, 1943. American and British troops had just moved from their conquest of North Africa to the conquest of the Mediterranean island of Sicily, just off the southern coast of Nazi Germany's Axis ally, Italy. The troops were now preparing to invade Italy proper. Roosevelt here was celebrating the collapse of the Fascist government of Benito Mussolini from the shock of the Allied conquest and invasion.

And, as usual, he did more. He reiterated the Allies' determination to fight on to "total victory" and the "unconditional surrender" of the Axis, which Roosevelt believed was imperative to prevent a third world war. He nodded in the direction of the United Nations, the new world body that he hoped would help keep the postwar peace. He applauded America's other major ally, Russia, a Communist country not wildly popular but one that had seriously wounded the Germans in titanic battles at Stalingrad and Kursk. He reminded listeners of the hard struggles to come and personalized the foe as not only "Herr Hitler" but "Tojo," the hard-line Japanese prime minister. Lastly, having emphasized the need for home-front sacrifice to sustain the fighting men, he proposed a major new postwar veterans' program, which materialized the following year as the "GI Bill," a package of educational, medical, and other benefits that touched the lives of millions and became, with social security and support for organized labor, one of the major legacies of the Roosevelt era.

Questions to Consider. Roosevelt's talks were famous at the time for their clear, simple language and easy-to-grasp examples and metaphors—their "chattiness." On the evidence of the excerpts below, was this reputation warranted? How did the president attempt to make his case that the battlefront and the home front were in some ways the same, all linked together in a common struggle? What was he trying to accomplish or forestall in stressing the challenges that lay ahead even more than the immediate triumphs? Where in the "chat" did he appear to acknowledge the existence of domestic political opposition? What seems to have been the nature of that opposition? Why did he go out of his way to give credit to the Russians? Why do you think he characterized the regimes of Germany and Japan as "gangs" for his domestic audience? Did he set up his proposal for a big new domestic program in an effective way?

★▪▪▪★▪▪▪★

A Fireside Chat (1943)

FRANKLIN D. ROOSEVELT

My fellow Americans. Over a year and a half ago I said this to the Congress: "The militarists in Berlin and Rome and Tokyo started this war. But the massed, angered forces of common humanity will finish it."

Samuel I. Rosenman, ed., *The Public Papers and Addresses of Franklin D. Roosevelt,* vol. II (Harper and Brothers, New York, 1950).

Today that prophecy is in the process of being fulfilled. The massed, angered forces of common humanity are on the march. They're going forward—on the Russian front, in the vast Pacific area, and into Europe—converging upon their ultimate objectives: Berlin and Tokyo.

I think the first crack in the Axis has come. The criminal, corrupt Fascist regime in Italy is going to pieces.

The pirate philosophy of the Fascists and the Nazis cannot stand adversity. The military superiority of the United Nations—on sea and land and in the air—has been applied in the right place and at the right time.

Hitler refused to send sufficient help to save Mussolini. In fact, Hitler's troops in Sicily stole the Italians' motor equipment, leaving Italian soldiers so stranded that they had no choice but to surrender. Once again the Germans betrayed their Italian allies, as they had done time and time again on the Russian front and in the long retreat from Egypt, through Libya and Tripoli, to the final surrender in Tunisia.

And so Mussolini came to the reluctant conclusion that the "jig was up"; he could see the shadow of the long arm of justice.

But he and his Fascist gang will be brought to book, and punished for their crimes against humanity. No criminal will be allowed to escape by the expedient of "resignation."

So our terms to Italy are still the same as our terms to Germany and Japan—"unconditional surrender." . . .

In every country conquered by the Fascists and the Nazis, or the Japanese militarists, the people have been reduced to the status of slaves or chattels.

It is our determination to restore these conquered peoples to the dignity of human beings, masters of their own fate, entitled to freedom of speech, freedom of religion, freedom from want, and freedom from fear.

We have started to make good on that promise.

I am sorry if I step on the toes of those Americans who, playing party politics at home, call that kind of foreign policy "crazy altruism" and "starry-eyed dreaming." . . .

It's a little over a year since we planned the North African campaign. It is six months since we planned the Sicilian campaign. I confess that I am of an impatient disposition, but I think that I understand and that most people understand the amount of time necessary to prepare for any major military or naval operation. We cannot just pick up the telephone and order a new campaign to start the next week.

For example, behind the invasion forces in North Africa, the invasion forces that went out of North Africa, were thousands of ships and planes guarding the long, perilous sea lanes, carrying the men, carrying the equipment and the supplies to the point of attack. And behind all these were the railroad lines and the highways here back home that carried the men and the munitions to the ports of embarkation—there were the factories and the mines and the farms here back home that turned out the materials—there were the training camps here back home where the men learned how to perform the strange and difficult and dangerous tasks which were to meet them on the beaches and in the deserts and in the mountains.

All this had to be repeated, first in North Africa and then in Sicily. Here in Sicily the factor of air attack was added—for we could use North Africa as the base for softening up the landing places and the lines of defense in Sicily and the lines of supply in Italy.

It is interesting for us to realize that every Flying Fortress that bombed harbor installations at, for example, Naples, bombed it from its base in North Africa, required 1,110 gallons of gasoline for each single flight and that this is the equal of about 375 "A" ration tickets—enough gas to drive your car five times across this continent. You will better understand your part in the war—and what gasoline rationing means—if you multiply this by the gasoline needs of thousands of planes and hundreds of thousands of jeeps and trucks and tanks that are now serving overseas. . . .

Those few Americans who grouse and complain about the inconveniences of life here in the United States should learn some lessons from the civilian populations of our allies—Britain and China and Russia—and of all the lands occupied by our common enemy.

The heaviest and most decisive fighting today is going on in Russia. I am glad that the British and we have been able to contribute somewhat to the great striking power of the Russian armies.

In 1941–42 the Russians were able to retire without breaking, to move many of their war plants from western Russia far into the interior, to stand together with complete unanimity in the defense of their homeland.

The success of the Russian armies has shown that it is dangerous to make prophecies about them—a fact which has been forcibly brought home to that mystic master of strategic intuition, Herr Hitler. . . .

In the Pacific, we are pushing the Japs around from the Aleutians to New Guinea. There too we have taken the initiative—and we are not going to let go of it.

It becomes clearer and clearer that the attrition, the whittling down process against the Japanese is working. The Japs have lost more planes and more ships than they have been able to replace. . . .

The same kind of careful planning that gained victory in North Africa and Sicily is required, if we are to make victory an enduring reality and do our share in building the kind of peaceful world that will justify the sacrifices made in this war.

The United Nations are substantially agreed on the general objectives for the postwar world. They are also agreed that this is not the time to engage in an international discussion of *all* the terms of peace and *all* the details of the future. Let us win the war first. We must not relax our pressure on the enemy by taking time out to define every boundary and settle every political controversy in every part of the world. The important thing, the all-important thing now is to get on with the war—and to win it.

While concentrating on military victory, we are not neglecting the planning of the things to come, the freedoms which we know will make for more decency and greater justice throughout the world.

Among many other things we are, today, laying plans for the return to civilian life of our gallant men and women in the armed services. They must not be demobilized into an environment of inflation and unemployment, to a place on a breadline, or on a corner selling apples. We must, this time, have plans ready—instead of waiting to do a hasty, inefficient, and ill-considered job at the last moment. . . .

Of course, the returning soldier and sailor and marine are a part of the problem of demobilizing the rest of the millions of Americans who have been working and living in a war economy since 1941. That larger objective of reconverting wartime America to a peacetime basis is one for which your government is laying plans to be submitted to the Congress for action.

But the members of the armed forces have been compelled to make greater economic sacrifice and every other kind of sacrifice than the rest of us, and they are entitled to definite action to help take care of their special problems.

The least to which they are entitled, it seems to me, is something like this:

First, mustering-out pay to every member of the armed forces and merchant marine when he or she is honorably discharged; mustering-out pay large enough in each case to cover a reasonable period of time between his discharge and the finding of a new job.

Secondly, in case no job is found after diligent search, then unemployment insurance if the individual registers with the United States Employment Service.

Third, an opportunity for members of the armed services to get further education or trade training at the cost of their government.

Fourth, allowance of credit to all members of the armed forces, under unemployment compensation and federal old-age and survivors' insurance, for their period of service. For these purposes they ought to be treated as if they had continued their employment in private industry.

Fifth, improved and liberalized provisions for hospitalization, for rehabilitation, for medical care of disabled members of the armed forces and the merchant marine.

And finally, sufficient pensions for disabled members of the armed forces. . . .

The plans we made for the knocking out of Mussolini and his gang have largely succeeded. But we still have to knock out Hitler and his gang, and Tojo and his gang. No one of us pretends that this will be an easy matter. . . .

We shall not settle for less than total victory. That is the determination of every American on the fighting front. That must be, and will be, the determination of every American here at home.

28

Destroyer of Worlds

American strategy in the Pacific war was to "island-hop" toward Japan, occupying undefended atolls where possible and taking others by amphibious assault where necessary. This oceanic march began in 1942 with a painful, costly victory at Guadalcanal, northeast of Australia. It culminated in 1945 at Okinawa, off southern Japan, in a gruesome fight that produced 150,000 casualties. Meanwhile, the United States had proved its new air capability with the victory of its carrier-based planes at Midway in 1942 and with long-range bombing of the Japanese mainland after 1943. Finally, as American soldiers grouped to invade Japan in mid-1945, President Harry S. Truman warned the Japanese that unless they surrendered by August 3 they would face "prompt and utter destruction." When they did not surrender, he ordered that an atomic bomb be dropped on Hiroshima on August 6 and another on Nagasaki on August 9.

The concept of the atomic bomb was brought to the United States by scientists fleeing Nazi Germany and Fascist Italy. In 1939, after suggestions from scientist Albert Einstein that the Germans might develop nuclear weapons, President Roosevelt authorized a National Defense Research Committee, which in turn led to the top-secret Manhattan Project for developing the bomb. By 1945, nuclear plants in Tennessee and Washington had produced enough fissionable material to construct a test bomb, which was exploded spectacularly in the New Mexico desert in July. One of the first decisions that President Truman faced upon succeeding Roosevelt in office concerned using the bomb against Japan. Why he ordered the use of the bomb continues to be debated. He claimed he did so to avoid a bloody land assault that would have cost many lives—American and Japanese. Some historians suggest he did so to demonstrate U.S. power to the Russians. Nevertheless, the effects of the bomb itself were soon clear. More than 100,000 Japanese died from the two blasts.

While on assignment in late 1945 and 1946, John Hersey, a journalist covering the Far East for major American periodicals, prepared an account of how the bomb affected individual Japanese. Though most Allied leaders regarded the atomic bomb as just another big bomb, the excerpts from Hersey's *Hiroshima* reprinted below make clear that in its capacity for devastation the bomb dwarfed all other weapons of war.

John Hersey was born in 1914 in Tientsin, China, to American missionary parents, and became a journalist in the late 1930s after study at Yale University and Cambridge University in England. His first major work was *Men on Bataan* (1942), based on a series of interviews. A stream of books based on interviews and news clippings soon followed, including *Into the Valley* (1943), about a company of marines on Guadalcanal, and *Hiroshima* (1946). Hersey won the Pulitzer Prize for *A Bell for Adano* (1944), a story about the American occupation of Italy.

Questions to Consider.   *Hiroshima* probably continues to be the most widely read and influential study of the effects of the dropping of the bomb. What clues in the excerpts below help explain this popularity? Is it strictly a consequence of Hersey's strategy of focusing on individuals? Might his style of writing also be a factor? Why does Hersey tell us about the blind soldiers? Is it the blindness that moves us, or the fact that these blind are soldiers? Why did Hersey choose to make two of his six main characters, Dr. Fujii and Dr. Sasaki, medical men? Why is one of the six, Father Kleinsorge, not Japanese? Some U.S. officials were upset, even angry, that *Hiroshima* was so popular. What passage in the excerpts do you think might have caused such official distress?

Hiroshima (1946)

JOHN HERSEY

The lot of Drs. Fujii, Kanda, and Machii right after the explosion—and, as these three were typical, that of the majority of the physicians and surgeons of Hiroshima—with their offices and hospitals destroyed, their equipment scattered, their own bodies incapacitated in varying degrees, explained why so many citizens who were hurt went untended and why so many who might have lived died. Of a hundred and fifty doctors in the city, sixty-five were already dead and most of the rest were wounded. Of 1,780 nurses, 1,654 were dead or too badly hurt to work. In the biggest hospital, that of the Red Cross, only six doctors out of thirty were able to function, and only ten nurses out of more than two hundred. The sole uninjured doctor on the Red

Hiroshima, Japan, two years after the dropping of the atomic bomb. After three years and $2 billion invested in secret research and production, the United States exploded the first atomic device at Alamogordo, New Mexico, on July 16, 1945. A scientist who was there said it was as if "the earth had opened and the skies had split or like the moment of creation when God said, 'Let there be light.'" Although the catastrophic power of the weapon was clear, President Truman never really considered not using it. The latest estimates indicate that a quarter of a million people died in the atomic attacks on Hiroshima and Nagasaki. (Corbis-Bettmann)

Cross Hospital staff was Dr. Sasaki. After the explosion, he hurried to a storeroom to fetch bandages. This room, like everything he had seen as he ran through the hospital, was chaotic—bottles of medicines thrown off shelves and broken, salves spattered on the walls, instruments strewn everywhere. He grabbed up some bandages and an unbroken bottle of mercurochrome, hurried back to the chief surgeon, and bandaged his cuts. Then he went out into the corridor and began patching up the wounded patients and the doctors and nurses there. He blundered so without his glasses that he took a pair off the face of a wounded nurse, and although they only approximately compensated for the errors of his vision, they were better than nothing. (He was to depend on them for more than a month.)

Dr. Sasaki worked without method, taking those who were nearest him first, and he noticed soon that the corridor seemed to be getting more and

more crowded. Mixed in with the abrasions and lacerations which most people in the hospital had suffered, he began to find dreadful burns. He realized
then that casualties were pouring in from outdoors. There were so many that
he began to pass up the lightly wounded; he decided that all he could hope
to do was to stop people from bleeding to death. Before long, patients lay and
crouched on the floors of the wards and the laboratories and all the other
rooms, and in the corridors, and on the stairs, and in the front hall, and under the portecochère, and on the stone front steps, and in the driveway and
courtyard, and for blocks each way in the streets outside. Wounded people
supported maimed people; disfigured families leaned together. Many people
were vomiting. A tremendous number of schoolgirls—some of those who
had been taken from their classrooms to work outdoors, cleaning fire lanes—
crept into the hospital. In a city of two hundred and forty-five thousand,
nearly a hundred thousand people had been killed or doomed at one blow; a
hundred thousand more were hurt. At least ten thousand of the wounded
made their way to the best hospital in town, which was altogether unequal to
such a trampling, since it had only six hundred beds, and they had all been
occupied. The people in the suffocating crowd inside the hospital wept and
cried, for Dr. Sasaki to hear, "*Sensei!* Doctor!" and the less seriously wounded
came and pulled at his sleeve and begged him to go to the aid of the worse
wounded. Tugged here and there in his stockinged feet, bewildered by the
numbers, staggered by so much raw flesh, Dr. Sasaki lost all sense of the profession and stopped working as a skillful surgeon and a sympathetic man;
he became an automaton, mechanically wiping, daubing, winding, wiping,
daubing, winding. . . .

The morning, again, was hot. Father Kleinsorge went to fetch water for the
wounded in a bottle and a teapot he had borrowed. He had heard that it was
possible to get fresh tap water outside Asano Park. Going through the rock
gardens, he had to climb over and crawl under the trunks of fallen pine trees;
he found he was weak. There were many dead in the gardens. At a beautiful
moon bridge, he passed a naked, living woman who seemed to have been
burned from head to toe and was red all over. Near the entrance to the park,
an Army doctor was working, but the only medicine he had was iodine,
which he painted over cuts, bruises, slimy burns, everything—and by now
everything he painted had pus on it. Outside the gate of the park, Father
Kleinsorge found a faucet that still worked—part of the plumbing of a vanished house—and he filled his vessels and returned. When he had given the
wounded the water, he made a second trip. This time, the woman by the
bridge was dead. On his way back with the water, he got lost on a detour
around a fallen tree, and as he looked for his way through the woods, he
heard a voice ask from the underbrush, "Have you anything to drink?" He
saw a uniform. Thinking there was just one soldier, he approached with the
water. When he had penetrated the bushes, he saw there were about twenty
men, and they were all in exactly the same nightmarish state: their faces were

wholly burned, their eyesockets were hollow, the fluid from their melted eyes had run down their cheeks. (They must have had their faces upturned when the bomb went off; perhaps they were anti-aircraft personnel.) Their mouths were mere swollen, pus-covered wounds, which they could not bear to stretch enough to admit the spout of the teapot. So Father Kleinsorge got a large piece of grass and drew out the stem so as to make a straw, and gave them all water to drink that way. One of them said, "I can't see anything." Father Kleinsorge answered, as cheerfully as he could, "There's a doctor at the entrance to the park. He's busy now, but he'll come soon and fix your eyes, I hope." . . .

Early that day, August 7th, the Japanese radio broadcast for the first time a succinct announcement that very few, if any, of the people most concerned with its content, the survivors in Hiroshima, happened to hear: "Hiroshima suffered considerable damage as the result of an attack by a few B-29s. It is believed that a new type of bomb was used. The details are being investigated." Nor is it probable that any of the survivors happened to be tuned in on a short-wave rebroadcast of an extraordinary announcement by the president of the United States, which identified the new bomb as atomic: "That bomb had more power than twenty thousand tons of TNT. It had more than two thousand times the blast power of the British Grand Slam, which is the largest bomb ever yet used in the history of warfare." Those victims who were able to worry at all about what had happened thought of it and discussed it in more primitive, childish terms—gasoline sprinkled from an airplane, maybe, or some combustible gas, or a big cluster of incendiaries, or the work of parachutists; but, even if they had known the truth, most of them were too busy or too weary or too badly hurt to care that they were the objects of the first great experiment in the use of atomic power, which (as the voices on the short wave shouted) no country except the United States, with its industrial know-how, its willingness to throw two billion gold dollars into an important wartime gamble, could possibly have developed. . . .

Dr. Sasaki and his colleagues at the Red Cross Hospital watched the unprecedented disease unfold and at last evolved a theory about its nature. It had, they decided, three stages. The first stage had been all over before the doctors even knew they were dealing with a new sickness; it was the direct reaction to the bombardment of the body, at the moment when the bomb went off, by neutrons, beta particles, and gamma rays. The apparently uninjured people who had died so mysteriously in the first few hours or days had succumbed in this first stage. It killed ninety-five per cent of the people within a half-mile of the center, and many thousands who were farther away. The doctors realized in retrospect that even though most of these dead had also suffered from burns and blast effects, they had absorbed enough radiation to kill them. The rays simply destroyed body cells—caused their nuclei to degenerate and broke their walls. Many people who did not die right away came down with nausea, headache, diarrhea, malaise, and fever, which lasted several days. Doctors could not be certain whether some of these symptoms were the result of radiation or nervous shock. The second stage set in ten or fifteen days after the bombing. Its first symptom was falling hair. Diarrhea and fever, which in some cases went as high as 106, came next. Twenty-five to thirty days after the explosion, blood disorders appeared: gums bled, the white-blood-cell count dropped sharply, and *petechiae* [eruptions] appeared on the skin and mucous membranes. The drop in the number of white blood corpuscles reduced the patient's capacity to resist infection, so open wounds were unusually slow in healing and many of the sick developed sore throats and mouths. The two key symptoms, on which the doctors came to base their prognosis, were fever and the lowered white-corpuscle count. If fever remained steady and high, the patient's chances for survival were poor. The white count almost always dropped below four thousand; a patient whose count fell below one thousand had little hope of living. Toward the end of the second stage, if the patient survived, anemia, or a drop in the red blood count, also set in. The third stage was the reaction that came when the body struggled to compensate for its ills—when, for instance, the white count not only returned to normal but increased to much higher than normal levels. In this stage, many patients died of complications, such as infections in the chest cavity. Most burns healed with deep layers of pink, rubbery scar tissue, known as keloid tumors. The duration of the disease varied, depending on the patient's constitution and the amount of radiation he had received. Some victims recovered in a week; with others the disease dragged on for months.

As the symptoms revealed themselves, it became clear that many of them resembled the effects of overdoses of X-ray, and the doctors based their therapy on that likeness. They gave victims liver extract, blood transfusions, and vitamins, especially B_1. The shortage of supplies and instruments hampered them. Allied doctors who came in after the surrender found plasma and penicillin very effective. Since the blood disorders were, in the long run, the predominant factor in the disease, some of the Japanese doctors evolved a theory as to the seat of the delayed sickness. They thought that perhaps gamma rays, entering the body at the time of the explosion, made the phosphorus in the victims' bones radioactive, and that they in turn emitted beta particles, which, though they could not penetrate far through flesh, could enter the bone marrow, where blood is manufactured, and gradually tear it down. Whatever its source, the disease had some baffling quirks. Not all the patients exhibited all the main symptoms. People who suffered flash burns were protected, to a considerable extent, from radiation sickness. Those who had lain quietly for days or even hours after the bombing were much less liable to get sick than those who had been active. Gray hair seldom fell out. And, as if nature were protecting man against his own ingenuity, the reproductive processes were affected for a time; men became sterile, women had miscarriages, menstruation stopped. . . .

A surprising number of the people of Hiroshima remained more or less indifferent about the ethics of using the bomb. Possibly they were too terrified by it to want to think about it at all. Many citizens of Hiroshima, however, continued to feel a hatred for Americans which nothing could possibly erase. "I see," Dr. Sasaki once said, "that they are holding a trial for war criminals in Tokyo just now. I think they ought to try the men who decided to use the bomb and they should hang them all."

Father Kleinsorge and the other German Jesuit priests, who as foreigners, could be expected to take a relatively detached view, often discussed the ethics of using the bomb. One of them, Father Siemes, who was out at Nagatsuka [Hiroshima suburb] at the time of the attack, wrote in a report to the Holy See in Rome: "Some of us consider the bomb in the same category as poison gas and were against its use on a civilian population. Others were of the opinion that in total war, as carried on in Japan, there was no difference between civilians and soldiers, and that the bomb itself was an effective force tending to end the bloodshed, warning Japan to surrender and thus to avoid total destruction. It seems logical that he who supports total war in principle cannot complain of a war against civilians. The crux of the matter is whether total war in its present form is justifiable, even when it serves a just purpose. Does it not have material and spiritual evil as its consequences which far exceed whatever good might result? When will our moralists give us a clear answer to this question?"

An anti-Vietnam riot. Confrontations during the Vietnam era were often emotional and violent. (Corbis-Bettmann)

CHAPTER FIVE

Protracted Conflict

29

REBUILDING EUROPE

Franklin D. Roosevelt fought World War II for internationalist ideals. Concerned to preserve and extend democracy, Roosevelt was equally determined to help create a new international order in which the United States would play a major role, as it had not after World War I. Roosevelt was therefore profoundly committed to the establishment of the United Nations, which he helped bring into being during the war and whose U.N. Relief and Rehabilitation Administration (largely supported by the United States) distributed millions of dollars of aid to war-torn regions of the world. He was also committed to using America's industrial resources to help the Allied countries wage total war, which he effected through the immense U.S. Lend-Lease program of wartime and postwar economic and military assistance.

Roosevelt died before the war ended, and both Lend-Lease and UNRRA ceased functioning in 1947. Yet Roosevelt's legacy of generous internationalism endured into the Truman administration, particularly as regards Europe, which American policymakers considered vital to U.S. interests. And postwar Europe was in fact in serious trouble, unable to rebuild or even feed itself, threatened, it seemed, by an adversarial Soviet Union, and facing economic collapse and political upheaval.

In 1947 the State Department urged President Truman to coordinate and expand the remaining U.S. aid efforts and use them to promote real revival rather than mere relief. In June Secretary of State George C. Marshall delivered an address at Harvard University outlining a major U.S. economic recovery program for Europe. Non-Communist Europe responded immediately and positively. Truman signed the measure into law in April 1948.

Aid began to flow almost immediately—over $12 billion over the next three years. The "Marshall Plan," as it came to be called, fed people, put coal and oil in furnaces, rebuilt factories and city services, furthered the economic integration of Europe, and laid the groundwork for the social democracy that characterized western Europe for the next half-century. The farsightedness of the plan stemmed partly from the fact that the Americans were rebuilding an industrialized Europe that would eventually compete with them. But they helped anyway, believing that a prosperous and stable Europe would be good for the United States. Moreover, since the plan required the Europeans to spend the assistance on American products, it boosted the U.S. economy as well. It may be that except for World War II itself, the Marshall Plan was the single most successful large-scale diplomatic initiative in American history.

George C. Marshall was born in Uniontown, Pennsylvania, in 1880. Marshall graduated from Virginia Military Institute in 1901, became an army officer, served in the Philippines, attended the army's General Staff School, and filled high staff posts during World War I. In 1939 Roosevelt appointed Marshall army chief of staff, responsible for organizing, training, supplying, and deploying U.S. troops. He held this post until 1945, becoming, in many eyes, the greatest chief of staff of any nation in World War II. Marshall served President Truman as secretary of state from 1947 to 1949 and as secretary of defense early in the Korean conflict. In 1953 he received the Nobel Prize for Peace for his work on European recovery. He died in Washington in 1959.

Questions to Consider. Marshall's task was to persuade the United States to break with its peacetime tradition of minimal foreign aid by emphasizing the importance of a stable Europe to world peace. Did he appeal mainly to altruism or to self-interest? Did he suggest anywhere that the task of helping Europe rebuild was going to be bigger than people expected? What factors might explain why Marshall, in this address, stressed the huge importance of trade between cities and the countryside? Was he perhaps sketching, among other things, a free-trade model for a future European economy? Did he expect the United States to make basic political and economic decisions for Europe as well as to provide assistance? The Marshall Plan has been called the last act of the Second World War and also the first act of the Cold War. How would George Marshall have characterized it? Why might he have decided to give this important policy statement at Harvard University? Why did he end it with a series of questions?

★━━★━━★

Harvard Commencement Address (1947)

GEORGE C. MARSHALL

I need not tell you that the world situation is very serious. . . . [But] the people of this country are distant from the troubled areas of the earth and it is

The New York Times, June 6, 1947. Reprinted by permission of The George C. Marshall Research Library.

hard for them to comprehend the plight and consequent reactions of the long-suffering peoples of Europe, and the effect of those reactions on their governments in connection with our efforts to promote peace in the world.

In considering the requirements for the rehabilitation of Europe, the physical loss of life, the visible destruction of cities, factories, mines, and railroads was correctly estimated, but it has become obvious during recent months that this visible destruction was probably less serious than the dislocation of the entire fabric of European economy. For the past ten years conditions have been highly abnormal. The feverish preparation for war and the more feverish maintenance of the war effort engulfed all aspects of national economies. Machinery has fallen into disrepair or is entirely obsolete. Under the arbitrary and destructive Nazi rule, virtually every possible enterprise was geared into the German war machine.

Long-standing commercial ties, private institutions, banks, insurance companies, and shipping companies disappeared through loss of capital, absorption through nationalization, or by simple destruction. In many countries, confidence in the local currency has been severely shaken. The breakdown of the business structure of Europe during the war was complete. Recovery has been seriously retarded by the fact that two years after the close of hostilities a peace settlement with Germany and Austria has not been agreed upon. But even given a more prompt solution of these difficult problems, the rehabilitation of the economic structure of Europe quite evidently will require a much longer time and greater effort than had been foreseen.

There is a phase of this matter which is both interesting and serious. The farmer has always produced the foodstuffs to exchange with the city dweller for the other necessities of life. This division of labor is the basis of modern civilization. At the present time it is threatened with breakdown. The town and city industries are not producing adequate goods to exchange with the food-producing farmer. Raw materials and fuel are in short supply. Machinery is lacking or worn out. The farmer or the peasant cannot find the goods for sale which he desires to purchase. So the sale of his farm produce for money, which he cannot use, seems to him an unprofitable transaction. He, therefore, has withdrawn many fields from crop cultivation and is using them for grazing. He feeds more grain to stock and finds for himself and his family an ample supply of food, however short he may be on clothing and the other ordinary gadgets of civilization. Meanwhile, people in the cities are short of food and fuel, and in some places approaching the starvation levels. So the governments are forced to use their foreign money and credits to procure these necessities abroad. This process exhausts funds which are urgently needed for reconstruction. Thus a very serious situation is rapidly developing which bodes no good for the world. The modern system of the division of labor upon which the exchange of products is based is in danger of breaking down.

The truth of the matter is that Europe's requirements for the next three or four years of foreign food and other essential products—principally from

America—are so much greater than her present ability to pay that she must have substantial additional help or face economic, social, and political deterioration of a very grave character.

The remedy seems to lie in breaking the vicious circle and restoring the confidence of the European people in the economic future of their own countries and of Europe as a whole. The manufacturer and the farmer throughout wide areas must be able and willing to exchange their products for currencies, the continuing value of which is not open to question. . . .

Our policy is directed not against any country or doctrine but against hunger, poverty, desperation, and chaos. Its purpose should be the revival of a working economy in the world so as to permit the emergence of political and social conditions in which free institutions can exist. Such assistance, I am convinced, must not be on a piecemeal basis as various crises develop. Any assistance that this government may render in the future should provide a cure rather than a mere palliative. Any government that is willing to assist in the task of recovery will find full cooperation, I am sure, on the part of the United States Government. Any government which maneuvers to block the recovery of other countries cannot expect help from us. Furthermore, governments, political parties, or groups which seek to perpetuate human misery in order to profit therefrom politically or otherwise will encounter the opposition of the United States.

It is already evident that, before the United States Government can proceed much further in its efforts to alleviate the situation and help start the European world on its way to recovery, there must be some agreement among the countries of Europe as to the requirements of the situation and the part those countries themselves will take in order to give proper effect to whatever action might be undertaken by this Government. It would be neither fitting nor efficacious for this Government to undertake to draw up unilaterally a program designed to place Europe on its feet economically. This is the business of the Europeans. The initiative, I think, must come from Europe. The role of this country should consist of friendly aid in the drafting of a European program and of later support of such a program so far as it may be practical for us to do so. The program should be a joint one, agreed to by a number [of], if not all, European nations. . . .

To my mind, it is of vast importance that our people reach some general understanding of what the complications really are, rather than react from a passion or a prejudice or an emotion of the moment. As I said more formally a moment ago, we are remote from the scene of these troubles. It is virtually impossible at this distance merely by reading, or listening, or even seeing photographs or motion pictures, to grasp at all the real significance of the situation. And yet the whole world of the future hangs on a proper judgment. It hangs, I think to a large extent on the realization of the American people, of just what are the various dominant factors. What are the reactions of the people? What are the justifications of those reactions? What are the sufferings? What is needed? What can best be done? What must be done?

30

SEEING REDS

In 1946 Joseph R. McCarthy defeated progressive Senator Robert M. La Follette, Jr., in the Republican primary in Wisconsin and went on to win election to the U.S. Senate that fall. During the primary contest he was supported by Wisconsin Communists who were infuriated by La Follette's pre–Pearl Harbor anti-interventionism and by his criticisms of Soviet dictator Joseph Stalin. Asked about the support the Communists were giving him against La Follette, McCarthy said airily, "The Communists have votes, too, don't they?" Four years later he became the leader of an impassioned crusade against Communism, and the word "McCarthyism" came to mean a reckless and demagogic assault on domestic dissent.

McCarthyism did not operate in a vacuum. Revelations of Communist spy activity in Canada, England, and the United States after World War II produced demands for counterespionage measures, and in 1947 President Truman inaugurated a loyalty program to ferret out Communists in government. Meanwhile, a series of "spy" cases hit the headlines: the trial and conviction of eleven Communist leaders under the Smith Act for conspiring to advocate the violent overthrow of the government; the conviction of former State Department official Alger Hiss, denounced as a Communist spy, for perjury; and the trial and execution of Julius and Ethel Rosenberg, government workers charged with passing atomic secrets to the Russians. For many Americans, the distinction between the expression of unpopular ideas and deliberate conspiratorial activity on behalf of a foreign power became increasingly blurred. In 1950, Senator McCarthy obliterated the distinction.

In a radio speech (excerpted below) given in Wheeling, West Virginia, in February 1950, McCarthy announced that he had in his hand a list of Communists in the State Department "known to the Secretary of State" and "still working and making policy." Overnight McCarthy became a national figure. Although he never showed anyone his famous "list" and was increasingly vague about the precise number of names it contained (205 or 81 or 57 or "a lot"), he came to exercise great influence in the U.S. Senate and in the nation. In July 1950, a Senate subcommittee headed by Maryland's Millard Tydings dismissed

McCarthy's charges as "a fraud and a hoax." But when Tydings, a conservative Democrat, ran for reelection that fall, McCarthy's insinuations that he was pro-Communist helped defeat him. Similar accusations helped defeat Connecticut Democrat William Benton in 1952.

Not every Republican admired Senator McCarthy or approved his tactics, even when they benefited Republican candidates. Margaret Chase Smith of Maine, the only woman in the U.S. Senate in 1950, had served with McCarthy on the Permanent Investigations Subcommittee of the Senate and had become perturbed by his lack of concern for the unfair damage the subcommittee might do to individuals' reputations. Smith became still more perturbed following McCarthy's West Virginia speech in February 1950 about Communists in the State Department. When the Democrats failed to rebut McCarthy's charges effectively, she determined to speak out. Six other Republican senators endorsed Smith's "Declaration of Conscience."

It would take more than a statement by a handful of Senate Republicans to halt Joe McCarthy. In 1951 McCarthy charged that George C. Marshall, President Truman's former secretary of state and of defense, was part of "a conspiracy so immense and infamy so black as to dwarf any previous venture in the history of man." During the 1952 presidential campaign McCarthy talked ominously of "twenty years of treason" under the Democrats. His followers identified Roosevelt's New Deal, Truman's Fair Deal, and, indeed, all efforts for social reform since the Great Depression as Communist inspired. In 1953, as chairman of the Senate Committee on Government Operations, McCarthy launched a series of investigations of federal agencies, including the Voice of America, the International Information Agency, and the Army Signal Corps installation at Fort Monmouth, New Jersey. When the army decided to fight back, McCarthyism reached its climax in a series of televised Senate hearings in the spring of 1954. During these hearings, the Wisconsin senator's accusations and defamations of character gradually alienated all but his most devoted followers. On July 30, Republican Senator Ralph Flanders of Vermont, who had not endorsed Margaret Chase Smith's 1950 Declaration, introduced a resolution of censure. In December, the Senate voted, 67 to 32, to censure McCarthy for his behavior.

Joseph R. McCarthy was born in Grand Chute, Wisconsin, in 1908 to middle-class Roman Catholic parents. He graduated from Marquette University and entered the legal profession in Wisconsin in 1935. Originally a Democrat, he won his first political race (for a local judgeship) as a Republican in 1939. After serving as a Marine from 1942 to 1944, he became a state Republican power with his defeat of La Follette in the 1946 senatorial race. McCarthy's strongest bases of support were Wisconsin's small business owners and voters of German heritage; they reelected him in 1952 and largely continued their support even after his fall from national popularity. He died at the Bethesda Naval Hospital in Maryland in 1957.

Questions to Consider. Why did McCarthy launch his attack in 1950 rather than in 1949 or 1951? What area of the world most concerned him and what had happened there to give his message impact? Why did he attack from an out-of-the-way place (Wheeling, West Virginia) rather than from Washington or even his home state, Wisconsin, and why, moreover, on the radio? What reasons might McCarthy have had for singling out the State Department for attack, rather than, for example, the Department of Defense or the Department of Justice? In view of the fact that seven twentieth-century presidents and even more secretaries of state had attended just four private colleges (Yale, Harvard, Princeton, and Amherst), was there a certain logic in men such as Mc-Carthy trying to link a Communist conspiracy with a conspiracy of "those who have had all the benefits"?

■══■══■

Lincoln Day Address (1950)

JOSEPH R. MCCARTHY

Ladies and gentlemen, tonight as we celebrate the one hundred and forty-first birthday of one of the greatest men in American history, I would like to be able to talk about what a glorious day today is in the history of the world. As we celebrate the birth of this man who with his whole heart and soul hated war, I would like to be able to speak of peace in our time, of war being out-lawed, and of worldwide disarmament. These would be truly appropriate things to be able to mention as we celebrate the birthday of Abraham Lincoln.

Five years after a world war has been won, men's hearts should anticipate a long peace, and men's minds should be free from the heavy weight that comes with war. But this is not such a period—for this is not a period of peace. This is a time of the "cold war." This is a time when all the world is split into two vast, increasingly hostile armed camps—a time of a great armaments race.

Today we are engaged in a final, all-out battle between Communistic atheism and Christianity. The modern champions of Communism have selected this as the time. And, ladies and gentlemen, the chips are down—they are truly down.

Six years ago, at the time of the first conference to map out the peace—Dumbarton Oaks—there was within the Soviet orbit 180 million people.

The Congressional Record, 81st Congress, v. 96, part 2 (February 20, 1950).

Lined up on the antitotalitarian side there were in the world roughly 1,625 million people. Today, only six years later, there are 800 million people under the absolute domination of Soviet Russia—an increase of over 400 percent. On our side, the figure has shrunk to around 500 million. In other words, in less than six years the odds have changed from 9 to 1 in our favor to 8 to 5 against us. This indicates the swiftness of the tempo of Communist victories and American defeats in the cold war. As one of our outstanding historical figures once said, "When a great democracy is destroyed, it will not be because of enemies from without, but rather because of enemies from within."

The truth of this statement is becoming terrifyingly clear as we see this country each day losing on every front. . . .

The reason why we find ourselves in a position of impotency is not because our only powerful potential enemy has sent men to invade our shores, but rather because of the traitorous actions of those who have been treated so well by this Nation. It has not been the less fortunate or members of minority groups who have been selling this Nation out, but rather those who have had all the benefits that the wealthiest nation on earth has had to offer—the finest homes, the finest college education, and the finest jobs in Government we can give.

This is glaringly true in the State Department. There the bright young men who are born with silver spoons in their mouths are the ones who have been worst. . . .

When Chiang Kai-shek was fighting our war, the State Department had in China a young man named John S. Service. His task, obviously, was not to work for the Communization of China. Strangely, however, he sent official reports back to the State Department urging that we torpedo our ally Chiang Kai-shek and stating, in effect, that Communism was the best hope for China.

Later, this man—John Service—was picked up by the Federal Bureau of Investigation for turning over to the Communists secret State Department information. Strangely, however, he was never prosecuted. However, Joseph Grew, the Under Secretary of State, who insisted on his prosecution, was forced to resign. Two days after Grew's successor, Dean Acheson, took over as Under Secretary of State, this man—John Service—who had been picked up by the FBI and who had previously urged that Communism was the best hope of China, was not only reinstated in the State Department but promoted. And finally, under Acheson, placed in charge of all placements and promotions.

Today, ladies and gentlemen, this man Service is on his way to represent the State Department and Acheson in Calcutta—by far and away the most important listening post in the Far East. . . .

This, ladies and gentlemen, gives you somewhat of a picture of the type of individuals who have been helping to shape our foreign policy. In my opinion the State Department, which is one of the most important government departments, is thoroughly infested with Communists.

I have in my hand 57 cases of individuals who would appear to be either card carrying members or certainly loyal to the Communist Party, but who nevertheless are still helping to shape our foreign policy.

One thing to remember in discussing the Communists in our Government is that we are not dealing with spies who get 30 pieces of silver to steal the blueprints of a new weapon. We are dealing with a far more sinister type of activity because it permits the enemy to guide and shape our policy. . . .

As you hear this story of high treason, I know that you are saying to yourself, "Well, why doesn't the Congress do something about it?" Actually, ladies and gentlemen, one of the important reasons for the graft, the corruption, the dishonesty, the disloyalty, the treason in high Government positions—one of the most important reasons why this continues is a lack of moral uprising on the part of the 140 million American people. In the light of history, however, this is not hard to explain.

It is the result of an emotional hangover and a temporary moral lapse which follows every war. It is the apathy to evil which people who have been subjected to the tremendous evils of war feel. As the people of the world see mass murder, the destruction of defenseless and innocent people, and all of the crime and lack of morals which go with war, they become numb and apathetic. It has always been thus after war.

However, the morals of our people have not been destroyed. They still exist. This cloak of numbness and apathy has only needed a spark to rekindle them. Happily, this spark has finally been supplied.

As you know, very recently the Secretary of State [Dean Acheson] proclaimed his loyalty to a man [Alger Hiss] guilty of what has always been considered as the most abominable of all crimes—of being a traitor to the people who gave him a position of great trust. The Secretary of State in attempting to justify his continued devotion to the man who sold out the Christian world to the atheistic world, referred to Christ's Sermon on the Mount as a justification and reason therefor, and the reaction of the American people to this would have made the heart of Abraham Lincoln happy.

When this pompous diplomat in striped pants, with a phony British accent, proclaimed to the American people that Christ on the Mount endorsed Communism, high treason, and betrayal of a sacred trust, the blasphemy was so great that it awakened the dormant indignation of the American people.

He has lighted the spark which is resulting in a moral uprising and will end only when the whole sorry mess of twisted, warped thinkers are swept from the national scene so that we may have a new birth of national honesty and decency in Government.

31

A QUESTION OF COMMAND

In 1950 the cold war between the United States and the Soviet Union turned suddenly hot in Korea, a peninsula abutting China near Japan. Korea had been freed from Japanese rule at the end of World War II, divided at the 38th parallel, and occupied by Russian troops in the north and American troops in the south. The Russians installed a friendly regime in North Korea and then withdrew; the United Nations, at U.S. urging, did the same in South Korea. On June 25, 1950, North Korean armies suddenly crossed the 38th parallel and launched a full-scale invasion of South Korea. President Truman, seeing the hand of China and therefore of the Soviet Union behind this move, promptly committed American troops to the defense of South Korea. He won the backing of the United Nations for his action and announced American determination to support anticommunist governments throughout East Asia. The Korean War lasted from June 1950 until the armistice of July 1953. Under United Nations auspices, sixteen nations participated in the conflict against North Korea. South Korea remained independent, but the Korean War cost the United States $22 billion and 34,000 dead.

The Korean War also prompted a major reassertion of the constitutional primacy of civilian rule in the U.S. government. The United Nations commander in the Korean theater was General Douglas MacArthur, one of the greatest U.S. heroes of World War II and the American proconsul in charge of transforming postwar Japanese society. Against the advice of the American joint chiefs of staff, MacArthur launched a brilliant amphibious landing behind Communist lines. He then recaptured the capital city of Seoul and moved far enough into North Korea to reach the border with China.

MacArthur had gambled that China would not commit troops to the conflict; President Truman's advisers feared it would. MacArthur was wrong. Massive Chinese forces poured across the border, pushing U.N. forces back down the peninsula. Embarrassed, MacArthur publicly called for President Truman to order massive air strikes on China. The president, fearing a long and costly land war with China, refused the general's request and asked him not to argue U.S. policy in the newspapers. MacArthur again called for air attacks on China, took a swipe at the American doctrine of limited (non-nuclear and geographically restricted) war, and implied that Truman was practicing appeasement. President Truman had had enough: On April 10, 1951, he fired MacArthur for insubordination. On April 11 he gave the following radio address to the American public. MacArthur returned home to an enormous ticker-tape parade, an invitation to address a joint session of Congress, and a brief flirtation with Republican Party kingpins. But Matthew Ridgway now commanded U.N. forces in Korea, Harry Truman was still president and commander in chief—and the long-established Constitutional subordination of military to civilian authority again held firm.

Harry S. Truman was born on a farm near Independence, Missouri, in 1884. After graduating from high school, he worked as a farmer and a bank clerk and, during World War I, saw action in France as a captain in the field artillery. On his return from the war he entered the clothing business and in 1922 went into politics. After serving as county judge and presiding judge of Jackson County, Missouri, he was elected senator in 1934 and served in the Senate until his election as vice-president in 1944. As a senator he supported Roosevelt's New Deal policies and won a national reputation as an enemy of favoritism and waste in defense spending. His presidency from 1945 to 1953 was characterized by futile efforts to ram progressive Fair Deal legislation through a conservative Congress and, increasingly, by an anticommunist domestic and foreign policy. He is popularly remembered for his integrity, combativeness, and sense of responsibility—"The buck," he said, "stops here." Truman never made a more politically risky decision than to fire Douglas MacArthur. He died at his home in Independence, Missouri, in 1972.

Questions to Consider. Americans of Truman's era, it has been said, had two overwhelming fears: Communism and war. How did Truman attempt to balance these two fears in his 1951 address? On which side did he finally come down most strongly? American policy makers of the 1950s have been accused of exaggerating the scope and unity of international Communism. Did Truman fall into this habit? Did the confrontation with MacArthur perhaps drive Truman to overcompensate? Truman's action preserved the primacy of civilian control of war policy; why did he not defend his actions on these grounds?

★═══★═══★

Address on Korea and MacArthur (1951)

HARRY S. TRUMAN

In the simplest terms, what we are doing in Korea is this:

We are trying to prevent a third world war.

I think most people in this country recognized that fact last June. And they warmly supported the decision of the Government to help the Republic of Korea against the Communist aggressors. Now, many persons, even some who applauded our decision to defend Korea, have forgotten the basic reason for our action. . . .

The aggression against Korea is the boldest and most dangerous move the Communists have yet made.

The attack on Korea was part of a greater plan for conquering all of Asia. . . .

They want to control all Asia from the Kremlin.

This plan of conquest is in flat contradiction to what we believe. We believe that Korea belongs to the Koreans. We believe that India belongs to the Indians. We believe that all the nations of Asia should be free to work out their affairs in their own way. This is the basis of peace in the Far East and it is the basis of peace everywhere else.

The whole Communist imperialism is back of the attack on peace in the Far East. It was the Soviet Union that trained and equipped the North Koreans for aggression. The Chinese Communists massed forty-four well-trained and well-equipped divisions on the Korean frontier. These were the troops they threw into battle when the North Korean Communists were beaten.

The question we have had to face is whether the Communist plan of conquest can be stopped without general war. Our Government and other countries associated with us in the United Nations believe that the best chance of stopping it without general war is to meet the attack in Korea and defeat it there.

That is what we have been doing. It is a difficult and bitter task.

But so far it has been successful.

So far, we have prevented World War III.

So far, by fighting a limited war in Korea, we have prevented aggression from succeeding, and bringing on a general war. And the ability of the whole free world to resist Communist aggression has been greatly improved. . . .

We do not want to see the conflict in Korea extended. We are trying to prevent a world war—not to start one. The best way to do that is to make it plain that we and the other free countries will continue to resist the attack.

But you may ask why can't we take other steps to punish the aggressor.

The New York Times, April 12, 1951.

General Douglas MacArthur. On June 29, 1950, the American government ordered combat troops into Korea under the command of General MacArthur. Three months later, MacArthur's forces engineered a brilliant landing behind North Korean lines and quickly overran the northern half of the country. This position proved untenable because, contrary to MacArthur's prediction, Chinese troops entered the war and pushed the Americans far into the south—one of the longest retreats in U.S. history. Here MacArthur, left, receives a decoration from President Harry S. Truman—who would soon strip him of his command for insubordination. (National Archives)

Why don't we bomb Manchuria and China itself? Why don't we assist Chinese Nationalist troops to land on the mainland of China?

If we were to do these things we would be running a very grave risk of starting a general war. If that were to happen, we would have brought about the exact situation we are trying to prevent.

If we were to do these things, we would become entangled in a vast conflict on the continent of Asia and our task would become immeasurably more difficult all over the world.

What would suit the ambitions of the Kremlin better than for our military forces to be committed to a full-scale war with Red China?

It may well be that, in spite of our best efforts, the Communists may spread the war. But it would be wrong—tragically wrong—for us to take the initiative in extending the war.

The dangers are great. Make no mistake about it. Behind the North Koreans and Chinese Communists in the front lines stand additional millions of Chinese soldiers. And behind the Chinese stand the tanks, the planes, the submarines, the soldiers, and the scheming rulers of the Soviet Union.

Our aim is to avoid the spread of the conflict. . . .

If the Communist authorities realize that they cannot defeat us in Korea, if they realize it would be foolhardy to widen the hostilities beyond Korea, then they may recognize the folly of continuing their aggression. A peaceful settlement may then be possible. The door is always open.

Then we may achieve a settlement in Korea which will not compromise the principles and purposes of the United Nations.

I have thought long and hard about this question of extending the war in Asia. I have discussed it many times with the ablest military advisers in the country. I believe with all my heart that the course we are following is the best course.

I believe that we must try to limit the war to Korea for these vital reasons: To make sure that the precious lives of our fighting men are not wasted, to see that the security of our country and the free world is not needlessly jeopardized, and to prevent a third world war.

A number of events have made it evident that General MacArthur did not agree with that policy. I have, therefore, considered it essential to relieve General MacArthur so that there would be no doubt or confusion as to the real purpose and aim of our policy.

It was with the deepest personal regret that I found myself compelled to take this action. General MacArthur is one of our greatest military commanders. But the cause of world peace is more important than any individual.

The change in commands in the Far East means no change whatever in the policy of the United States. We will carry on the fight in Korea with vigor and determination in an effort to bring the war to a speedy and successful conclusion. . . .

Real peace can be achieved through a settlement based on the following factors:

One: The fighting must stop.

Two: Concrete steps must be taken to insure that the fighting will not break out again.

Three: There must be an end to the aggression.

A settlement founded upon these elements would open the way for the unification of Korea and the withdrawal of all foreign forces.

32

THE MILITARY-INDUSTRIAL COMPLEX

During Dwight D. Eisenhower's eight years as president, the United States ended the Korean War and moved to replace expensive conventional armaments with "cheap" nuclear weapons. Moreover, though the Eisenhower administration landed troops briefly in Lebanon, sent military aid to Indochina, and helped overthrow radical governments in Iran and Guatemala, the United States managed to stay out of war in other parts of the world. There was intense cold war. But there was also peace.

Despite all the years of peace under Eisenhower, the United States in 1960 still kept 2,500,000 military personnel on active duty, poured $51 billion into the defense budget—10 percent of the entire gross national product—and threw every scientific resource into creating sophisticated weapons systems. So striking was this development that President Eisenhower, himself a former general and a probusiness Republican, felt compelled in his 1961 farewell address to warn the public against the rise of a "military-industrial complex" in the land. Since military spending never in fact receded after Eisenhower, the concept and the phrase entered permanently into the political vocabulary, thus becoming somewhat ironic Eisenhower legacies to the people.

Born in Texas in 1890, Dwight D. Eisenhower grew up in Kansas in modest circumstances. A West Point graduate of 1915, he served at various army posts in the United States and Asia and under General Douglas MacArthur during the 1930s; his abilities were also perceived by General George Marshall, and he won promotion to brigadier general in 1941. Commander of the Allied forces in western Europe, he oversaw Allied invasions of North Africa, Italy, and France during World War II, demonstrating impressive diplomatic and administrative skills, and returned to America in late 1945 as a five-star general and a vastly popular hero. It was largely these skills and this reputation, plus his disarming grin and the irresistible slogan "I like Ike," that propelled him to landslide presidential victories in 1952 and 1956. After 1961, Eisenhower eased quickly into retirement and discovered that, much like his nemesis Harry Truman, he had become one of America's beloved political figures. He died in Washington, D.C., in 1969.

Questions to Consider. Two aspects of President Eisenhower's striking address deserve special attention. First, Eisenhower was warning not only against the influence of the military and the arms industry, as represented by huge military budgets, but also against the rise of a scientific-technological elite, as symbolized by the growing control of scholarship by Washington. Of these two tendencies, which did he seem to see as the greater threat? Second, although Eisenhower said plainly that these forces—the military-industrial and the scientific-technological—represented a danger to our liberties and democratic processes, he was vague about how exactly the forces did endanger them and especially about what might, in a concrete way, be done to prevent such threats. Was Eisenhower, a former general, perhaps tacitly urging that soldiers and defense contractors be restricted in their political activities—in campaign contributions, for example, or lobbying efforts—or that defense budgets be scrutinized and slimmed down with special rigor? How realistic were these hints? What connection, if any, was he making at the end of his speech between disarmament and democracy?

★═══★═══★

Farewell Address (1961)

DWIGHT D. EISENHOWER

A vital element in keeping the peace is our military establishment. Our arms must be mighty, ready for instant action, so that no potential aggressor may be tempted to risk his own destruction.

Our military organization today bears little relation to that known by any of my predecessors in peacetime, or indeed by the fighting men of World War II or Korea.

Until the latest of our world conflicts, the United States had no armaments industry. American makers of plowshares could, with time and as required, make swords as well. But now we can no longer risk emergency improvisation of national defense; we have been compelled to create a permanent armaments industry of vast proportions. Added to this, three and a half million men and women are directly engaged in the defense establishment. We annually spend on military security more than the net income of all United States corporations.

This conjunction of an immense military establishment and a large arms industry is new in the American experience. The total influence—economic, political, even spiritual—is felt in every city, every statehouse, every office of the federal government. We recognize the imperative need for this development.

The New York Times, January 18, 1961.

B-52 strategic bombers in mass production at a Boeing company plant in the state of Washington, about 1955. Military production largely built and sustained the mid-century economy of the West Coast. Aerospace was one of the three new sectors, along with petrochemicals and electronics, that built and sustained the postwar economy of the United States. (Courtesy of The Boeing Company)

Yet we must not fail to comprehend its grave implications. Our toil, resources, and livelihood are all involved; so is the very structure of our society.

In the councils of government, we must guard against the acquisition of unwarranted influence, whether sought or unsought, by the military-industrial complex. The potential for the disastrous rise of misplaced power exists and will persist.

We must never let the weight of this combination endanger our liberties or democratic processes. We should take nothing for granted. Only an alert and knowledgeable citizenry can compel the proper meshing of the huge industrial and military machinery of defense with our peaceful methods and goals, so that security and liberty may prosper together.

Akin to, and largely responsible for the sweeping changes in our industrial-military posture, has been the technological revolution during recent decades.

In this revolution, research has become central; it also becomes more formalized, complex, and costly. A steadily increasing share is conducted for, by, or at the discretion of, the federal government. . . .

The prospect of domination of the nation's scholars by federal employment, project allocations, and the power of money is ever present—and is gravely to be regarded.

Yet, in holding scientific research and discovery in respect, as we should, we must also be alert to the equal and opposite danger that public policy could itself become the captive of a scientific-technological elite.

It is the task of statesmanship to mold, to balance, and to integrate these and other forces, new and old, within the principles of our democratic system— ever aiming toward the supreme goals of our free society.

Another factor in maintaining balance involves the element of time. As we peer into society's future, we—you and I, and our government—must avoid the impulse to live only for today, plundering, for our own ease and convenience, the precious resources of tomorrow. We cannot mortgage the material assets of our grandchildren without risking the loss also of their political and spiritual heritage. We want democracy to survive for all generations to come, not to become the insolvent phantom of tomorrow.

Down the long lane of the history yet to be written America knows that this world of ours, ever growing smaller, must avoid becoming a community of dreadful fear and hate, and be, instead, a proud confederation of mutual trust and respect.

Such a confederation must be one of equals. The weakest must come to the conference table with the same confidence as do we, protected as we are by our moral, economic, and military strength. That table, though scarred by many past frustrations, cannot be abandoned for the certain agony of the battlefield.

Disarmament, with mutual honor and confidence, is a continuing imperative. Together we must learn how to compose differences, not with arms, but with intellect and decent purpose. Because this need is so sharp and apparent I confess that I lay down my official responsibilities in this field with a definite sense of disappointment. As one who has witnessed the horror and the lingering sadness of war—as one who knows that another war could utterly destroy this civilization which has been so slowly and painfully built over thousands of years—I wish I could say tonight that a lasting peace is in sight.

Happily, I can say that war has been avoided. Steady progress toward our ultimate goal has been made. But, so much remains to be done. As a private citizen, I shall never cease to do what little I can to help the world advance along that road. . . .

33

The Defense of Freedom

Although the New Frontier of President John F. Kennedy had a significant domestic component centering on civil rights and social welfare programs, Kennedy's primary emphasis, as his inaugural address, reprinted below, makes clear, was on the development of a vigorous foreign policy. Kennedy perceived the Soviet threat in much the same way that Richard M. Nixon, his Republican opponent, had perceived it during the 1960 presidential campaign: as ubiquitous and unremitting and therefore to be countered at every turn. But Kennedy's views held significant differences from the policy pursued by the Eisenhower administration.

Kennedy was more willing than Eisenhower to increase defense spending; he was also more skeptical about the value of responding to revolutions in the Third World by threatening thermonuclear war. Departing from the policies of his predecessor, Kennedy moved toward a doctrine of "flexible response" that stressed conventional forces over atomic weapons and emphasized international propaganda and public relations over armaments. At once idealistic and demanding, like the 1961 inaugural address itself, Kennedy's views led to the signing of treaties with the Soviet Union that banned atmospheric nuclear testing and to the establishment of emergency communications between the White House and the Kremlin. But these same views also led to the sending of more and more military personnel to South Vietnam, to prevent Ho Chi Minh, the Communist leader of North Vietnam, from unifying Vietnam under his rule.

John F. Kennedy was born in 1917 to a wealthy Irish-American family. After graduating with honors from Harvard in 1940, he served for a time as secretary to his father, who was then U.S. ambassador to Great Britain. *Why England Slept*—his best-selling book on British military policies during the 1930s—was published in 1940. During World War II he served in the U.S. Navy and won the Navy and Marine Corps Medal for his heroism. After the war he entered politics in Massachusetts, winning election to the House of Representatives in 1946 and to the Senate in 1952. His book *Profiles in Courage,* published in 1956, won the Pulitzer Prize, and in 1960 he narrowly bested Richard Nixon in a contest for the presidency. The youngest man and the only Roman

Catholic ever elected president, Kennedy projected an image of intelligence, vitality, and sophistication. Worldwide mourning occurred after he was assassinated in Dallas, Texas, on November 22, 1963.

Questions to Consider. Some historians have argued that in this address Kennedy formally shifted the focus of the cold war from Europe to the nonaligned or economically underdeveloped part of the world. Do you agree or disagree? If you agree, do you also believe there was a connection between this shift and Kennedy's emphasis on feeding and clothing the world—on winning by doing good? Was there also a connection between this shift and Kennedy's preference for invoking human rights instead of democracy? Historians have also read the address as an unprecedented fusion of "adversarialism" with "universalism." Again, do you agree or disagree? Was this fusion connected with Kennedy's sense of facing an "hour of maximum danger" in which Americans might have to "pay any price" for liberty?

★━━★━━★

Inaugural Address (1961)

JOHN F. KENNEDY

We observe today not a victory of party but a celebration of freedom—symbolizing an end as well as a beginning—signifying renewal as well as change. For I have sworn before you and Almighty God the same solemn oath our forbears prescribed nearly a century and three-quarters ago.

The world is very different now. For man holds in his mortal hands the power to abolish all forms of human poverty and all forms of human life. And yet the same revolutionary beliefs for which our forbears fought are still at issue around the globe—the belief that the rights of man come not from the generosity of the state but from the hand of God.

We dare not forget today that we are the heirs of that first revolution. Let the word go forth from this time and place, to friend and foe alike, that the torch has been passed to a new generation of Americans—born in this century, tempered by war, disciplined by a hard and bitter peace, proud of our ancient heritage—and unwilling to witness or permit the slow undoing of those human rights to which this nation has always been committed, and to which we are committed today at home and around the world.

Let every nation know, whether it wishes us well or ill, that we shall pay any price, bear any burden, meet any hardship, support any friend, oppose any foe to assure the survival and the success of liberty.

The New York Times, January 21, 1961.

John F. Kennedy. Kennedy, with his wife, Jacqueline, sitting at his side, during the presidential inauguration, 1961. (Paul Schutzer/TimeLife Picture/Getty Images)

This much we pledge—and more.

To those old allies whose cultural and spiritual origins we share, we pledge the loyalty of faithful friends. United, there is little we cannot do in a host of co-operative ventures. Divided, there is little we can do—for we dare not meet a powerful challenge at odds and split asunder.

To those new states whom we welcome to the ranks of the free, we pledge our word that one form of colonial control shall not have passed away merely to be replaced by a far more iron tyranny. We shall not always expect to find them supporting our view. But we shall always hope to find them strongly supporting their own freedom—and to remember that, in the past, those who foolishly sought power by riding the back of the tiger ended up inside.

To those people in the huts and villages of half the globe struggling to break the bonds of mass misery, we pledge our best efforts to help them help themselves, for whatever period is required—not because the Communists may be doing it, not because we seek their votes, but because it is right. If a free society cannot help the many who are poor, it cannot save the few who are rich.

To our sister republics south of our border, we offer a special pledge—to convert our good words into good deeds—in a new alliance for progress—to assist free men and free governments in casting off the chains of poverty. But this peaceful revolution of hope cannot become the prey of hostile powers. Let all our neighbors know that we shall join with them to oppose aggression or subversion anywhere in the Americas. And let every other power know that this hemisphere intends to remain the master of its own house.

To that world assembly of sovereign states, the United Nations, our last best hope in an age where the instruments of war have far outpaced the instruments of peace, we renew our pledge of support—to prevent it from becoming merely a forum for invective—to strengthen its shield of the new and the weak—and to enlarge the area in which its writ may run.

Finally, to those nations who would make themselves our adversary, we offer not a pledge but a request: that both sides begin anew the quest for peace, before the dark powers of destruction unleashed by science engulf all humanity in planned or accidental self-destruction.

We dare not tempt them with weakness. For only when our arms are sufficient beyond doubt can we be certain beyond doubt that they will never be employed.

But neither can two great and powerful groups of nations take comfort from our present course—both sides overburdened by the cost of modern weapons, both rigidly alarmed by the steady spread of the deadly atom, yet both racing to alter that uncertain balance of terror that stays the hand of mankind's final war.

So let us begin anew—remembering on both sides that civility is not a sign of weakness, and sincerity is always subject to proof. Let us never negotiate out of fear. But let us never fear to negotiate.

Let both sides explore what problems unite us instead of belaboring those problems which divide us.

Let both sides, for the first time, formulate serious and precise proposals for the inspection and control of arms—and bring the absolute power to destroy other nations under the absolute control of all nations.

Let both sides seek to invoke the wonders of science instead of its terror. Together let us explore the stars, conquer the deserts, eradicate disease, tap the ocean depths, and encourage the arts and commerce.

Let both sides unite to heed in all corners of the earth the command of Isaiah—to "undo the heavy burdens . . . [and] let the oppressed go free."

And if a beachhead of co-operation may push back the jungle of suspicion, let both sides join in creating a new endeavor, not a new balance of power, but a new world of law, where the strong are just and the weak secure and the peace preserved.

All this will not be finished in the first one hundred days. Nor will it be finished in the first one thousand days, nor in the life of this administration, nor even perhaps in our lifetime on this planet. But let us begin.

In your hands, my fellow citizens, more than mine, will rest the final success or failure of our course. Since this country was founded, each generation of Americans has been summoned to give testimony to its national loyalty. The graves of young Americans who answered the call to service surround the globe.

Now the trumpet summons us again—not as a call to bear arms, though arms we need—not as a call to battle, though embattled we are—but a call to bear the burden of a long twilight struggle, year in and year out, "rejoicing in hope, patient in tribulation"—a struggle against the common enemies of man: tyranny, poverty, disease, and war itself.

Can we forge against these enemies a grand and global alliance, North and South, East and West, that can assure a more fruitful life for all mankind? Will you join in that historic effort?

In the long history of the world, only a few generations have been granted the role of defending freedom in its hour of maximum danger. I do not shrink from this responsibility—I welcome it. I do not believe that any of us would exchange places with any other people or any other generation. The energy, the faith, the devotion which we bring to this endeavor will light our country and all who serve it—and the glow from that fire can truly light the world.

And so, my fellow Americans: ask not what your country can do for you— ask what you can do for your country.

My fellow citizens of the world: ask not what America will do for you, but what together we can do for the freedom of man.

Finally, whether you are citizens of America or citizens of the world, ask of us here the same high standards of strength and sacrifice which we ask of you. With a good conscience our only sure reward, with history the final judge of deeds, let us go forth to lead the land we love, asking His blessing and His help, but knowing that here on earth God's work must truly be our own.

34

Blank Check

American involvement in Vietnam began modestly enough with a promise in 1945 to help France restore colonial rule there. The United States backed France because Ho Chi Minh, the leader of the struggle for Vietnamese independence, was a Communist. American policy makers were more impressed by Ho's Communism than by his nationalism; they viewed him as a tool of the Kremlin, although he had the backing of many non-Communists in Indochina who wanted freedom from French control. In 1954, Ho's forces defeated the French, and the French decided to withdraw from Vietnam. At this point the United States stepped in, backed a partition of Vietnam, and gave aid to the South Vietnamese government in Saigon. American policy continued to be based on the belief that Communism in Vietnam was inspired by China or the Soviet Union, if not both. If Vietnam went Communist, Washington warned, other countries in Asia might topple like so many dominoes, and Communist influence in the world would grow at the expense of America's.

U.S. military personnel entered the Vietnamese conflict between North and South under Presidents Eisenhower and Kennedy. American bombers began raiding North Vietnam in 1965, after the reelection of Kennedy's successor, Lyndon B. Johnson. By 1969, American troops in South Vietnam numbered around 550,000, and American planes had dropped more bombs in Vietnam than had been dropped on Germany and Japan during World War II. Yet the Vietcong (the South Vietnamese insurgents), aided by North Vietnamese military units, seemed stronger than ever. International opinion had now turned against the United States.

A key episode in Lyndon Johnson's escalation came with the so-called Tonkin Gulf incident. On August 2, 1964, the U.S.S. *Maddox*, an American destroyer supporting South Vietnamese commando raids against North Vietnam, came under attack by enemy patrol boats. The attackers suffered heavy damage; the *Maddox* was unharmed. Two days later the *Maddox* and another U.S. destroyer again moved into North Vietnamese waters. Although the weather was bad, sonar equipment indicated enemy torpedoes. When the captain of the *Maddox* later questioned members of his crew, no one could recall any enemy attacks, and subsequent investigations of the incident likewise turned up no evidence of hostile fire. The American destroyers nevertheless reportedly leveled heavy fire against North Vietnamese patrol boats. President Johnson, despite the questionable evidence and without admitting that U.S. ships were supporting raids against the North, ordered air strikes on North Vietnamese naval bases and announced on television that he was retaliating for "unprovoked" attacks. U.S. planes would now, he said, bomb North Vietnam.

On August 5, Johnson, in the address excerpted below, asked Congress to give him authority to repel "any armed attack against the forces of the United States and to prevent further aggression." The resolution passed the House by 466 to 0 and passed the Senate by 88 to 2. The resolution, as Johnson eventually argued, was tantamount to a declaration of war—which Congress has not voted against any country since December 1941. Under its auspices, the president authorized not only the carpet-bombing of North Vietnam but the American buildup to over a half-million combat troops. Its effect in 1964 was to preempt criticism from Republican presidential candidate Barry Goldwater, a hawk on foreign policy, help raise Johnson's approval rating in the polls from 42 percent to 72 percent, and contribute to a major victory in that fall's election.

Born in the poor hill country of central Texas in 1908, Lyndon Johnson worked his way through Southwest Texas State Teachers College in San Marcos and went to Washington as assistant to a local congressman in 1931. An intensely ambitious and ardent New Deal Democrat, Johnson began his political career with his election to fill a congressional vacancy in 1937. He was elected to the U.S. Senate in 1948. Unmatched at arranging the compromises and distributing the favors and money on which congressional politics rested, he became Senate minority leader in 1953 and majority leader in 1955, when the Democrats regained control of the Senate. As the vice-presidential nominee in 1960, he helped John F. Kennedy carry enough Southern states to become president; he became president himself upon Kennedy's assassination in 1963. As president, Johnson helped enact the most sweeping civil rights legislation of the century, but he also dramatically escalated a fundamentally unpopular war. Faced with widespread opposition to his policies, he declined to run for reelection in 1968. He died in San Antonio in 1973.

Questions to Consider. On what grounds did Johnson defend the American presence in Vietnam? How did he deal with the problematic nature of the evidence of North Vietnamese attacks on U.S. ships? Johnson wanted authorization not only for limited retaliation over this specific incident but to attack North Vietnam on a large scale over a long period of time. How did he move in this address from the particular incident to the general goal? What parts of the speech might have been especially effective in undercutting Barry Goldwater's criticism of the Democrats as "soft on Communism"? Was Johnson demanding, in effect, a declaration of war? If so, why didn't he ask for that?

★══★══★

Message on the Gulf of Tonkin (1964)

LYNDON B. JOHNSON

Last night I announced to the American people that the North Vietnamese regime had conducted further deliberate attacks against U.S. naval vessels operating in international waters, and that I had therefore directed air action against gun boats and supporting facilities used in these hostile operations. This air action has now been carried out with substantial damage to the boats and facilities. Two U.S. aircraft were lost in the action.

After consultation with the leaders of both parties in the Congress, I further announced a decision to ask the Congress for a Resolution expressing the unity and determination of the United States in supporting freedom and in protecting peace in Southeast Asia.

These latest actions of the North Vietnamese regime have given a new and grave turn to the already serious situation in Southeast Asia. Our commitments in that area are well known to the Congress. They were first made in 1954 by President Eisenhower. They were further defined in the Southeast Asia Collective Defense Treaty approved by the Senate in February 1955.

This Treaty with its accompanying protocol obligates the United States and other members to act in accordance with their Constitutional processes to meet Communist aggression against any of the parties or protocol states.

Our policy in Southeast Asia has been consistent and unchanged since 1954. I summarized it on June 2 in four simple propositions:

1. *America keeps her word.* Here as elsewhere, we must and shall honor our commitments.
2. *The issue is the future of Southeast Asia as a whole.* A threat to any nation in that region is a threat to all, and a threat to us.
3. *Our purpose is peace.* We have no military, political or territorial ambitions in the area.
4. *This is not just a jungle war, but a struggle for freedom on every front of*

The New York Times, August 6, 1964.

human activity. Our military and economic assistance to South Vietnam and Laos in particular has the purpose of helping these countries to repel aggression and strengthen their independence.

The threat to the free nations of Southeast Asia has long been clear. The North Vietnamese regime has constantly sought to take over South Vietnam and Laos. This Communist regime has violated the Geneva Accords for Vietnam. It has systematically conducted a campaign of subversion, which includes the direction, training, and supply of personnel and arms for the conduct of guerrilla warfare in South Vietnamese territory. In Laos, the North Vietnamese regime has maintained military forces, used Laotian territory for infiltration into South Vietnam, and most recently carried out combat operations—all in direct violation of the Geneva Agreements of 1962.

In recent months, the actions of the North Vietnamese regime have become steadily more threatening. In May, following new acts of Communist aggression in Laos, the United States undertook reconnaissance flights over Laotian territory, at the request of the Government of Laos. These flights had the essential mission of determining the situation in territory where Communist forces were preventing inspection by the International Control Commission. When the Communists attacked these aircraft, I responded by furnishing escort fighters with instructions to fire when fired upon. Thus, these latest North Vietnamese attacks on our naval vessels are not the first direct attack on armed forces of the United States.

As President of the United States I have concluded that I should now ask the Congress, on its part, to join in affirming the national determination that all such attacks will be met, and that the U.S. will continue in its basic policy of assisting the free nations of the area to defend their freedom.

As I have repeatedly made clear, the United States intends no rashness, and seeks no wider war. We must make it clear to all that the United States is united in its determination to bring about the end of Communist subversion and aggression in the area. We seek the full and effective restoration of the international agreements signed in Geneva in 1954, with respect to South Vietnam, and again in Geneva in 1962, with respect to Laos.

I recommend a Resolution expressing the support of the Congress for all necessary action to protect our armed forces and to assist nations covered by the SEATO Treaty. At the same time, I assure the Congress that we shall continue readily to explore any avenues of political solution that will effectively guarantee the removal of Communist subversion and the preservation of the independence of the nations of the area.

The Resolution could well be based upon similar resolutions enacted by the Congress in the past—to meet the threat to Formosa in 1955, to meet the threat to the Middle East in 1957, and to meet the threat in Cuba in 1962. It could state in the simplest terms the resolve and support of the Congress for action to deal appropriately with attacks against our armed forces and to defend freedom and preserve peace in Southeast Asia in accordance with the obligations of the United States under the Southeast Asia Treaty. I urge the Congress to enact such a Resolution promptly and thus to give convincing evidence to the aggressive Communist nations, and to the world as a whole, that our policy in Southeast Asia will be carried forward—and that the peace and security of the area will be preserved.

The events of this week would in any event have made the passage of a Congressional Resolution essential. But there is an additional reason for doing so at a time when we are entering on three months of political campaigning. Hostile nations must understand that in such a period the United States will continue to protect its national interests, and that in these matters there is no division among us.

35

AGONY IN ASIA

The escalation of American involvement in Vietnam provoked perhaps the greatest wartime opposition in American history. By the end of 1965, the first draft card burnings had occurred. Students in major universities throughout the country had organized "teach-ins" (named after the civil rights "sit-ins") to discuss the nature of the war and had held the first antiwar march on Washington. By 1967, protest rallies were drawing hundreds of thousands, and evasion of the draft among middle-class students was widespread. Some of the country's most prominent leaders, including the Reverend Martin Luther King, Jr., were vehemently criticizing the Johnson administration for its Vietnam policy. The speech reprinted below, which King delivered at Riverside Church in New York City, stresses the links between international violence and domestic violence, war spending and social poverty, and the suppression of independence movements abroad and minority aspirations at home.

Martin Luther King's stance had special force because of his stature as an advocate of peace and human rights. Born in Atlanta, Georgia, in 1929, the son of a Baptist clergyman, King entered college at the age of fifteen. He eventually received a doctorate in theology from Boston University. In 1954 he was called to the ministry of a church in Montgomery, Alabama, and in 1955 he became a leader in the successful effort to integrate the local bus system. Calling on this experience and on his philosophy of nonviolence, King was soon promoting demonstrations against segregation throughout the South. In August 1963 he spoke to 250,000 people in the nation's capital on behalf of black voting rights, the first so-called March on Washington and a model for later antiwar protests. In 1964 he won the Nobel Peace Prize. In April 1968, having broken with the Johnson administration over the Vietnam War and on the eve of a vast "Poor People's Campaign" for economic justice, King was assassinated in Memphis, Tennessee. The death of the apostle of nonviolence triggered massive race riots in the nation's cities. His funeral attracted 150,000 mourners. The inscription on his tombstone, taken from his 1963 Washington speech, reads: "Free at Last, Free at Last, Thank God Almighty, I'm Free at Last."

Questions to Consider. Of the seven reasons King gave for deciding to "break silence" over Vietnam, which—as measurable by the rank and emphasis he gave them and by his rhetorical style—seem to have mattered most to him? Note how King inveighed first against racial injustice, then against violence, and finally against both. Was he right to link the two so closely? Would any perceptive critic of injustice have done so, or did this reflect King's particular way of seeing things and his personal experience in the civil rights movement? Many historians believe this speech marked a sharp political shift by King away from the struggle for civil rights and toward a broader struggle for economic justice and social transformation. Is there evidence for this interpretation in the speech? Why do you suppose King waited until 1967 to launch a public attack on American policy in Vietnam? Why was he careful to call his silence, rather than his attack, a "betrayal"?

★═══★═══★

A Time to Break Silence (1967)

MARTIN LUTHER KING, JR.

I come to this magnificent house of worship tonight because my conscience leaves me no other choice. I join with you in this meeting because I am in deepest agreement with the aims and work of the organization which has brought us together: Clergy and Laymen Concerned About Vietnam. The recent statement of your executive committee are the sentiments of my own heart and I found myself in full accord when I read its opening lines: "A time comes when silence is betrayal." That time has come for us in relation to Vietnam. . . .

Over the past two years, as I have moved to break the betrayal of my own silences and to speak from the burnings of my own heart, as I have called for radical departures from the destruction of Vietnam, many persons have questioned me about the wisdom of my path. At the heart of their concerns this query has often loomed large and loud: Why are you speaking about the war, Dr. King? Why are you joining the voices of dissent? Peace and civil rights don't mix, they say. Aren't you hurting the cause of your people, they ask? And when I hear them, though I often understand the source of their concern, I am nevertheless greatly saddened, for such questions mean that the inquirers have not really known me, my commitment or my calling. Indeed, their questions suggest that they do not know the world in which they live.

Wartime remembrance. Another soldier returns from Vietnam. (© 1969 Constantine Manos/Magnum Photos)

In the light of such tragic misunderstanding, I deem it of signal importance to try to state clearly, and I trust concisely, why I believe that the path from Dexter Avenue Baptist Church—the church in Montgomery, Alabama, where I began my pastorate—leads clearly to this sanctuary tonight. . . .

Since I am a preacher by trade, I suppose it is not surprising that I have seven major reasons for bringing Vietnam into the field of my moral vision. There is at the outset a very obvious and almost facile connection between the war in Vietnam and the struggle I, and others, have been waging in America. A few years ago there was a shining moment in that struggle. It seemed as if there was a real promise of hope for the poor—both black and white—through the Poverty Program. There were experiments, hopes, new beginnings. Then came the build-up in Vietnam and I watched the program broken and eviscerated as if it were some idle political plaything of a society gone mad on war, and I knew that America would never invest the necessary funds or energies in rehabilitation of its poor so long as adventures like Vietnam continued to draw men and skills and money like some demonic destructive suction tube. So I was increasingly compelled to see the war as an enemy of the poor and to attack it as such.

Perhaps the more tragic recognition of reality took place when it became clear to me that the war was doing far more than devastating the hopes of the poor at home. It was sending their sons and their brothers and their husbands to fight and to die in extraordinarily high proportions relative to the rest of the population. We were taking the black young men who had been crippled by our society and sending them 8,000 miles away to guarantee liberties in Southeast Asia which they had not found in Southwest Georgia and East Harlem. So we have been repeatedly faced with the cruel irony of watching negro and white boys on TV screens as they kill and die together for a nation that has been unable to seat them together in the same schools. So we watch them in brutal solidarity burning the huts of a poor village, but we realize that they would never live on the same block in Detroit. I could not be silent in the face of such cruel manipulation of the poor.

My third reason moves to an even deeper level of awareness, for it grows out of my experience in the ghettos of the north over the last three years—especially the last three summers. As I have walked among the desperate, rejected and angry young men I have told them that Molotov cocktails and rifles would not solve their problems. I have tried to offer them my deepest compassion while maintaining my conviction that social change comes most meaningfully through nonviolent action. But they asked—and rightly so—what about Vietnam? They asked if our own nation wasn't using massive doses of violence to solve its problems, to bring about the changes it wanted. Their questions hit home, and I knew that I could never again raise my voice against the violence of the oppressed in the ghettos without having first spoken clearly to the greatest purveyor of violence in the world today—my own government. For the sake of those boys, for the sake of this government, for the sake of the hundreds of thousands trembling under our violence, I cannot be silent.

For those who ask the question, "Aren't you a Civil Rights leader?" and thereby mean to exclude me from the movement for peace, I have this further answer. In 1957 when a group of us formed the Southern Christian Leadership Conference, we chose as our motto: "To save the soul of America." We were convinced that we could not limit our vision to certain rights for black people, but instead affirmed the conviction that America would never be free or saved from itself unless the descendants of its slaves were loosed completely from the shackles they still wear. In a way we were agreeing with Langston Hughes, that black bard of Harlem, who had written earlier:

> *O, yes*
> *I say it plain,*
> *America never was America to me,*
> *And yet I swear this oath—*
> *America will be!*[1]

Now, it should be incandescently clear that no one who has any concern for the integrity and life of America today can ignore the present war. If America's soul becomes totally poisoned, part of the autopsy must read Vietnam. It can never be saved so long as it destroys the deepest hopes of men the world over. So it is that those of us who are yet determined that America will be are led down the path of protest and dissent, working for the health of our land.

As if the weight of such a commitment to the life and health of America were not enough, another burden of responsibility was placed upon me in 1964; and I cannot forget that the Nobel Prize for Peace was also a commission—a commission to work harder than I had ever worked before for "the brotherhood of man." This is a calling that takes me beyond national allegiances, but even if it were not present I would yet have to live with the meaning of my commitment to the ministry of Jesus Christ. To me the relationship of this ministry to the making of peace is so obvious that I sometimes marvel at those who ask me why I am speaking against the war. Could it be that they do not know that the good news was meant for all men—for Communists and capitalists, for their children and ours, for black and for white, for revolutionary and conservative? Have they forgotten that my ministry is in obedience to the one who loved his enemies so fully that he died for them? What can I say to the "Viet Cong" or to Castro or to Mao as a faithful minister of this one? Can I threaten them with death or must I not share with them my life?

Finally, as I try to delineate for you and for myself the road that leads from Montgomery to this place I would have offered all that was most valid if I simply said that I must be true to my conviction that I share with all men the calling to be a son of the Living God. Beyond the calling of race or nation or creed is this vocation of sonship and brotherhood, and because I believe that the Father is deeply concerned especially for his suffering and helpless and outcast children, I come tonight to speak for them. . . .

1. From *The Collected Poems of Langston Hughes* by Langston Hughes. Copyright © 1994 by The Estate of Langston Hughes. Used by permission of Alfred A. Knopf, a division of Random House, Inc.

And as I ponder the madness of Vietnam and search within myself for ways to understand and respond to compassion my mind goes constantly to the people of that peninsula. I speak now not of the soldiers of each side, not of the junta in Saigon, but simply of the people who have been living under the curse of war for almost three continuous decades now. I think of them too because it is clear to me that there will be no meaningful solution there until some attempt is made to know them and hear their broken cries. . . .

They languish under our bombs and consider us—not their fellow Vietnamese—the real enemy. They move sadly and apathetically as we herd them off the land of their fathers into concentration camps where minimal social needs are rarely met. They know they must move or be destroyed by our bombs. So they go—primarily women and children and the aged.

They watch as we poison their water, as we kill a million acres of their crops. They must weep as the bulldozers roar through their areas preparing to destroy the precious trees. They wander into the hospitals, with at least twenty casualties from American firepower for one "Viet Cong"-inflicted injury. So far we may have killed a million of them—mostly children. They wander into the towns and see thousands of the children, homeless, without clothes, running in packs on the streets like animals. They see the children degraded by our soldiers as they beg for food. They see the children selling their sisters to our soldiers, soliciting for their mothers.

What do the peasants think as we ally ourselves with the landlords and as we refuse to put any action into our many words concerning land reform? What do they think as we test out our latest weapons on them, just as the Germans tested out new medicine and new tortures in the concentration camps of Europe? Where are the roots of the independent Vietnam we claim to be building? Is it among these voiceless ones?

We have destroyed their two most cherished institutions: the family and the village. We have destroyed their land and their crops. We have cooperated in the crushing of the nation's only non-communist revolutionary political force—the unified Buddhist Church. We have supported the enemies of the peasants of Saigon. We have corrupted their women and children and killed their men. What liberators! . . .

At this point I should make it clear that while I have tried in these last few minutes to give a voice to the voiceless on Vietnam and to understand the arguments of those who are called enemy, I am as deeply concerned about our own troops there as anything else. For it occurs to me that what we are submitting them to in Vietnam is not simply the brutalizing process that goes on in any war where armies face each other and seek to destroy. We are adding cynicism to the process of death, for they must know after a short period there that none of the things we claim to be fighting for are really involved. Before long they must know that their government has sent them into a struggle among Vietnamese, and the more sophisticated surely realize that we are on the side of the wealthy and the secure while we create a hell for the poor.

Somehow this madness must cease. We must stop now. I speak as a child of God and brother to the suffering poor of Vietnam. I speak for those whose land is being laid waste, whose homes are being destroyed, whose culture is being subverted. I speak for the poor of America who are paying the double price of smashed hopes at home and death and corruption in Vietnam. I speak as a citizen of the world, for the world as it stands aghast at the path we have taken. I speak as an American to the leaders of my own nation. The great initiative in this war is ours. The initiative to stop it must be ours. . . .

In 1957 a sensitive American official overseas said that it seemed to him that our nation was on the wrong side of a world revolution. During the past ten years we have seen emerge a pattern of suppression which now has justified the presence of U.S. military "advisers" in Venezuela. This need to maintain social stability for our investments accounts for the counterrevolutionary action of American forces in Guatemala. It tells why American helicopters are being used against guerrillas in Colombia and why American napalm and green beret forces have already been active against rebels in Peru. It is with such activity in mind that the words of the late John F. Kennedy come back to haunt us. Five years ago he said, "Those who make peaceful revolution impossible will make violent revolution inevitable."

Increasingly, by choice or by accident, this is the role our nation has taken—the role of those who make peaceful revolution impossible by refusing to give up the privileges and the pleasures that come from the immense profits of overseas investment.

I am convinced that if we are to get on the right side of the world revolution, we as a nation must undergo a radical revolution of values. We must rapidly begin the shift from a "thing-oriented" society to a "person-oriented" society. When machines and computers, profit motives and property rights are considered more important than people, the giant triplets of racism, materialism, and militarism are incapable of being conquered.

A true revolution of values will soon cause us to question the fairness and justice of many of our past and present policies. On the one hand we are called to play the Good Samaritan on life's roadside; but that will be only an initial act. One day we must come to see that the whole Jericho Road must be transformed so that men and women will not be constantly beaten and robbed as they make their journey on Life's highway. True compassion is more than flinging a coin to a beggar; it is not haphazard and superficial. It comes to see that an edifice which produces beggars needs restructuring. A true revolution of values will soon look uneasily on the glaring contrast of poverty and wealth. With righteous indignation, it will look across the seas and see individual capitalists of the West investing huge sums of money in Asia, Africa and South America, only to take the profits out with no concern for the social betterment of the countries, and say: "This is not just." It will look at our alliance with the landed gentry of Latin America and say: "This is not just." The Western arrogance of feeling that it has everything to teach others and nothing to learn from them is not just. A true revolution of values will lay hands on the world order and say of war: "This way of settling differences is not just."

Now let us begin. Now let us rededicate ourselves to the long and bitter—but beautiful—struggle for a new world. This is the calling of the sons of God, and our brothers wait eagerly for our response. Shall we say the odds are too great? Shall we tell them the struggle is too hard? Will our message be that the forces of American life militate against their arrival as full men, and we send our deepest regrets? Or will there be another message, of longing, of hope, of solidarity with their yearnings, of commitment to their cause, whatever the cost? The choice is ours, and though we might prefer it otherwise we must choose in this crucial moment of human history.

Martin Luther King, Jr., in prayer with Ralph Abernathy (behind King's left shoulder) and other supporters of the Southern Christian Leadership Conference. (Corbis-Bettmann)

CHAPTER SIX

Movements for Change

36

DESEGREGATION

Racial segregation was a fact of life everywhere in the South until the middle of the twentieth century. Organizations such as the National Association for the Advancement of Colored People (NAACP) and the Congress of Racial Equality (CORE) fought hard against segregation and its handmaiden, disfranchisement of blacks. But in 1896 the Supreme Court had ruled in *Plessy* v. *Ferguson* that separate facilities for blacks and whites were legal, and there seemed little recourse from this decree, especially given the unsympathetic racial views of the national government in this period. Only in 1947 did some tentative preliminary change come with the integration of major-league baseball for commercial reasons, the integration of the armed forces by presidential order, and the integration of Southern law schools by a Supreme Court decision that year arguing that such schools were inherently unequal because they denied opportunities to those excluded.

Then, in 1954, in an NAACP lawsuit entitled *Brown* v. *The Board of Education of Topeka,* the Supreme Court extended its reasoning from law schools to the entire segregated school system, thereby reversing the "separate-but-equal" doctrine some sixty years after its adoption. Written by Chief Justice Earl Warren on behalf of a unanimous Court, at first this momentous decision, reprinted below, was met with bitter resentment and resistance from most Southern whites. Yet it marked the beginning of the end for legally segregated schools in the nation. Together with the massive civil rights movement led by Martin Luther King, Jr., and others, it outlawed all segregated public facilities, whether buses, beaches, lunch counters, voting booths, or schools.

Earl Warren was born in Los Angeles in 1891. After he was graduated from the University of California at Berkeley, he practiced law in the San Francisco area until joining the army during World War I. In the 1920s Warren embarked on a successful political career in California, serving as district attorney, state attorney general, and governor. His only electoral defeat came as Republican vice-presidential candidate in 1948. When President Eisenhower appointed him chief justice in 1953, Warren was considered a rather traditional Republican moderate. His leadership of the Court, however, brought an unexpected burst of judicial activism that strengthened not only minority rights but also the rights of voters, trial defendants, and witnesses before congressional committees. Warren resigned from the Court in 1969 and died in Washington in 1974.

Questions to Consider. Note, in this decision, that Warren virtually disregarded what had once seemed so crucial—the actual differences between the races. Note, too, that Warren read very large public purposes into the bountiful commitment of local governments to public education: good citizenship, values, training, and social adjustment. Were these two factors—colorblindness and purposeful public education— enough to account for the Court's 1954 decision? If so, why did Warren introduce psychological studies into his argument? Was it merely a reflection of the findings of modern social science? In what other areas besides education might modern courts attempt to use the equal protection clause of the Fourteenth Amendment as construed by the Warren Court?

★━━━★━━━★

Brown v. The Board of Education of Topeka (1954)

EARL WARREN

These cases come to us from the States of Kansas, South Carolina, Virginia, and Delaware. They are premised on different facts and different local conditions, but a common legal question justifies their consideration together in this consolidated opinion.

In approaching this problem, we cannot turn the clock back to 1868 when the Amendment was adopted, or even to 1896 when *Plessy* v. *Ferguson* was written. We must consider public education in the light of its full development and its present place in American life throughout the Nation. Only in this way can it be determined if segregation in public schools deprives these plaintiffs of the equal protection of the laws.

Today, education is perhaps the most important function of state and local governments. Compulsory school attendance laws and the great expenditures for education both demonstrate our recognition of the importance of education to our democratic society. It is required in the performance of our most basic public responsibilities, even service in the armed forces. It is the very foundation of good citizenship. Today it is a principal instrument in awakening

Brown v. *The Board of Education of Topeka,* 347 U.S. 483 (1954).

Elizabeth Eckford approaching Little Rock's Central High School during the integration crisis of 1957. The crowd began to curse and yell, "Lynch her! Lynch her!" A national guardsman blocked her entrance into the school with his rifle. Faced with this, Eckford retreated back down the street away from the mob. But a week later, under the protection of U.S. Army troops, she finally attended, and integrated, Central High School. (Alfred Eisenstaedt/TimeLife Pictures/Getty Images)

the child to cultural values, in preparing him for later professional training, and in helping him to adjust normally to his environment. In these days, it is doubtful that any child may reasonably be expected to succeed in life if he is denied the opportunity of an education. Such an opportunity, where the state has undertaken to provide it, is a right which must be made available to all on equal terms.

We come then to the question presented: Does segregation of children in public schools solely on the basis of race, even though the physical facilities and other "tangible" factors may be equal, deprive the children of the minority group of equal educational opportunities? We believe that it does.

In *Sweatt* v. *Painter*, . . . in finding that a segregated law school for Negroes could not provide them equal educational opportunities, this Court relied in large part on "those qualities which are incapable of objective measurement but which make for greatness in a law school." In *McLaurin* v. *Oklahoma State*

Regents, . . . the Court, in requiring that a Negro admitted to a white graduate school be treated like all other students, again resorted to intangible considerations: ". . . his ability to study, to engage in discussions and exchange views with other students, and, in general, to learn his profession." Such considerations apply with added force to children in grade and high schools. To separate them from others of similar age and qualifications solely because of their race generates a feeling of inferiority as to their status in the community that may affect their hearts and minds in a way unlikely ever to be undone. The effect of this separation on their educational opportunities was well stated by a finding in the Kansas case by a court which nevertheless felt compelled to rule against the Negro plaintiffs:

> Segregation of white and colored children in public schools has a detrimental effect upon the colored children. The impact is greater when it has the sanction of the law; for the policy of separating the races is usually interpreted as denoting the inferiority of the Negro group. A sense of inferiority affects the motivation of a child to learn. Segregation with the sanction of the law, therefore, has a tendency to retard the educational and mental development of Negro children and to deprive them of some of the benefits they would receive in a racially integrated school system.

Whatever may have been the extent of psychological knowledge at the time of *Plessy* v. *Ferguson*, this finding is amply supported by modern authority. Any language in *Plessy* v. *Ferguson* contrary to this finding is rejected.

We conclude that in the field of public education the doctrine of "separate but equal" has no place. Separate educational facilities are inherently unequal. Therefore, we hold that the plaintiffs and others similarly situated for whom the actions have been brought are, by reason of the segregation complained of, deprived of the equal protection of the laws guaranteed by the Fourteenth Amendment. . . .

37

SAVING THE HABITAT

Although occasionally writers such as Henry David Thoreau celebrated the beauty and power of nature, modern environmentalism began only late in the nineteenth century, as cities and industry grew so rapidly that they flattened and contaminated nature even as railroads increased access to it. In 1872 Congress created the first national park, Yellowstone, and twenty years later, after prodding by a new environmental organization, the Sierra Club, Congress enabled the president to set up wilderness areas. Theodore Roosevelt promoted more rational uses of scarce timber and mining resources after 1900. Franklin D. Roosevelt initiated important conservation projects, including the Tennessee Valley Authority and the Civilian Conservation Corps, during the Depression.

Environmentalism as a mass movement arose chiefly in the 1960s as people began to worry about not only the despoliation of wilderness but also the pollution of air, drinking water, and food and the wholesale annihilation of plant and animal species. In part this was because of a series of horror stories: polluted rivers spontaneously catching fire, poisons detected in human tissues and mothers' milk, acid rain destroying lakes and streams, massive coastal oil spills, air too "smoggy" to breathe safely. But the writings of scientists and naturalists, from Paul Erlich's *The Population Bomb* to Barry Commoner's *The Closing Circle*, played a part as well.

No book was more important in creating modern environmental consciousness than Rachel Carson's *Silent Spring*. Carson was mainly concerned about DDT, a chemical used in World War II to kill malaria-bearing mosquitoes and then by farmers against agricultural pests. Carson's book addressed, for virtually the first time, the dangers of heavy use of pesticides such as DDT, noting that DDT caused cancer and leukemia in eagles, trout, and other animals, including undoubtedly humans. DDT had also practically wiped out bird populations in some areas. Hence "springs" were now "silent" where birds had sung. Carson indicted consumers for using toxic products. More controversially, she indicted businesses for carelessly manufacturing and heavily advertising such products.

Congress responded to Carson and others with the Clean Air, Clean Water, and Endangered Species Acts and by establishing the Environmental Protection Agency. And these measures mostly worked. By the mid-1990s, even though species and woodlands still vanished and cancer rates remained high, levels of DDT and some other cancer-causing compounds were down sharply, as were soot, carbon monoxide, and sulfur dioxide emissions. Energy usage grew only a fifth as fast as the overall economy. America's water supply was the cleanest in the industrial world.

Rachel Carson was born in Springdale, Pennsylvania, in 1907. Showing an early interest in nature, she studied biology at Pennsylvania College for Women and various graduate schools, and in 1936 joined the U.S. Bureau of Fisheries, where she remained until 1952. Carson's first three books, about life in and around the seas, were brilliant fusions of scientific accuracy and elegant prose. One, *The Sea Around Us*, became a best seller and was translated into thirty languages. *Silent Spring*, her last book, was also a best seller but prompted bitter criticism, especially from large-scale producers and users who argued that pesticides increased productivity and therefore living standards. No one, though, refuted her facts and case histories. Carson died in Silver Spring, Maryland, in 1964.

Questions to Consider. Why did Carson call the 1950s "the age of poisons"? Was her proposal to label consumer pesticides with a skull and crossbones practical? Why did she emphasize household products so much, including gardening materials? What was happening in American society in the 1950s that might have prompted this focus on the household and home? What specific measures did Carson propose to protect society from agricultural chemicals? Which of these measures would be most likely to arouse resistance?

Silent Spring (1962)

RACHEL CARSON

So thoroughly has the age of poisons become established that anyone may walk into a store and, without questions being asked, buy substances of far greater death-dealing power than the medicinal drug for which he may be

Rachel Carson. (Alfred Eisenstaedt/TimeLife Pictures/Getty Images)

required to sign a "poison book" in the pharmacy next door. A few minutes' research in any supermarket is enough to alarm the most stouthearted customer—provided, that is, he has even a rudimentary knowledge of the chemicals presented for his choice.

If a huge skull and crossbones were suspended above the insecticide department the customer might at least enter it with the respect normally accorded death-dealing materials. But instead the display is homey and cheerful, and, with the pickles and olives across the aisle and the bath and laundry soaps adjoining, the rows upon rows of insecticides are displayed. Within easy reach of a child's exploring hand are chemicals in *glass* containers. If dropped to the floor by a child or careless adult everyone nearby could be splashed with the same chemical that has sent spraymen using it into convulsions. These hazards of course follow the purchaser right into his home. A can of a mothproofing material containing DDD [dichloro-diphenyl-dichloroethane], for example, carries in very fine print the warning that its contents are under pressure and that it may burst if exposed to heat or open flame. A common insecticide for household use, including assorted uses in the kitchen, is chlordane. Yet the Food and Drug Administration's chief pharmacologist has declared the hazard of living in a house sprayed with chlordane to be "very great." Other household preparations contain the even more toxic dieldrin.

Use of poisons in the kitchen is made both attractive and easy. Kitchen shelf paper, white or tinted to match one's color scheme, may be impregnated with insecticide, not merely on one but on both sides. Manufacturers offer us do-it-yourself booklets on how to kill bugs. With push-button ease, one may send a fog of dieldrin into the most inaccessible nooks and crannies of cabinets, corners, and baseboards.

If we are troubled by mosquitoes, chiggers, or other insect pests on our persons we have a choice of innumerable lotions, creams, and sprays for application to clothing or skin. Although we are warned that some of these will dissolve varnish, paint, and synthetic fabrics, we are presumably to infer that the human skin is impervious to chemicals. To make certain that we shall at all times be prepared to repel insects, an exclusive New York store advertises a pocket-sized insecticide dispenser, suitable for the purse or for beach, golf, or fishing gear.

Gardening is now firmly linked with the super poisons. Every hardware store, garden-supply shop, and supermarket has rows of insecticides for every conceivable horticultural situation. Those who fail to make wide use of this array of lethal sprays and dusts are by implication remiss, for almost every newspaper's garden page and the majority of the gardening magazines take their use for granted.

So extensively are even the rapidly lethal organic phosphorus insecticides applied to lawns and ornamental plants that in 1960 the Florida State Board of Health found it necessary to forbid the commercial use of pesticides in residential areas by anyone who had not first obtained a permit and met certain requirements. A number of deaths from parathion had occurred in Florida before this regulation was adopted.

Little is done, however, to warn the gardener or homeowner that he is handling extremely dangerous materials. On the contrary, a constant stream of new gadgets makes it easier to use poisons on lawn and garden—and increase the gardener's contact with them. One may get a jar-type attachment for the garden hose, for example, by which such extremely dangerous chemicals as chlordane or dieldrin are applied as one waters the lawn. Such a device is not only a hazard to the person using the hose; it is also a public menace. The *New York Times* found it necessary to issue a warning on its garden page to the effect that unless special protective devices were installed poisons might get into the water supply by back siphonage. Considering the number of such devices that are in use, and the scarcity of warnings such as this, do we need to wonder why our public waters are contaminated?

As an example of what may happen to the gardener himself, we might look at the case of a physician—an enthusiastic sparetime gardener—who began using DDT and then malathion on his shrubs and lawn, making regular weekly applications. Sometimes he applied the chemicals with a hand spray, sometimes with an attachment to his hose. In doing so, his skin and clothing were often soaked with spray. After about a year of this sort of thing, he suddenly collapsed and was hospitalized. Examination of a biopsy specimen of fat showed an accumulation of 23 parts per million of DDT. There was extensive nerve damage, which his physicians regarded as permanent. As time went on he lost weight, suffered extreme fatigue, and experienced a peculiar muscular weakness, a characteristic effect of malathion. All of these persisting effects were severe enough to make it difficult for the physician to carry on his practice. . . .

Among the general population with no known gross exposures to insecticides it may be assumed that much of the DDT stored in fat deposits has entered the body in food. To test this assumption, a scientific team from the United States Public Health Service sampled restaurant and institutional meals. *Every meal sampled contained DDT.* From this the investigators concluded, reasonably enough, that "few if any foods can be relied upon to be entirely free of DDT."

The quantities in such meals may be enormous. In a separate Public Health Service study, analysis of prison meals disclosed such items as stewed dried fruit containing 69.6 parts per million and bread containing 100.9 parts per million of DDT!

In the diet of the average home, meats and any products derived from animal fats contain the heaviest residues of chlorinated hydrocarbons. This is because these chemicals are soluble in fat. Residues on fruits and vegetables tend to be somewhat less. These are little affected by washing—the only remedy is to remove and discard all outside leaves of such vegetables as lettuce or cabbage, to peel fruit and to use no skins or outer covering whatever. Cooking does not destroy residues.

Milk is one of the few foods in which no pesticide residues are permitted by Food and Drug Administration regulations. In actual fact, however, residues turn up whenever a check is made. They are heaviest in butter and other manufactured dairy products. A check of 461 samples of such products in 1960 showed that a third contained residues, a situation which the Food and Drug Administration characterized as "far from encouraging." . . .

The fact that every meal we eat carries its loads of chlorinated hydrocarbons is the inevitable consequence of the almost universal spraying or dusting of agricultural crops with these poisons. If the farmer scrupulously follows the instructions on the labels, his use of agricultural chemicals will produce no residues larger than are permitted by the Food and Drug Administration. Leaving aside for the moment the question whether these legal residues are as "safe" as they are represented to be, there remains the well-known fact that farmers very frequently exceed the prescribed dosages, use the chemical too close to the time of harvest, use several insecticides where one would do, and in other ways display the common human failure to read the fine print.

Even the chemical industry recognizes the frequent misuse of insecticides and the need for education of farmers. One of its leading trade journals recently declared that "many users do not seem to understand that they may exceed insecticide tolerances if they use higher dosages than recommended. And haphazard use of insecticides on many crops may be based on farmers' whims."

The files of the Food and Drug Administration contain records of a disturbing number of such violations. A few examples will serve to illustrate the disregard of directions: a lettuce farmer who applied not one but eight different insecticides to his crop within a short time of harvest, a shipper who had used the deadly parathion on celery in an amount five times the recommended maximum, growers using endrin—most toxic of all the chlorinated hydrocarbons—on lettuce although no residue was allowable, spinach sprayed with DDT a week before harvest.

There are also cases of chance or accidental contamination. Large lots of green coffee in burlap bags have become contaminated while being transported by vessels also carrying a cargo of insecticides. Packaged foods in warehouses are subjected to repeated aerosol treatments with DDT, lindane, and other insecticides, which may penetrate the packaging materials and occur in measurable quantities on the contained foods. The longer the food remains in storage, the greater the danger of contamination.

To the question "But doesn't the government protect us from such things?" the answer is, "Only to a limited extent." The activities of the Food and Drug Administration in the field of consumer protection against pesticides are severely limited by two facts. The first is that it has jurisdiction only over foods shipped in interstate commerce; foods grown and marketed within a state are entirely outside its sphere of authority, no matter what the violation. The second and critically limiting fact is the small number of inspectors on its staff—fewer than 600 men for all its varied work. According to a Food and Drug official, only an infinitesimal part of the crop products moving in interstate commerce—far less than 1 per cent—can be checked with existing facilities, and this is not enough to have statistical significance. As for food produced and sold within a state, the situation is even worse, for most states have woefully inadequate laws in this field. . . .

What is the solution? The first necessity is the elimination of tolerances on the chlorinated hydrocarbons, the organic phosphorus group, and other highly toxic chemicals. It will immediately be objected that this will place an intolerable burden on the farmer. But if, as is now the presumable goal, it is possible to use chemicals in such a way that they leave a residue of only 7 parts per million (the tolerance for DDT), or of 1 part per million (the tolerance for parathion), or even of only 0.1 part per million as is required for dieldrin on a great variety of fruits and vegetables, then why is it not possible, with only a little more care, to prevent the occurrence of any residues at all?

This, in fact, is what is required for some chemicals such as heptachlor, endrin, and dieldrin on certain crops. If it is considered practical in these instances, why not for all?

But this is not a complete or final solution, for a zero tolerance on paper is of little value. At present, as we have seen, more than 99 per cent of the interstate food shipments slip by without inspection. A vigilant and aggressive Food and Drug Administration, with a greatly increased force of inspectors, is another urgent need.

This system, however—deliberately poisoning our food, then policing the result—is too reminiscent of Lewis Carroll's White Knight who thought of "a plan to dye one's whiskers green, and always use so large a fan that they could not be seen." The ultimate answer is to use less toxic chemicals so that the public hazard from their misuse is greatly reduced. Such chemicals already exist: the pyrethrins, rotenone, ryania, and others derived from plant substances. Synthetic substitutes for the pyrethrins have recently been developed [so that an otherwise critical shortage can be averted]. Public education as to the nature of the chemicals offered for sale is sadly needed. The average purchaser is completely bewildered by the array of available insecticides, fungicides, and weed killers, and has no way of knowing which are the deadly ones, which reasonably safe. . . .

Until a large-scale conversion to these methods has been made, we shall have little relief from a situation that, by any common-sense standards, is intolerable. As matters stand now, we are in little better position than the guests of the Borgias.

38

NONVIOLENCE AND PROTEST

When the Supreme Court ordered public schools desegregated in 1954, the country's leading civil rights organizations—the NAACP, CORE, and the National Urban League—were all situated in the North. They drew their strength mainly from teachers, journalists, lawyers, students, businesspeople, and other persons who made up the tiny black middle class, and challenged racial oppression mostly through lawsuits and political lobbying. The initiatives of these organizations might affect Southern blacks and change the lives of black rural and urban workers, who made up most of the black population, because most blacks still lived in the South and did manual labor. But the organizations themselves were not based on this Southern black majority and so were unable to involve these African Americans in the civil rights struggle or to mount direct challenges to racial injustice in the section of the country where it mattered most.

By the late 1950s the situation was changing. In part this resulted from efforts to implement the *Brown* decision, particularly in New Orleans, Louisiana, and Little Rock, Arkansas. There militant whites met black students with violence, prompting not only federal intervention but black demonstrations in support of desegregation. Southern NAACP chapters now grew rapidly, giving that organization a regional strength it had not enjoyed before. Even more important were the direct actions against segregated public facilities led by the Reverend Martin Luther King, Jr., and the civil rights group he founded in 1957, the Southern Christian Leadership Conference (SCLC). The first of these actions was precipitated by an incident in Montgomery, Alabama, in December 1955, when a woman named Rosa Parks refused to move to a seat at the back of the bus, where bus regulations required blacks to sit. When Parks was arrested, Montgomery blacks, acting under King's general leadership, began a boycott of the bus system that involved unprecedented mass meetings in local black churches and lasted until the city finally desegregated its public transportation a year later. This success spurred similar actions elsewhere against the racial caste system and propelled King and the SCLC to the forefront of civil rights protest.

In the early 1960s the CORE sent "freedom riders" on bus trips into the South to find out whether interstate bus facilities were integrated. A new group, the Student Nonviolent Coordinating Committee (SNCC), organized sit-ins in segregated cafes, stand-ins at segregated theaters, and swim-ins at segregated beaches. Then in early 1963, King and the SCLC organized boycotts and marches in the industrial city of Birmingham, Alabama, during which thousands of black men, women, and children were beaten, shot at, attacked by dogs, sprayed with hoses, and imprisoned. Among the imprisoned was King; while in jail, in answer to an "open letter" by several white clergymen, he wrote a statement, reprinted below, on the goals and methods of the civil rights movement and the SCLC's controversial philosophy of nonviolent protest. The Birmingham protests ended after important city business and civic leaders pledged to begin the process of local desegregation.

Questions to Consider.   King organized his famous letter around points that local ministers had raised in an open letter critical of the demonstrations. Do you find his responses compelling? Is his explanation of the philosophy of nonviolence adequate? King himself acknowledged that many in the black community, especially in the North, found nonviolence too passive, deferential, and submissive. Were they likely to find his letter satisfactory? To defend lawbreaking, King divided laws into two categories and attempted to explain why he advocated breaking unjust laws and opposed breaking just ones. Is his distinction valid? Finally, what evidence can you find in the style of the letter that it was written in jail? by a minister?

★━━★━━★

Letter from Birmingham Jail (1963)

MARTIN LUTHER KING, JR.

My Dear Fellow Clergymen:

While confined here in the Birmingham city jail, I came across your recent statement calling my present activities "unwise and untimely." . . .

I think I should indicate why I am here in Birmingham, since you have been influenced by the view which argues against "outsiders coming in." I have the honor of serving as president of the Southern Christian Leadership Conference, an organization operating in every southern state, with head-

March on Washington. In August 1963, some 250,000 demonstrators gathered at the foot of the Lincoln Memorial to press the federal government for action on the civil rights front. Highlighted by Martin Luther King's dramatic "I have a dream" speech envisioning a land without prejudice, the march was notable in three ways in addition to its size. First, it was integrated. Second, it was orderly. Third, it had a limited goal: congressional action to protect constitutional rights. It was practically the last of the great demonstrations of the 1960s with all these characteristics. (AP/Wide World)

quarters in Atlanta, Georgia. We have some eighty-five affiliated organizations across the South, and one of them is the Alabama Christian Movement for Human Rights. Frequently we share staff, educational and financial resources with our affiliates. Several months ago the affiliate here in Birmingham asked us to be on call to engage in a nonviolent direct-action program if such were deemed necessary. We readily consented, and when the hour came we lived up to our promise. So I, along with several members of my staff, am here because I was invited here. I am here because I have organizational ties here.

But more basically, I am in Birmingham because injustice is here. Just as the prophets of the eighth century B.C. left their villages and carried their "thus saith the Lord" far beyond the boundaries of their home towns, and just as the Apostle Paul left his village of Tarsus and carried the gospel of Jesus Christ to the far corners of the Greco-Roman world, so am I compelled to carry the gospel of freedom beyond my own home town. Like Paul, I must constantly respond to the Macedonian call for aid.

Moreover, I am cognizant of the interrelatedness of all communities and states. I cannot sit idly by in Atlanta and not be concerned about what happens in Birmingham. Injustice anywhere is a threat to justice everywhere. We are caught in an inescapable network of mutuality, tied in a single garment of destiny. Whatever affects one directly, affects all indirectly. Never again can we afford to live with the narrow, provincial "outside agitator" idea. Anyone who lives inside the United States can never be considered an outsider anywhere within its bounds.

You deplore the demonstrations taking place in Birmingham. But your statement, I am sorry to say, fails to express a similar concern for the conditions that brought about the demonstrations. I am sure that none of you would want to rest content with the superficial kind of social analysis that deals merely with effects and does not grapple with underlying causes. It is unfortunate that demonstrations are taking place in Birmingham, but it is even more unfortunate that the city's white power structure left the Negro community with no alternative.

In any nonviolent campaign there are four basic steps: collection of the facts to determine whether injustices exist; negotiation; self-purification; and direct action. We have gone through all these steps in Birmingham. There can be no gainsaying the fact that racial injustice engulfs this community. Birmingham is probably the most thoroughly segregated city in the United States. Its ugly record of brutality is widely known. Negroes have experienced grossly unjust treatment in the courts. There have been more unsolved bombings of Negro homes and churches in Birmingham than in any other city in the nation. These are the hard, brutal facts of the case. On the basis of these conditions, Negro leaders sought to negotiate with the city fathers. But the latter consistently refused to engage in good-faith negotiation. . . .

As in so many past experiences, our hopes had been blasted, and the shadow of deep disappointment settled upon us. We had no alternative except to prepare for direct action, whereby we would present our very bodies as a means of laying our case before the conscience of the local and the national community. Mindful of the difficulties involved, we decided to undertake a process of self-purification. We began a series of workshops on nonviolence, and we repeatedly asked ourselves: "Are you able to accept blows without retaliating?" "Are you able to endure the ordeal of jail?" We decided to schedule our direct-action program for the Easter season, realizing that except for Christmas, this is the main shopping period of the year. . . .

You may well ask: "Why direct action? Why sit-ins, marches and so forth? Isn't negotiation a better path?" You are quite right in calling for negotiation. Indeed, this is the very purpose of direct action. Nonviolent direct action seeks to create such a crisis and foster such a tension that a community which has constantly refused to negotiate is forced to confront the issue. It seeks so to dramatize the issue that it can no longer be ignored. My citing the creation of tension as part of the work of the nonviolent-resister may sound rather shocking. But I must confess that I am not afraid of the word "tension." I have earnestly opposed violent tension, but there is a type of constructive, nonviolent tension which is necessary for growth. Just as Socrates [Greek philosopher] felt that it was necessary to create a tension in the mind so that individuals could rise from the bondage of myths and half-truths to the un-fettered realm of creative analysis and objective appraisal, so must we see the need for nonviolent gadflies to create the kind of tension in society that will help men rise from the dark depths of prejudice and racism to the majestic heights of understanding and brotherhood.

The purpose of our direct-action program is to create a situation so crisis-packed that it will inevitably open the door to negotiation. I therefore con-cur with you in your call for negotiation. Too long has our beloved Southland been bogged down in a tragic effort to live in monologue rather than dialogue. . . .

We know through painful experience that freedom is never voluntarily given by the oppressor; it must be demanded by the oppressed. Frankly, I have yet to engage in a direct-action campaign that was "well timed" in the view of those who have not suffered unduly from the disease of segregation. For years now I have heard the word "Wait!" It rings in the ear of every Ne-gro with piercing familiarity. This "Wait" has almost always meant "Never." We must come to see, with one of our distinguished jurists, that "justice too long delayed is justice denied."

We have waited for more than 340 years for our constitutional and God-given rights. The nations of Asia and Africa are moving with jetlike speed to-ward gaining political independence, but we still creep at horse-and-buggy pace toward gaining a cup of coffee at a lunch counter. Perhaps it is easy for those who have never felt the stinging darts of segregation to say, "Wait." But when you have seen vicious mobs lynch your mothers and fathers at will and drown your sisters and brothers at whim; when you have seen hate-filled po-licemen curse, kick and even kill your black brothers and sisters; when you see the vast majority of your twenty million Negro brothers smothering in an airtight cage of poverty in the midst of an affluent society; when you sud-denly find your tongue twisted and your speech stammering as you seek to explain to your six-year-old daughter why she can't go to the public amuse-ment park that has just been advertised on television, and see tears welling up in her eyes when she is told that Funtown is closed to colored children, and see ominous clouds of inferiority beginning to form in her little men-tal sky, and see her beginning to distort her personality by developing an unconscious bitterness toward white people; when you have to concoct an answer for a five-year-old son who is asking: "Daddy, why do white people treat colored people so mean?"; when you take a cross-country drive and find it necessary to sleep night after night in the uncomfortable corners of your automobile because no motel will accept you; when you are humiliated day in and day out by nagging signs reading "white" and "colored"; when your first name becomes "nigger," your middle name becomes "boy" (however old you are) and your last name becomes "John," and your wife and mother are never given the respected title "Mrs."; when you are harried by day and haunted by night by the fact that you are a Negro, living constantly at tiptoe stance, never quite knowing what to expect next, and are plagued with inner fears and outer resentments; when you are forever fighting a degenerating sense of "nobodiness"—then you will understand why we find it difficult to wait. There comes a time when the cup of endurance runs over, and men are no longer willing to be plunged into the abyss of despair. I hope, sirs, you can understand our legitimate and unavoidable impatience.

You express a great deal of anxiety over our willingness to break laws. This is certainly a legitimate concern. Since we so diligently urge people to obey the Supreme Court's decision of 1954 [*Brown* v. *The Board of Education of Topeka*] outlawing segregation in the public schools, at first glance it may seem rather paradoxical for us consciously to break laws. One may well ask: "How can you advocate breaking some laws and obeying others?" The answer lies in the fact that there are two types of laws: just and unjust. I would be the first to advocate obeying just laws. One has not only a legal but a moral responsibility to obey just laws. Conversely, one has a moral responsibility to disobey unjust laws. I would agree with St. Augustine that "an unjust law is no law at all."

Now, what is the difference between the two? How does one determine whether a law is just or unjust? A just law is a man-made code that squares with the moral law or the law of God. An unjust law is a code that is out of harmony with the moral law. To put it in the terms of St. Thomas Aquinas [Catholic theologian]: An unjust law is a human law that is not rooted in eternal law and natural law. Any law that uplifts human personality is just. Any law that degrades human personality is unjust. All segregation statutes are unjust because segregation distorts the soul and damages the personality. It gives the segregator a false sense of superiority and the segregated a false sense of inferiority. Segregation, to use the terminology of the Jewish philosopher Martin Buber, substitutes an "I-it" relationship for an "I-thou" relationship and ends up relegating persons to the status of things. Hence segregation is not only politically, economically and sociologically unsound, it is morally wrong and sinful. Paul Tillich [Protestant theologian] has said that sin is separation. Is not segregation an existential expression of man's tragic separation, his awful estrangement, his terrible sinfulness? Thus it is that I can urge men to obey the 1954 decision of the Supreme Court, for it is morally right; and I can urge them to disobey segregation ordinances, for they are morally wrong. . . .

I hope you are able to see the distinction I am trying to point out. In no sense do I advocate evading or defying the law, as would the rabid segregationist. That would lead to anarchy. One who breaks an unjust law must do so openly, lovingly, and with a willingness to accept the penalty. I submit that an individual who breaks a law that conscience tells him is unjust, and who willingly accepts the penalty of imprisonment in order to arouse the conscience of the community over its injustice, is in reality expressing the highest respect for the law. . . .

In your statement you assert that our actions, even though peaceful, must be condemned because they precipitate violence. But is this a logical assertion? Isn't this like condemning a robbed man because his possession of money precipitated the evil act of robbery? Isn't this like condemning Socrates because his unswerving commitment to truth and his philosophical inquiries precipitated the act by the misguided populace in which they made him drink hemlock? Isn't this like condemning Jesus because his unique God-consciousness and never-ceasing devotion to God's will precipitated the evil act of crucifixion? We must come to see that, as the federal courts have consistently affirmed, it is wrong to urge an individual to cease his efforts to gain his basic constitutional rights because the quest may precipitate violence. Society must protect the robbed and punish the robber. . . .

You speak of our activity in Birmingham as extreme. At first I was rather disappointed that fellow clergymen would see my nonviolent efforts as those of an extremist. I began thinking about the fact that I stand in the middle of two opposing forces in the Negro community. One is a force of complacency, made up in part of Negroes who, as a result of long years of oppression, are so drained of self-respect and a sense of "somebodiness" that they have adjusted to segregation; and in part of a few middle-class Negroes who, because of a degree of academic and economic security and because in some ways they profit by segregation, have become insensitive to the problems of the masses. The other force is one of bitterness and hatred, and it comes perilously close to advocating violence. It is expressed in the various black nationalist groups that are springing up across the nation, the largest and best-known being Elijah Muhammad's Muslim movement. Nourished by the Negro's frustration over the continued existence of racial discrimination, this movement is made up of people who have lost faith in America, who have absolutely repudiated Christianity, and who have concluded that the white man is an incorrigible "devil."

I have tried to stand between these two forces, saying that we need emulate neither the "do-nothingism" of the complacent nor the hatred and despair of the black nationalist. For there is the more excellent way of love and nonviolent protest. I am grateful to God that, through the influence of the Negro church, the way of nonviolence became an integral part of our struggle. . . .

. . . [T]hough I was initially disappointed at being categorized as an extremist, as I continued to think about the matter I gradually gained a measure of satisfaction from the label. Was not Jesus an extremist for love: "Love your enemies, bless them that curse you, do good to them that hate you, and pray for them which despitefully use you, and persecute you." Was not Amos an extremist for justice: "Let justice roll down like waters and righteousness like an ever-flowing stream." Was not Paul an extremist for the Christian gospel: "I bear in my body the marks of the Lord Jesus." Was not Martin Luther an extremist: "Here I stand: I cannot do otherwise, so help me God." And John Bunyan: "I will stay in jail to the end of my days before I make a butchery of my conscience." And Abraham Lincoln: "This nation cannot survive half slave and half free." And Thomas Jefferson: "We hold these truths to be self-evident, that all men are created equal . . ." So the question is not whether we will be extremists, but what kind of extremists we will be. Will we be extremists for hate or for love? Will we be extremists for the preservation of injustice or for the extension of justice? . . .

Before closing I feel impelled to mention one other point in your statement that has troubled me profoundly. You warmly commended the Birmingham police force for keeping "order" and "preventing violence." I doubt that you would have so warmly commended the police force if you had seen its dogs sinking their teeth into unarmed, nonviolent Negroes. I doubt that you would so quickly commend the policemen if you were to observe their ugly and inhumane treatment of Negroes here in the city jail; if you were to watch them push and curse old Negro women and young Negro girls; if you were to see them slap and kick old Negro men and young boys; if you were to observe them, as they did on two occasions, refuse to give us food because we wanted to sing our grace together. I cannot join you in your praise of the Birmingham police department. . . .

I wish you had commended the Negro sit-inners and demonstrators of Birmingham for their sublime courage, their willingness to suffer and their amazing discipline in the midst of great provocation. One day the South will recognize its real heroes. They will be the James Merediths,[1] with the noble sense of purpose that enables them to face jeering and hostile mobs, and with the agonizing loneliness that characterizes the life of the pioneer. They will be old, oppressed, battered Negro women, symbolized in a seventy-two-year-old woman in Montgomery, Alabama, who rose up with a sense of dignity and with her people decided not to ride segregated buses, and who responded with ungrammatical profundity to one who inquired about her weariness: "My feets is tired, but my soul is at rest." They will be the young high school and college students, the young ministers of the gospel and a host of their elders, courageously and nonviolently sitting in at lunch counters and willingly going to jail for conscience' sake. One day the South will know that when these disinherited children of God sat down at lunch

---

1. James Meredith was the first black student at the University of Mississippi. His efforts to enter the university in 1962 were met by white demonstrations and violence.—*Eds.*

counters, they were in reality standing up for what is best in the American dream and for the most sacred values in our Judaeo-Christian heritage, thereby bringing our nation back to those great wells of democracy which were dug deep by the founding fathers in their formulation of the Constitution and the Declaration of Independence.

Never before have I written so long a letter. I'm afraid it is much too long to take your precious time. I can assure you that it would have been much shorter if I had been writing from a comfortable desk, but what else can one do when he is alone in a narrow jail cell, other than write long letters, think long thoughts and pray long prayers?

39

WOMEN'S LIBERATION

After its bright triumph of the early 1920s, interest in the movement for women's rights lagged, then gathered new steam in the 1950s. This resurgence resulted partly from a trend in the workforce: 27 percent of adult women worked outside the home in 1940, 33 percent in 1960, and 50 percent in 1980. With so many women in the workforce, they gradually made their concerns heard: equal pay for equal work, managerial positions in heretofore all-male administrations, elimination of sexual and physical harassment. Working wives, it turned out, often strained traditional male-dominant marriages, and both the divorce rate and the need for new child-care arrangements increased. Also, married or not, working women saw their lives focusing less exclusively on children and domesticity. They therefore looked increasingly to modern birth control devices and to abortion. (The Supreme Court declared abortion legal in 1973.) From 1960 to 1980, the birth rate decreased 50 percent.

But if these trends provided the underpinnings for the modern women's movement, true feminism—the struggle for women's liberation—came only with the addition of "consciousness raising" to these socioeconomic tendencies. Here, too, there was a crucial underlying trend: many more women were college-educated than ever before. In 1940 approximately 15 percent of American women had completed at least one year of college, and women earned about one-fourth of all bachelor's degrees given by U.S. colleges. By 1960, about 20 percent of all women had gone to college, and women earned one-third of all bachelor's degrees. By 1990, the percentage of women attending college was over 45 percent and women earned nearly half of all U.S. bachelor's degrees.

In part, Betty Friedan was addressing these millions of educated but underemployed women in her pathbreaking *The Feminine Mystique,* published in 1963 and excerpted below. Friedan attacked the mass media for brainwashing women into models of domesticity. The National Organization for Women (NOW), created in 1966 with Friedan's support, pressed for eliminating all discriminatory legal sexual distinctions. A half-century after the suffrage amendment, politics witnessed major gains for women. They became governors in numerous states, including Texas, one of the three largest. Female senators were elected from several states, including Florida, another of the three largest. Mayors in many of the nation's largest cities, including Chicago and Houston, were women. They held three cabinet positions under Jimmy Carter and one each under Reagan and Bush. Two women were appointed Supreme Court justices, and one ran as a Democratic Party vice-presidential candidate. Women were commonplace in the American military forces in the two Persian Gulf wars, although not initially in official combat roles.

Betty Friedan was born in 1921 in Illinois and attended Smith College and the University of California at Berkeley. In the early 1960s Friedan was a wife and mother who, having lost her job as a newspaper reporter, was contributing to popular magazines. Noticing that editors frequently cut her references to women's careers in favor of more material on homemaking, she began to analyze the housewife fantasy and to interview housewives themselves. The result was *The Feminine Mystique* (1963), an instant best seller that catapulted its author to the forefront of the women's movement and earned her countless offers to lecture and teach. Friedan was the founding president of the National Organization for Women from 1966 to 1970 and also helped found the National Women's Political Caucus and the National Association to Repeal Abortion Laws. None of it was easy. "A lot of people," she recalled, "treated me like a leper."

Questions to Consider. Betty Friedan argued in *The Feminine Mystique* that American women suffered from a "problem that has no name." What was that problem? Was she the first to discover it? What were her methods of investigating and reporting it? Why did it have no name? Did Friedan name it? Would all American women have responded to Friedan's arguments? What kinds of women would have been most likely to respond? How revolutionary was her message? What social or political measures would be required to deal effectively with this problem?

★━━★━━★

The Feminine Mystique (1963)

BETTY FRIEDAN

The suburban housewife—she was the dream image of the young American women and the envy, it was said, of women all over the world. The American

A balding Jock Semple of the Boston Athletic Association accosts Karen Switzer of Syracuse in an effort to enforce the BAA's rule barring women from running in the Boston Marathon, 1967. In the late 1960s there were still few opportunities for women to participate in serious sports at any level, a situation that changed significantly only with the passage of federal antidiscrimination legislation. (© Bettmann/Corbis)

housewife—freed by science and labor-saving appliances from the drudgery, the dangers of childbirth and the illnesses of her grandmother. She was healthy, beautiful, educated, concerned only about her husband, her children, her home. She had found true feminine fulfillment. As a housewife and mother, she was respected as a full and equal partner to man in his world. She was free to choose automobiles, clothes, appliances, supermarkets; she had everything that women ever dreamed of.

In the fifteen years after World War II, this mystique of feminine fulfillment became the cherished and self-perpetuating core of contemporary American culture. Millions of women lived their lives in the image of those pretty pictures of the American suburban housewife, kissing their husbands goodbye in front of the picture window, depositing their stationwagonsful of children at school, and smiling as they ran the new electric waxer over the spotless kitchen floor. They baked their own bread, sewed their own and their children's clothes, kept their new washing machines and dryers running all day. They changed the sheets on the beds twice a week instead of once, took the rug-hooking class in adult education, and pitied their poor frustrated mothers, who had dreamed of having a career. Their only dream was to be perfect wives and mothers; their highest ambition to have five children and a beautiful house, their only fight to get and keep their husbands. They had no thought for the unfeminine problems of the world outside the home; they wanted the men to make the major decisions. They gloried in their role as women, and wrote proudly on the census blank: "Occupation: housewife."

For over fifteen years, the words written for women, and the words women used when they talked to each other, while their husbands sat on the other side of the room and talked shop or politics or septic tanks, were about problems with their children, or how to keep their husbands happy, or improve their children's school, or cook chicken or make slipcovers. Nobody argued whether women were inferior or superior to men; they were simply different. Words like *emancipation* and *career* sounded strange and embarrassing; no one had used them for years. . . .

But on an April morning in 1959, I heard a mother of four, having coffee with four other mothers in a suburban development fifteen miles from New York, say in a tone of quiet desperation, "the problem." And the others knew, without words, that she was not talking about a problem with her husband, or her children, or her home. Suddenly they realized they all shared the same problem, the problem that has no name. They began, hesitantly, to talk about it. Later, after they had picked up their children at nursery school and taken them home to nap, two of the women cried, in sheer relief, just to know they were not alone. . . .

Just what was this problem that has no name? What were the words women used when they tried to express it? Sometimes a woman would say "I feel empty somehow . . . incomplete." Or she would say, "I feel as if I don't exist." Sometimes she blotted out the feeling with a tranquilizer. Sometimes she thought the problem was with her husband, or her children, or that what she really needed was to redecorate her house, or move to a better neighborhood, or have an affair, or another baby. Sometimes, she went to a doctor with symptoms she could hardly describe: "A tired feeling . . . I get so angry with the children it scares me . . . I feel like crying without any reason." (A Cleveland doctor called it "the housewife's syndrome.") A number of women told me about great bleeding blisters that break out on their hands and arms. "I call it the housewife's blight," said a family doctor in Pennsylvania. "I see it so often lately in these young women with four, five and six children who bury themselves in their dishpans. But it isn't caused by detergent and it isn't cured by cortisone." . . .

In 1960, the problem that has no name burst like a boil through the image of the happy American housewife. In the television commercials the pretty housewives still beamed over their foaming dishpans and *Time's* cover story on "The Suburban Wife, an American Phenomenon" protested: "Having too good a time . . . to believe that they should be unhappy." But the actual unhappiness of the American housewife was suddenly being reported—from the *New York Times* and *Newsweek* to *Good Housekeeping* and CBS Television

("The Trapped Housewife"), although almost everybody who talked about it found some superficial reason to dismiss it. . . .

Of the growing thousands of women currently getting private psychiatric help in the United States, the married ones were reported dissatisfied with their marriages, the unmarried ones suffering from anxiety and, finally, depression. Strangely, a number of psychiatrists stated that, in their experience, unmarried women patients were happier than married ones. So the door of all those pretty suburban houses opened a crack to permit a glimpse of uncounted thousands of American housewives who suffered alone from a problem that suddenly everyone was talking about, and beginning to take for granted, as one of those unreal problems in American life that can never be solved—like the hydrogen bomb. . . .

I do not accept the answer that there is no problem because American women have luxuries that women in other times and lands never dreamed of; part of the strange newness of the problem is that it cannot be understood in terms of the age-old material problems of man: poverty, sickness, hunger, cold. The women who suffer this problem have a hunger that food cannot fill. . . .

Are the women who finished college, the women who once had dreams beyond housewifery, the ones who suffer the most? According to the experts they are, but . . . housewives of all educational levels suffer the same feeling of desperation.

The fact is that no one today is muttering angrily about "women's rights," even though more and more women have gone to college. In a recent study of all the classes that have graduated from Barnard College, a significant minority of earlier graduates blamed their education for making them want "rights," later classes blamed their education for giving them career dreams, but recent graduates blamed the college for making them feel it was not enough simply to be a housewife and mother; they did not want to feel guilty if they did not read books or take part in community activities. But if education is not the cause of the problem, the fact that education somehow festers in these women may be a clue.

If the secret of feminine fulfillment is having children, never have so many women, with the freedom to choose, had so many children, in so few years, so willingly. If the answer is love, never have women searched for love with such determination. And yet there is a growing suspicion that the problem may not be sexual, though it must somehow be related to sex. I have heard from many doctors evidence of new sexual problems between man and wife—sexual hunger in wives so great their husbands cannot satisfy it. . . .

Can the problem that has no name be somehow related to the domestic routine of the housewife? When a woman tries to put the problem into words, she often merely describes the daily life she leads. What is there in this recital of comfortable domestic detail that could possibly cause such a feeling of desperation? Is she trapped simply by the enormous demands of her role as modern housewife: wife, mistress, mother, nurse, consumer, cook, chauffeur; expert on interior decoration, child care, appliance repair, furniture refinishing, nutrition, and education? . . .

If I am right, the problem that has no name stirring in the minds of so many American women today is not a matter of loss of femininity or too much education, or the demands of domesticity. It is far more important than anyone recognizes. It is the key to these other new and old problems which have been torturing women and their husbands and children, and puzzling their doctors and educators for years. It may well be the key to our future as a nation and a culture. We can no longer ignore that voice within women that says: "I want something more than my husband and my children and my home."

40

THE RIGHT TO VOTE

Lyndon Johnson would have been "a tough can-do president," said a disappointed Lady Bird Johnson after her husband had lost the 1960 Democratic presidential nomination to John F. Kennedy. Johnson then stepped down as majority leader of the Senate, ran for vice president with Kennedy, helped carry enough Southern states to put Kennedy in the White House—and became president himself in November 1963 when Kennedy was assassinated. Once in office, Johnson, confident of his ability to influence Congress and eager to pursue and expand Kennedy's unfinished initiatives, told his staff, "Get me those bills. We've got a window here that's going to close pretty quickly." The country was about to discover what Lady Bird was talking about.

In 1964 Johnson engineered a major corporate tax reduction. He followed this up with a historic Civil Rights Act, passed over bitter Southern objections, that banned segregation in public facilities and outlawed most employment discrimination; and the Economic Opportunity Act authorizing funds for a "war on poverty" and an office to co-ordinate such programs as Head Start and Upward Bound, for children and adolescents across the nation, and VISTA, a kind of "domestic peace corps." The next year Johnson really hit his stride, with the Elementary and Secondary Education Act, the first general federal program for schools in U.S. history; the Medical Care Act supporting medical insurance for the elderly and health funds for welfare recipients; a major housing act supplementing low-income rents; a major federal loan program for needy college students; and the establishment of the National Endowments for the Arts and the Humanities. These "Great Society" initiatives concluded in 1966 with subsidies for urban housing, recreational facilities, and mass-transit projects and unprecedented consumer safety acts.

Amid this plethora of federal legislation, none was more urgent or far-reaching than the Voting Rights Act of 1965, which President Johnson introduced to Congress in the televised speech excerpted below. One consequence of the failure of Republican Reconstruction after the Civil War had been that African Americans were prevented throughout the South from registering to vote or casting their ballots. Without the vote, black citizens and their allies could not ward off segregation, lynching, and other measures of racial subjugation, which almost inevitably followed. By the beginning of the twentieth century only one potential black voter in ten was registered; in states such as Georgia, Alabama, Mississippi, and Louisiana, the figure was less than one in twenty. Even by 1964, after years of civil rights agitation and some federal election monitoring, only a fourth of eligible black voters were registered.

The passage of the 1965 Voting Rights Act, which authorized federal examiners to register qualified voters and struck down literacy tests and other exclusionary devices, changed all this. Within five years two-thirds of the eligible black voters of the former Confederate states were registered. And when they voted, they overwhelmingly deserted the party of Lincoln for the party of Lyndon Johnson. Southern whites, particularly white males, meanwhile moved the other way, leading for the first time to Republican domination of the "Solid South," a shift that constituted the most important political realignment in modern American history. Even so, most Southern states remained competitive in federal elections thanks to the new black voters, and in state and local races black candidates began to win, thus redressing the region's long imbalance of political representation and power.

Questions to Consider. Lyndon Johnson was not known as an orator who could touch people's emotions. Yet many listeners who heard this speech found it uncharacteristically eloquent. What devices did Johnson use in this address to give it rhetorical power? What was there about this topic that seemed to demand and require eloquence? What different audiences did Johnson hope to reach? Was he speaking more to African Americans or to the general public? How did he use his own life experiences to strengthen his appeal? Do you find this effective? Did he believe that voting rights alone would suffice? White Southerners, including many of Johnson's Senate colleagues, detested this speech more than any of his other initiatives, including the Civil Rights Act. Why did they? Most other Americans welcomed it. Would they welcome it, and all it implied, as much today?

The American Promise (1965)

LYNDON B. JOHNSON

I speak tonight for the dignity of man and the destiny of democracy.

I urge every member of both parties, Americans of all religions and of all colors, from every section of this country, to join me in that cause. . . .

Our mission is at once the oldest and the most basic of this country: to right wrong, to do justice, to serve man.

In our time we have come to live with moments of great crisis. Our lives have been marked with debate about great issues; issues of war and peace, issues of prosperity and depression. But rarely in any time does an issue lay bare the secret heart of America itself. Rarely are we met with a challenge, not to our growth or abundance, our welfare or our security, but rather to the values and the purposes and the meaning of our beloved Nation.

The issue of equal rights for American Negroes is such an issue. And should we defeat every enemy, should we double our wealth and conquer the stars, and still be unequal to this issue, then we will have failed as a people and as a nation.

For with a country as with a person, "What is a man profited, if he shall gain the whole world, and lose his own soul?"

There is no Negro problem. There is no Southern problem. There is no Northern problem. There is only an American problem. And we are met here tonight as Americans—not as Democrats or Republicans—we are met here as Americans to solve that problem.

This was the first nation in the history of the world to be founded with a purpose. The great phrases of that purpose still sound in every American heart, North and South: "All men are created equal"—"government by consent of the governed"—"give me liberty or give me death." Well, those are not just clever words, or those are not just empty theories. In their name Americans have fought and died for two centuries, and tonight around the world they stand there as guardians of our liberty, risking their lives.

Those words are a promise to every citizen that he shall share in the dignity of man. This dignity cannot be found in a man's possessions; it cannot be found in his power, or in his position. It really rests on his right to be treated as a man equal in opportunity to all others. It says that he shall share in freedom, he shall choose his leaders, educate his children, and provide for his family according to his ability and his merits as a human being.

To apply any other test—to deny a man his hopes because of his color or race, his religion or the place of his birth—is not only to do injustice, it is to deny America and to dishonor the dead who gave their lives for American freedom.

Public Papers of the Presidents: Lyndon B. Johnson, 1965, no. 107.

Our fathers believed that if this noble view of the rights of man was to flourish, it must be rooted in democracy. The most basic right of all was the right to choose your own leaders. The history of this country, in large measure, is the history of the expansion of that right to all of our people.

Many of the issues of civil rights are very complex and most difficult. But about this there can and should be no argument. Every American citizen must have an equal right to vote. There is no reason which can excuse the denial of that right. There is no duty which weighs more heavily on us than the duty we have to ensure that right.

Yet the harsh fact is that in many places in this country men and women are kept from voting simply because they are Negroes.

Every device of which human ingenuity is capable has been used to deny this right. The Negro citizen may go to register only to be told that the day is wrong, or the hour is late, or the official in charge is absent. And if he persists, and if he manages to present himself to the registrar, he may be disqualified because he did not spell out his middle name or because he abbreviated a word on the application.

And if he manages to fill out an application he is given a test. The registrar is the sole judge of whether he passes this test. He may be asked to recite the entire Constitution, or explain the most complex provisions of State law. And even a college degree cannot be used to prove that he can read and write.

For the fact is that the only way to pass these barriers is to show a white skin.

Experience has clearly shown that the existing process of law cannot overcome systematic and ingenious discrimination. No law that we now have on the books—and I have helped to put three of them there—can ensure the right to vote when local officials are determined to deny it. . . .

Wednesday I will send to Congress a law designed to eliminate illegal barriers to the right to vote.

The broad principles of that bill will be in the hands of the Democratic and Republican leaders tomorrow. After they have reviewed it, it will come here formally as a bill. I am grateful for this opportunity to come here tonight at the invitation of the leadership to reason with my friends, to give them my views, and to visit with my former colleagues.

I have had prepared a more comprehensive analysis of the legislation which I had intended to transmit to the clerk tomorrow but which I will submit to the clerks tonight. But I want to really discuss with you now briefly the main proposals of this legislation.

This bill will strike down restrictions to voting in all elections—Federal, State, and local—which have been used to deny Negroes the right to vote.

This bill will establish a simple, uniform standard which cannot be used, however ingenious the effort, to flout our Constitution.

It will provide for citizens to be registered by officials of the United States Government if the State officials refuse to register them.

It will eliminate tedious, unnecessary lawsuits which delay the right to vote.

Finally, this legislation will ensure that properly registered individuals are not prohibited from voting. . . .

But even if we pass this bill, the battle will not be over. [This] is part of a far larger movement which reaches into every section and State of America. It is the effort of American Negroes to secure for themselves the full blessings of American life.

Their cause must be our cause too. Because it is not just Negroes, but really it is all of us, who must overcome the crippling legacy of bigotry and injustice.

And we shall overcome.

As a man whose roots go deeply into Southern soil I know how agonizing racial feelings are. I know how difficult it is to reshape the attitudes and the structure of our society.

But a century has passed, more than a hundred years, since the Negro was freed. And he is not fully free tonight. . . .

The time of justice has now come. I tell you that I believe sincerely that no force can hold it back. It is right in the eyes of man and God that it should come. And when it does, I think that day will brighten the lives of every American.

For Negroes are not the only victims. How many white children have gone uneducated, how many white families have lived in stark poverty, how many white lives have been scarred by fear, because we have wasted our energy and our substance to maintain the barriers of hatred and terror?

So I say to all of you here, and to all in the Nation tonight, that those who appeal to you to hold on to the past do so at the cost of denying you your future.

This great, rich, restless country can offer opportunity and education and hope to all: black and white, North and South, sharecropper and city dweller. These are the enemies: poverty, ignorance, disease. They are the enemies and not our fellow man, not our neighbor. And these enemies too, poverty, disease and ignorance, we shall overcome. . . .

The bill that I am presenting to you will be known as a civil rights bill. But, in a larger sense, most of the program I am recommending is a civil rights program. Its object is to open the city of hope to all people of all races.

Because all Americans just must have the right to vote. And we are going to give them that right.

All Americans must have the privileges of citizenship regardless of race. And they are going to have those privileges of citizenship regardless of race.

But I would like to caution you and remind you that to exercise these privileges takes much more than just legal right. It requires a trained mind and a healthy body. It requires a decent home, and the chance to find a job, and the opportunity to escape from the clutches of poverty.

Of course, people cannot contribute to the Nation if they are never taught to read or write, if their bodies are stunted from hunger, if their sickness goes untended, if their life is spent in hopeless poverty just drawing a welfare check.

So we want to open the gates to opportunity. But we are also going to give all our people, black and white, the help that they need to walk through those gates.

My first job after college was as a teacher in Cotulla, Texas, in a small

Mexican-American school. Few of them could speak English, and I couldn't speak much Spanish. My students were poor and they often came to class without breakfast, hungry. They knew even in their youth the pain of prejudice. They never seemed to know why people disliked them. But they knew it was so, because I saw it in their eyes. I often walked home late in the afternoon, after the classes were finished, wishing there was more that I could do. But all I knew was to teach them the little that I knew, hoping that it might help them against the hardships that lay ahead.

Somehow you never forget what poverty and hatred can do when you see its scars on the hopeful face of a young child.

I never thought then, in 1928, that I would be standing here in 1965. It never even occurred to me in my fondest dreams that I might have the chance to help the sons and daughters of those students and to help people like them all over this country.

But now I do have that chance—and I'll let you in on a secret—I mean to use it. And I hope that you will use it with me. . . .

Above the pyramid on the great seal of the United States it says—in Latin—"God has favored our undertaking."

God will not favor everything that we do. It is rather our duty to divine His will. But I cannot help believing that He truly understands and that He really favors the undertaking that we begin here tonight.

41

A Turn to Militancy

The civil rights movement began in earnest with *Brown* v. *The Board of Education of Topeka* in 1954 and the Montgomery bus boycott in 1955. For the next few years two groups provided the movement with leadership: the NAACP, which worked mainly through the courts and enjoyed a national membership; and the Southern Christian Leadership Conference (SCLC), based in the Southern churches and using the tactics of nonviolent demonstrations and boycotts. Though differing in methods, the two organizations shared important characteristics. Their chief objective was the integration of public facilities, including schools. And while they both had predominantly black membership, they also accepted white support and participation.

In the early 1960s, however, the civil rights movement began to change. Its primary focus moved from efforts to integrate public facilities to efforts to secure black voting rights. This brought fierce white resistance and much violence, particularly during the "freedom summers" of 1964 and 1965, when black and white college students ran voter registration campaigns in various parts of the South. The violence and the racially selective nature of the registration drives in turn sparked a reaction among young black activists against white participation in the movement. The new militant black position—articulated by the Student Nonviolent Coordinating Committee (SNCC) in the following 1966 position paper—gained plausibility from the outbreak of rioting in the Negro slums of Northern cities and from the example of dark-skinned liberation struggles in the Third World. After 1966, then, the civil rights movement became increasingly ethnocentric, militant, and fragmented. By 1970 it hardly existed in its original form.

SNCC was founded in 1960 at a conference called by Martin Luther King, Jr., who imbued its early members with his philosophy of nonviolence. The decisive shift occurred early in 1966 when Stokely Carmichael, the principal author of the position paper reprinted below, became chairman. Carmichael was born in 1941 on the West Indian island of Trinidad. After moving with his family to New York City, he lived first in mostly black Harlem and then in the mostly white Bronx, attended the High School of Science in the Bronx and Howard University in

Washington, D.C., and went to jail twenty-seven times during the Southern civil rights campaigns. Under Carmichael, SNCC dropped "Nonviolent" from its name, and its leaders urged angry blacks to undertake a militant black power position. Carmichael himself later married singer Miriam Makeba and moved to West Africa, where he took the name Kwame Touré and announced, "Africa is my home. I'm staying."

Questions to Consider. The SNCC paper on black power prompted quick, vigorous debate. Those distressed by the statement characterized it as belligerent, damaging, and despairing. Sympathizers called it necessary, determined, and reasonable. Does one set of adjectives seem more accurate than the other in assessing this statement? (Recently, scholars have used both sets of adjectives simultaneously in judging it!) Consider, too, the following points. Was it accurate to say in 1966 that no black could ever "represent" Americans and no white could ever "relate" to blacks? Did the paper propose to change this or accept it as a fact of life? Why were there so many references to popular culture in so political a paper? Why did the paper conclude by stressing the task of "identification"? Where did SNCC expect to find new sources of identity?

Black Power (1966)

STOKELY CARMICHAEL

The myth that the Negro is somehow incapable of liberating himself, is lazy, etc., came out of the American experience. In the books that children read, whites are always "good" (good symbols are white), blacks are "evil" or seen as savages in movies, their language is referred to as a "dialect," and black people in this country are supposedly descended from savages.

Any white person who comes into the movement has these concepts in his mind about black people if only subconsciously. He cannot escape them because the whole society has geared his subconscious in that direction.

Miss America coming from Mississippi has a chance to represent all of America, but a black person from either Mississippi or New York will never represent America. So that white people coming into the movement cannot relate to the black experience, cannot relate to the word "black," cannot relate to the "nitty gritty," cannot relate to the experience that brought such a word into being, cannot relate to chitterlings, hog's head cheese, pig feet, hamhocks, and cannot relate to slavery, because these things are not a part of their experience. They also cannot relate to the black religious experience, nor to the black church unless, of course, this church has taken on white manifestations.

Negroes in this country have never been allowed to organize themselves because of white interference. As a result of this, the stereotype has been reinforced that blacks cannot organize themselves. The white psychology that blacks have to be watched, also reinforces this stereotype. Blacks, in fact, feel intimidated by the presence of whites, because of their knowledge of the power that whites have over their lives. One white person can come into a meeting of black people and change the complexion of that meeting, whereas one black person would not change the complexion of that meeting unless he was an obvious Uncle Tom. People would immediately start talking about "brotherhood," "love," etc.; race would not be discussed.

If people must express themselves freely, there has to be a climate in which they can do this. If blacks feel intimidated by whites, then they are not liable to vent the rage that they feel about whites in the presence of whites—especially not the black people whom we are trying to organize, i.e. broad masses of black people. A climate has to be created whereby blacks can express themselves. The reason that whites must be excluded is not that one is antiwhite, but because the efforts that one is trying to achieve cannot succeed because whites have an intimidating effect. Oftentimes the intimidating effect is in direct proportion to the amount of degradation that black people have suffered at the hands of white people. How do blacks relate to other blacks as such? How do we react to Willie Mays as against Mickey Mantle? What is our reponse to Mays hitting a home run against Mantle performing the same deed? One has to come to the conclusion that it is because of black participation in baseball. Negroes still identify with the Dodgers because of Jackie Robinson's efforts with the Dodgers. Negroes would instinctively champion all-black teams if they opposed all-white or predominantly white teams. The same principle operates for the movement as it does for baseball: a mystique must be created whereby Negroes can identify with the movement.

Thus an all-black project is needed in order for the people to free themselves. This has to exist from the beginning. This relates to what can be called "coalition politics." There is no doubt in our minds that some whites are just as disgusted with this system as we are. But it is meaningless to talk about coalition if there is no one to align ourselves with, because of the lack of organization in the white communities. There can be no talk of "hooking up" unless black people organize blacks and white people organize whites. If these conditions are met then perhaps at some later date—and if we are going in the same direction—talks about exchange of personnel, coalition, and other meaningful alliances can be discussed.

These facts do not mean that whites cannot help. They can participate on a voluntary basis. We can contract work out to them, but in no way can they participate on a policy-making level.

The charge may be made that we are "racists," but whites who are sensitive to our problems will realize we must determine our own destiny.

In an attempt to find a solution to our dilemma, we propose that our organization (S.N.C.C.) should be black-staffed, black-controlled and black-financed. We do not want to fall into a similar dilemma that other civil rights organizations have fallen into. If we continue to rely upon white financial support we will find ourselves entwined in the tentacles of the white power complex that controls this country. It is also important that a black organization (devoid of cultism) be projected to our people so that it can be demonstrated that such organizations are viable.

More and more we see black people in this country being used as a tool of the white liberal establishment. Liberal whites have not begun to address themselves to the real problem of black people in this country; witness their bewilderment, fear and anxiety when nationalism is mentioned concerning black people. An analysis of their (white liberal) reaction to the word alone (nationalism) reveals a very meaningful attitude of whites of any ideological persuasion toward blacks in this country. It means previous solutions to black problems in this country have been made in the interests of those whites dealing with these problems and not in the best interests of black people in this country. Whites can only subvert our true search and struggle for self-determination, self-identification, and liberation in this country. Re-evaluation of the white and black roles must NOW take place not so that black people play but rather black people define white people's roles.

Too long have we allowed white people to interpret the importance and meaning of the cultural aspects of our society. We have allowed them to tell us what was good about our Afro-American music, art and literature. How many black critics do we have on the "jazz" scene? How can a white person who is not a part of the black psyche (except in the oppressor's role) interpret the meaning of the blues to us who are manifestations of the songs themselves? It must also be pointed out that on whatever level of contact that blacks and whites come together, that meeting or confrontation is not on the level of the whites. This only means that our everyday contact with whites is a reinforcement of the myth of white supremacy. Whites are the ones who must try to raise themselves to our humanistic level. We are not, after all, the ones who are responsible for a genocidal war in Vietnam; we are not the ones who are responsible for neocolonialism in Africa and Latin America; we are not the ones who held a people in animalistic bondage over 400 years. We reject the American dream as defined by white people and must work to construct an American reality defined by Afro-Americans.

One of the criticisms of white militants and radicals is that when we view the masses of white people we view the over-all reality of America, we view the racism, the bigotry, and the distortion of personality, we view man's inhumanity to man; we view in reality 180 million racists. The sensitive white intellectual and radical who is fighting to bring about change is conscious of this fact, but does not have the courage to admit this. When he admits this reality, then he must also admit his involvement because he is a part of the collective white America. It is only to the extent that he recognizes this that he will be able to change his reality.

Another concern is how does the white radical view the black community and how does he view the poor white community in terms of organizing. So far we have found that most white radicals have sought to escape the horrible reality of America by going into the black community and attempting to organize black people while neglecting the organization of their own people's racist communities. How can one clean up someone else's yard when one's own yard is untidy?

A thorough re-examination must be made by black people concerning the contributions that we have made in shaping this country. If this re-examination and re-evaluation is not made and black people are not given their proper due and respect, then the antagonisms and contradictions are going to become more and more glaring, more and more intense until a national explosion may result.

When people attempt to move from these conclusions it would be faulty reasoning to say they are ordered by racism, because, in this country and in the West, racism has functioned as a type of white nationalism when dealing with black people. We all know the habit that this has created throughout the world and particularly among nonwhite people in this country.

Therefore any re-evaluation that we must make will, for the most part, deal with identification. Who are black people, what are black people; what is their relationship to America and the world?

It must be repeated that the whole myth of "Negro citizenship," perpetuated by the white elite, has confused the thinking of radical and progressive blacks and whites in this country. The broad masses of black people react to American society in the same manner as colonial peoples react to the West in Africa and Latin America, and had the same relationship—that of the colonized toward the colonizer.

42

Life and Choice

Except for a brief "baby boom" period after 1945, the number of children born to the average American woman has steadily decreased since the early nineteenth century. She had seven children on average in the early 1800s, four in the late 1800s, three in the early 1900s, two in the late 1900s. In the nineteenth century, the chief methods for limiting births were primitive contraception, abstinence, and, especially, abortion. In the early twentieth century, however, abortion became illegal in most states, and abstinence in marriage was less acceptable to husbands and wives. Improved contraception and delays in first marriages therefore became increasingly important birth-limiting measures. The falling birthrate since 1960 has come chiefly from a dramatic improvement in contraceptive techniques, especially contraceptive sterilization, the pill, the intrauterine device, and the vaginal sponge. Less important but still significant has been a rise in abortion rates, most notably in the five years that followed the historic 1973 Supreme Court decision in *Roe* v. *Wade,* which ruled restrictive state abortion laws unconstitutional.

Roe v. *Wade* reflected major changes in American society. These included advances in birth control technology, a desire to limit family size, and, especially, increased attention to the rights of women. One of these rights, according to modern feminists, is "reproductive freedom," of which abortion on demand was a crucial part. *Roe* v. *Wade* also typified a notable long-term shift in how the Supreme Court has viewed constitutional "rights"—or at least the question of which rights are the truly vital ones. In theory, all rights in the Constitution are of equal value, but over the years the Court, reflecting changes in social values, has always cherished some rights as more important than others. In the nation's early days, private property was given special consideration; later this came to include the rights of businesses and liberty of contract. Then, in the 1930s and 1940s, economic rights lost pride of place to the rights enumerated in the First Amendment. Later, the right to vote and to attend racially integrated schools was judged to be of fundamental importance. With the *Roe* v. *Wade* decision, so was the right to privacy.[1]

Justice Harry Blackmun's decision, which invalidated the statutes of thirty states that forbade abortions except to save the mother's life, sparked bitter controversy. "Prolife" forces, most affiliated with religious denominations and uncompromisingly opposed to abortion, denounced the ruling. They called for a constitutional amendment defining human life as beginning at conception, picketed abortion clinics, and successfully urged Congress to curtail most Medicaid funds for abortions. Meanwhile, "prochoice" advocates organized in support of the right of a woman (rather than the state) to choose whether or not to have an abortion. They also supported doctors' rights to perform abortions and poor women's rights to obtain them. By the 1980s, a political candidate's position on abortion could make or break a campaign, just as a Supreme Court nominee's position on *Roe* v. *Wade* could make or break a Court nomination.

Harry Blackmun, author of the *Roe* v. *Wade* decision, was born in Illinois in 1908. He grew up in the Minneapolis-St. Paul area and then headed east to attend Harvard College and Harvard Law School. Blackmun returned to Minneapolis to open a private practice before moving to Rochester, Minnesota, as legal counsel for the world-famous Mayo Clinic. A hard-working, serious-minded, moderate Republican, he was first appointed to the federal judiciary by President Dwight Eisenhower in 1959. Blackmun, a boyhood friend of Chief Justice Warren Burger, was promoted to the Supreme Court in 1970 after the Senate had rejected Richard Nixon's first two nominations to fill a recent vacancy. Although Blackmun was initially perceived as Burger's "Minnesota twin," the *Roe* v. *Wade* ruling (from which Justices Byron White and William Rehnquist dissented) marked the beginning of his drift away from the conservative Burger wing of the Court toward the more liberal wing associated with Justice William Brennan.

Questions to Consider. On what two constitutional grounds did the appellant seek to overturn restrictive Texas abortion laws? Of the three reasons commonly given to justify restricting abortions since the nineteenth century, which did Blackmun consider most important? Where in the Constitution did he find grounds for the right to privacy claimed by the appellant? Did Blackmun consider a woman's right to privacy a guarantee of an absolute right to abortion? The State of Texas (the appellee) argued that states could restrict abortion because the state has a "compelling interest" in protecting the right of an unborn fetus under the provisions of the Fourteenth Amendment. How did Blackmun deal

---

1. In *Rust* v. *Sullivan* (1991) the Supreme Court decided that medical personnel in family planning clinics receiving federal funds may not mention abortion or abortion facilities to clients.—*Eds.*

with this argument? Why did he call Texas's position "one theory of life"? Why did Blackmun discuss "trimesters" and "viability" at such length? If medical technology were to shift the point of viability from the third to the second trimester, would that undercut the force of *Roe* v. *Wade*?

★━━★━━★

Roe v. *Wade* (1973)

HARRY BLACKMUN

The principal thrust of appellant's attack on the Texas statutes is that they improperly invade a right, said to be possessed by the pregnant woman, to choose to terminate her pregnancy. Appellant would discover this right in the concept of personal "liberty" embodied in the Fourteenth Amendment's Due Process Clause; or in personal, marital, familial, and sexual privacy said to be protected by the Bill of Rights.

It perhaps is not generally appreciated that the restrictive criminal abortion laws in effect in a majority of States today are of relatively recent vintage. Those laws, generally proscribing abortion or its attempt at any time during pregnancy except when necessary to preserve the pregnant woman's life, are not of ancient or even of common law origin. Instead, they derive from statutory changes effected, for the most part, in the latter half of the nineteenth century. . . .

Three reasons have been advanced to explain historically the enactment of criminal abortion laws in the nineteenth century and to justify their continued existence.

It has been argued occasionally that these laws were the product of a Victorian social concern to discourage illicit sexual conduct. Texas, however, does not advance this justification in the present case, and it appears that no court or commentator has taken the argument seriously. . . .

A second reason is concerned with abortion as a medical procedure. When most criminal abortion laws were first enacted, the procedure was a hazardous one for the woman. . . . Modern medical techniques have altered this situation. Appellants refer to medical data indicating that abortion in early pregnancy, that is, prior to the end of first trimester, although not without its risk, is now relatively safe. . . . The State retains a definite interest in protecting the woman's own health and safety when an abortion is proposed at a late stage of pregnancy.

The third reason is the State's interest—some phrase it in terms of duty— in protecting prenatal life. Some of the argument for this justification rests on the theory that a new human life is present from the moment of conception.

Roe v. *Wade*, 410 U.S. 113 (1973).

The State's interest and general obligation to protect life then extends, it is argued, to prenatal life. Only when the life of the pregnant mother herself is at stake, balanced against the life she carries within her, should the interest of the embryo or fetus not prevail. Logically, of course, a legitimate State interest in this area need not stand or fall on acceptance of the belief that life begins at conception or at some other point prior to live birth. In assessing the State's interest, recognition may be given to the less rigid claim that as long as at least *potential* life is involved, the State may assert interests beyond the protection of the pregnant woman alone. . . .

The Constitution does not explicitly mention any right of privacy. In a line of decisions, however, going back perhaps as far as *Union Pacific R. Co.* v. *Botsford* (1891), the Court has recognized that a right of personal privacy, or a guarantee of certain areas or zones of privacy, does exist under the Constitution. . . . These decisions make it clear that only personal rights that can be deemed "fundamental" or "implicit in the concept of ordered liberty," are included in this guarantee of personal privacy. They also make it clear that the right has some extension to activities relating to marriage, procreation, contraception. . . .[1]

This right of privacy, whether it be founded in the Fourteenth Amendment's concept of personal liberty and restrictions upon state action, as we feel it is, or, as the District Court determined, in the Ninth Amendment's reservation of rights to the people, is broad enough to encompass a woman's decision whether or not to terminate her pregnancy. The detriment that the State would impose upon the pregnant woman by denying this choice altogether is apparent. Specific and direct harm medically diagnosable even in early pregnancy may be involved. Maternity, or additional offspring, may force upon the woman a distressful life and future. Psychological harm may be imminent. Mental and physical health may be taxed by child care. There is also the distress, for all concerned, associated with the unwanted child, and there is the problem of bringing a child into a family already unable, psychologically and otherwise, to care for it. In other cases, as in this one, the additional difficulties and continuing stigma of unwed motherhood may be involved. All these are factors the woman and her responsible physician necessarily will consider in consultation. . . .

On the basis of elements such as these, appellants argue that the woman's right is absolute and that she is entitled to terminate her pregnancy at whatever time, in whatever way, and for whatever reason she alone chooses. With this we do not agree. Appellant's arguments that Texas either has no valid interest at all in regulating the abortion decision, or no interest strong enough to support any limitation upon the woman's sole determination, is unpersuasive. The Court's decisions recognizing a right of privacy also acknowledge that some state regulation in areas protected by that right is appropriate. As

---

1. References to prior court decisons have been omitted.—*Eds.*

noted above, a State may properly assert important interests in safeguarding health, in maintaining medical standards, and in protecting potential life. At some point in pregnancy, these respective interests become sufficiently compelling to sustain regulation of the factors that govern the abortion decision. The privacy right involved, therefore, cannot be said to be absolute. In fact, it is not clear to us that the claim . . . that one has an unlimited right to do with one's body as one pleases bears a close relationship to the right of privacy previously articulated in the Court's decisions. The Court has refused to recognize an unlimited right of this kind in the past.

We therefore conclude that the right of personal privacy includes the abortion decision, but that this right is not unqualified and must be considered against state interests in regulation. . . .

Appellee [the state of Texas] argues that the State's determination to recognize and protect prenatal life from and after conception constitutes a compelling state interest. We do not agree fully. . . .

The Constitution does not define "person" in so many words. Section 1 of the Fourteenth Amendment contains three references to "person." The first, in defining "citizens," speaks of "persons born or naturalized in the United States." The word also appears both in the Due Process Clause and in the Equal Protection Clause. "Person" is used in other places in the Constitution. . . . But in nearly all these instances, the use of the word is such that it has application only postnatally. None indicates, with any assurance, that it has any possible prenatal application. All this, together with our observation, that throughout the major portion of the nineteenth century prevailing legal abortion practices were far freer than they are today, persuades us that the word "person," as used in the Fourteenth Amendment, does not include the unborn. . . .

Texas urges that, apart from the Fourteenth Amendment, life begins at conception and is present throughout pregnancy, and that, therefore, the State has a compelling interest in protecting that life from and after conception. We need not resolve the difficult question of when life begins. When those trained in the respective disciplines of medicine, philosophy, and theology are unable to arrive at any consensus, the judiciary, at this point in the development of man's knowledge, is not in a position to speculate as to the answer.

In view of all this, we do not agree that, by adopting one theory of life, Texas may override the rights of the pregnant woman that are at stake. We repeat, however, that the State does have an important and legitimate interest in preserving and protecting the health of the pregnant woman, whether she be a resident of the State or a nonresident who seeks medical consultation and treatment there, and that it has still *another* important and legitimate interest in protecting the potentiality of human life. These interests are separate and distinct. Each grows in substantiality as the woman approaches term and, at a point during pregnancy, each becomes "compelling."

With respect to the State's important and legitimate interest in the health of the mother, the "compelling" point, in the light of present medical knowledge, is at approximately the end of the first trimester. This is so because of the now established medical fact, referred to above . . . that until the end of the first trimester mortality in abortion is less than mortality in normal childbirth. It follows that, from and after this point, a State may regulate the abortion procedure to the extent that the regulation reasonably relates to the preservation and protection of maternal health. Examples of permissible state regulation in this area are requirements as to the qualifications of the person who is to perform the abortion; as to the licensure of that person; as to the facility in which the procedure is to be performed, that is, whether it must be a hospital or may be a clinic or some other place of less-than-hospital status; as to the licensing of the facility; and the like.

This means, on the other hand, that, for the period of pregnancy prior to this "compelling" point, the attending physician, in consultation with his patient, is free to determine, without regulation by the State, that in his medical judgment the patient's pregnancy should be terminated. If that decision is reached, the judgment may be effectuated by an abortion free of interference by the State.

With respect to the State's important and legitimate interest in potential life, the "compelling" point is at viability. This is so because the fetus then presumably has the capability of meaningful life outside the mother's womb. State regulation protective of fetal life after viability thus has both logical and biological justifications. If the State is interested in protecting fetal life after viability, it may go so far as to proscribe abortion during that period except when it is necessary to preserve the life or health of the mother.

Measured against these standards, the Texas Penal Code, in restricting legal abortions to those "procured or attempted by medical advice for the purpose of saving the life of the mother," sweeps too broadly.

To summarize and to repeat:

A state criminal abortion statute of the current Texas type, that excepts from criminality only a *life saving* procedure on behalf of the mother, without regard to pregnancy stage and without recognition of the other interests involved, is violative of the Due Process Clause of the Fourteenth Amendment.

(a) For the stage prior to approximately the end of the first trimester, the abortion decision and its effectuation must be left to the medical judgment of the pregnant woman's attending physician.

(b) For the stage subsequent to approximately the end of the first trimester, the State, in promoting its interest in the health of the mother, may, if it chooses, regulate the abortion procedure in ways that are reasonably related to maternal health.

(c) For the stage subsequent to viability the State, in promoting its interest in the potentiality of human life, may, if it chooses, regulate, and even proscribe, abortion except where it is necessary, in appropriate medical judgment, for the preservation of the life or health of the mother.

43

CRISIS OF THE PRESIDENCY

On June 17, 1972, five men were arrested for rifling the files and tapping the telephones of the Democratic National Committee (DNC) in the Watergate office building in Washington, D.C. Thus was born the Watergate affair that transfixed the nation for the next two years. All five burglars, it turned out, were former agents of the Central Intelligence Agency (CIA). Two of the men, James McCord and G. Gordon Liddy, were currently working for the Committee to Re-elect the President (CRP, or, popularly, CREEP), an independent organization supporting President Richard Nixon's bid for reelection. McCord and Liddy had connections with another former CIA agent, E. Howard Hunt, who, like Liddy, now served as a White House aide. The other burglars were Cubans who had been associated with the Bay of Pigs operation in Cuba.

After the trial and conviction of the five burglars, McCord broke silence by indicating, first, that the head of CRP himself, none other than former attorney general John N. Mitchell, had approved the break-in and, second, that White House agents had paid "hush money" to the burglars. Newspaper reporters, the Federal Bureau of Investigation, and a special Senate committee on campaign practices opened investigations and soon learned that CRP had used extortionist tactics to raise an illegal slush fund from corporations for the 1972 presidential campaign, and that CRP had used this fund to pay for burglaries, wiretaps, forgeries, phony demonstrations, and other "dirty tricks" to discredit and punish Nixon critics.

By the summer of 1973 it was clear that President Nixon's closest aides, including advisers H. R. Haldeman and John D. Ehrlichman and counsel John W. Dean, had tried to interfere with the Watergate investigations and were withholding valuable evidence, notably tapes of White House conversations during the period under question. When the Senate committee, wondering who (including President Nixon) knew what, requested access to the tapes, Nixon pleaded executive privilege and refused to release them; and when Archibald Cox, a special Watergate prosecutor whom Nixon had appointed, asked for the tapes, the president ordered Cox's dismissal, even though several Justice Department officials resigned in protest.

During the next few months more than thirty former Nixon advisers were indicted for federal crimes, including Dean, Ehrlichman, Haldeman, Mitchell, and former secretary of commerce and CRP finance chairman Maurice Stans. The House Judiciary Committee began preparing articles of impeachment against the president. On August 4, 1974, the Supreme Court ordered Nixon to release the tapes. Investigators, hoping to unearth the "smoking pistol" (direct evidence, if it existed, that the president himself had authorized the cover-up), were eager to examine them.

The tapes did indeed provide such evidence. According to a June 1972 conversation, Nixon knew of the Watergate break-in forty-eight hours after it happened. He also withheld evidence, authorized bribes, and used the FBI and the CIA to thwart congressional investigators. A September 1972 tape showed Nixon's intent, in the aftermath of Watergate, to use the FBI and the Justice Department against the administration's enemies. In March 1973, in response to legal counsel John Dean's concern about washing money—"the sort of thing Mafia people can do"—for paying blackmail, Nixon replied that the money could be obtained. The Watergate scandal came gradually to cover a wide array of wrongdoing: favors in exchange for campaign contributions, misuse of public funds, the deceiving of Congress about the secret bombing of Indochina, and illegal surveillance and espionage of political opponents and journalists. On August 9 Richard Nixon announced his resignation from the presidency.

The House Judiciary Committee ultimately triggered Nixon's resignation by voting to recommend to the full House of Representatives that Nixon be impeached. The vote was by a 2–1 margin. Many Republicans joined the Democratic majority in support of impeachment, although some did not, including future Senate majority leader Trent Lott of Mississippi.

Senator Sam Ervin, chair of the Senate Select Committee to investigate the Watergate allegations, was born in North Carolina in 1897 to Scots-Irish stock. Ervin attended the University of North Carolina, won medals for valor in World War I, earned a law degree at Harvard in 1922, and returned to North Carolina to practice law. He served on the state supreme court from 1948 to 1954, when he ran successfully for the U.S. Senate, a post he held for twenty years. Ervin was a strict constitutionalist who opposed both civil rights legislation and the Equal Rights Amendment, which pleased conservatives. But he also opposed prayer in the schools and giving police "no knock" authority to enter people's homes, which pleased liberals. At the time of Watergate, Sam Ervin was an elderly Southern Democrat with melodramatic eyebrows, a "country courtly" manner, a thorough knowledge of the Constitution, a habit of quoting from the Bible and Shakespeare, and a knack for telling folksy stories. He said the burglars who broke into the DNC headquarters had "the same mentality as the Gestapo," and that they sought not jewels or money but our "most precious heritage: the right to vote in a free election." He died in Winston-Salem, North Carolina, in 1985.

Questions to Consider. Of the list of misdeeds that Sam Ervin summarized in the document that follows, which seem to you to be most serious and threatening to the constitutional order? Would you say that they all carry equal weight? Why did Sam Ervin and other members of the Senate and House, all experienced politicians, think that the Watergate affair represented much more than just "politics as usual"? Senate Majority Leader Mike Mansfield, who appointed Ervin to chair the Select Committee on Watergate, called him the only person who could have handled this assignment: to conduct lengthy televised hearings on the possible effort of the president to subvert the democratic process. What was there about Ervin that might have made him especially suitable for this task?

★━━━★━━━★

Statement on the Impeachment of Richard Nixon (1974)

SAM ERVIN

Watergate was a conglomerate of various illegal and unethical activities in which various officers and employees of the Nixon reelection committees and various White House aides of President Nixon participated in varying ways and degrees to accomplish these successive objectives:

1. To destroy, insofar as the Presidential election of 1972 was concerned, the integrity of the process by which the President of the United States is nominated and elected.
2. To hide from law enforcement officers, prosecutors, grand jurors, courts, the news media, and the American people the identities and wrongdoing of those officers and employees of the Nixon reelection committees, and those White House aides who had undertaken to

The New York Times, June 29, 1974.

destroy the integrity of the process by which the President of the United States is nominated and elected.

To accomplish the first of these objectives, the participating officers and employees of the reelection committees and the participating White House aides of President Nixon engaged in one or more of these things:

1. They exacted enormous contributions—usually in cash—from corporate executives by impliedly implanting in their minds the impressions that the making of the contributions was necessary to insure that the corporations would receive governmental favors, or avoid governmental disfavors, while President Nixon remained in the White House. A substantial portion of the contributions were made out of corporate funds in violation of a law enacted by Congress a generation ago.
2. They hid substantial parts of these contributions in cash in safes and secret deposits to conceal their sources and the identities of those who had made them.
3. They disbursed substantial portions of these hidden contributions in a surreptitious manner to finance the bugging and the burglary of the offices of the Democratic National Committee in the Watergate complex in Washington for the purpose of obtaining political intelligence; and to sabotage by dirty tricks, espionage, and scurrilous and false libels and slanders the campaigns and the reputations of honorable men, whose only offenses were that they sought the nomination of the Democratic Party for President and the opportunity to run against President Nixon for that office in the Presidential election of 1972.
4. They deemed the departments and agencies of the Federal Government to be the political playthings of the Nixon administration rather than impartial instruments for serving the people, and undertook to induce them to channel Federal contracts, grants, and loans to areas, groups, or individuals so as to promote the reelection of the President rather than to further the welfare of the people.
5. They branded as enemies of the President individuals and members of the news media who dissented from the President's policies and opposed his reelection, and conspired to urge the Department of Justice, the Federal Bureau of Investigation, the Internal Revenue Service, and the Federal Communications Commission to pervert the use of their legal powers to harass them for so doing.
6. They borrowed from the Central Intelligence Agency disguises which E. Howard Hunt used in political espionage operations, and photographic equipment [of] White House employees known as the "Plumbers" and their hired confederates . . .
7. They assigned to E. Howard Hunt, who was at the time a White

House consultant occupying an office in the Executive Office Building, the gruesome task of falsifying State Department documents
which they contemplated using in their altered state to discredit the
Democratic Party by defaming the memory of former President John
Fitzgerald Kennedy, who as the hapless victim of an assassin's bullet
had been sleeping in the tongueless silence of the dreamless dust for
9 years.

8. They used campaign funds to hire saboteurs to forge and dissemi-
nate false and scurrilous libels of honorable men running for the
Democratic Presidential nomination in Democratic Party primaries.

During the darkness of the early morning of June 17, 1972, James W. Mc-
Cord, the security chief of the John Mitchell committee, and four residents of
Miami, Fla., were arrested by Washington police while they were burglariz-
ing the offices of the Democratic National Committee in the Watergate complex to obtain political intelligence. At the same time, the four residents of
Miami had in their possession more than fifty $100 bills which were subse-
quently shown to be a part of campaign contributions made to the Nixon reelection committees.

On September 15, 1972, these five burglars, E. Howard Hunt, and Gordon
Liddy, general counsel of the Stans committee, were indicted by the grand
jury on charges arising out of the bugging and burglary of the Watergate.

They were placed on trial upon these charges before Judge John Sirica,
and a petit jury in the U.S. District Court for the District of Columbia in January 1973. At that time, Hunt and the four residents of Miami pleaded guilty,
and McCord and Liddy were found guilty by the petit jury. None of them
took the witness stand during the trial.

The arrest of McCord and the four residents of Miami created consterna-
tion in the Nixon reelection committees and the White House. Thereupon,
various officers and employees of the Nixon reelection committees and various White House aides undertook to conceal from law-enforcement officers,
prosecutors, grand jurors, courts, the news media, and the American people
the identities and activities of those officers and employees of the Nixon reelection committees and those White House aides who had participated in
any way in the Watergate affair.

Various officers and employees of the Nixon reelection committees and
various White House aides engaged in one or more of these acts to make the
concealment effective and thus obstruct the due administration of justice:

1. They destroyed the records of the Nixon reelection committees ante-
dating the bugging and the burglary.

2. They induced the Acting Director of the FBI, who was a Nixon ap-
pointee, to destroy the State Department documents which E. Howard Hunt had been falsifying.

3. They obtained from the Acting Director of the FBI copies of scores of

interviews conducted by FBI agents in connection with their investigation of the bugging and the burglary, and were enabled thereby to coach their confederates to give false and misleading statements to the FBI.

4. They sought to persuade the FBI to refrain from investigating the sources of the campaign funds which were used to finance the bugging and the burglary.

5. They intimidated employees of the Nixon reelection committees and employees of the White House by having their lawyers present when these employees were being questioned by agents of the FBI, and thus deterred these employees from making full disclosures to the FBI.

6. They lied to agents of the FBI, prosecutors, and grand jurors who undertook to investigate the bugging and the burglary, and to Judge Sirica and the petit jurors who tried the seven original Watergate defendants in January 1973. . . . .

8. They persuaded the Department of Justice and the prosecutors to refrain from asking Donald Segretti, their chief hired saboteur, any questions involving Herbert W. Kalmbach, the Preident's personal attorney, who was known by them to have paid Segretti for dirty tricks he perpetrated upon honorable men seeking the Democratic Presidential nomination, and who was subsequently identified before the Senate Select Committee as one who played a major role in the secret delivery of hush money to the seven original Watergate defendants.

9. They made cash payments totaling hundreds of thousands of dollars out of campaign funds in surreptitious ways to the seven original Watergate defendants as hush money to buy their silence and keep them from revealing their knowledge of the identities of the officers and employees of the Nixon reelection committees and the White House aides who had participated in the Watergate.

10. They gave assurances to some of the original seven defendants that they would receive Presidential clemency after serving short portions of their sentences if they refrained from divulging the identities and activities of the officers and employees of the Nixon reelection committees and the White House aides who had participated in the Watergate affair.

11. They made arrangements by which the attorneys who represented the seven original Watergate defendants received their fees in cash from moneys which had been collected to finance President Nixon's reelection campaign. . . . .

13. They inspired massive efforts on the part of segments of the news media friendly to the administration to persuade the American people that most of the members of the Select Committee named by the Senate to investigate the Watergate were biased and irresponsible

men motivated solely by desires to exploit the matters they investigated for personal or partisan advantage, and that the allegations in the press that Presidential aides had been involved in the Watergate were venomous machinations of a hostile and unreliable press bent on destroying the country's confidence in a great and good President.

President Ronald Reagan. Ronald Reagan gestures as he speaks to the National
Association of Evangelicals. (© Bettmann/Corbis)

CHAPTER SEVEN

Modern Times

44

BUSINESS UNLEASHED

Ronald Reagan first made his mark in politics with a televised appeal in 1964 on behalf of conservative Senator Barry Goldwater, the Republican presidential candidate. Reagan argued a position popular with the Sunbelt and the suburbs, where Republicans were beginning to show strength—that high taxes, social programs, and regulations were strangling individual freedom and threatening to drag the country "down to the ant heap of totalitarianism." He also showed himself to be a brilliant speaker—relaxed, confident, earnest, and poised, with a warm voice, a gift for turning a phrase, and a knack for seeming simultaneously friendly and determined. The speech failed to rescue Goldwater's foundering campaign, but it did launch Reagan's own political career, which led first to the California governor's mansion and then to the White House.

Reagan's major victory in the presidential election of 1980 can be traced to several sources. The Democratic candidate, incumbent Jimmy Carter, was widely perceived as a weak president, unable to lift the country from a lingering economic slump or to rescue American diplomatic hostages from the clutches of Moslem fundamentalists in Iran. But Reagan was himself a strong candidate, promising repeatedly (as he had on Goldwater's behalf sixteen years before) to cut taxes, deregulate business, balance the federal budget, and increase military spending—in brief, to restore unregulated capitalism and global supremacy, the twin pillars of the American system. That some of these promises appeared contradictory, mutually exclusive, or impossible was no problem, Reagan argued. According to "supply-side economics," which Reagan popularized, the country could accomplish these ends simply by cutting taxes enough to trigger massive investment and rapid growth, thus generating higher tax revenues despite lower tax rates. Reagan's Republican rival, George Bush, dismissed this notion as "voodoo economics." Nevertheless, Reagan's form of voodoo proved enormously popular with the American business community, which aggressively supported and financed his candidacy. President Reagan's inaugural address, excerpted below, signaled his determination to follow through on his campaign promises.

Born in 1914, Ronald Reagan won initial fame in Hollywood, where he worked in films and was president of the Screen Actors' Guild. During the 1950s he appeared on television and did publicity for General Electric Company. A two-term governor of California, he was by 1980 both a seasoned politician and a seasoned actor—photogenic, comfortable before the cameras, and possessing a mellifluous, compelling voice. No president since Franklin D. Roosevelt, with whom Reagan often compared himself, used the electronic media so effectively or to such political advantage. His critics labeled him "the Teflon president" because he managed for years to escape unscathed from scandal or policy gaffes. But his friends called him "the Great Communicator," perhaps the finest of the century.

Questions to Consider. What was the nature of the "crisis" that Reagan saw in the United States in 1981? How did this crisis manifest itself at the government level? Why did Reagan say "government is the problem"? Did the president propose specific steps to deal with this? What steps did he propose for forcing government to live "within its means"? How, given these principles, was it possible for Reagan to oversee the biggest increase in the federal deficit to that date in American history?

★━━★━━★

First Inaugural Address (1981)

RONALD REAGAN

These United States are confronted with an economic affliction of great proportions. We suffer from the longest and one of the worst sustained inflations in our national history. It distorts our economic decisions, penalizes thrift, and crushes the struggling young and the fixed-income elderly alike. It threatens to shatter the lives of millions of our people.

Idle industries have cast workers into unemployment, causing human misery and personal indignity. Those who do work are denied a fair return for their labor by a tax system which penalizes successful achievement and keeps us from maintaining full productivity.

But great as our tax burden is, it has not kept pace with public spending. For decades, we have piled deficit upon deficit, mortgaging our future and our children's future for the temporary convenience of the present. To continue this long trend is to guarantee tremendous social, cultural, political, and economic upheavals.

The New York Times, January 21, 1981.

The winning team. President-elect Ronald Reagan and Vice-President-elect George Bush at their first post-election news conference, November 7, 1980, after demolishing the Democratic ticket in the wake of the Iran hostage crisis. (Wide World)

You and I as individuals can, by borrowing, live beyond our means, but only for a limited period of time. Why, then, should we think that collectively, as a nation, we are not bound by that same limitation? . . .

In this present crisis, government is not the solution to our problem. Government is the problem.

From time to time, we have been tempted to believe that society has become too complex to be managed by self-rule, that government by an elite group is superior to government for, by, and of the people. But if no one among us is capable of governing himself, then who among us has the capacity to govern someone else?

All of us together, in and out of government, must bear the burden. The solutions we seek must be equitable, with no one group singled out to pay a higher price.

We hear much of special interest groups. Our concern must be for a special interest group that has been too long neglected. It knows no sectional boundaries or ethnic and racial divisions, and it crosses political party lines.

It is made up of men and women who raise our food, patrol our streets, man our mines and our factories, teach our children, keep our homes, and heal us when we are sick—professionals, industrialists, shopkeepers, clerks, cabbies, and truckdrivers. They are, in short, "We the people," this breed called Americans. . . .

So, as we begin, let us take inventory. We are a nation that has a government—not the other way around. And this makes us special among the nations of the earth. Our government has no power except that granted it by the people. It is time to check and reverse the growth of government, which shows signs of having grown beyond the consent of the governed.

It is my intention to curb the size and influence of the federal establishment and to demand recognition of the distinction between the powers granted to the federal government and those reserved to the states or to the people.

All of us need to be reminded that the federal government did not create the states; the states created the federal government.

So there will be no misunderstanding, it is not my intention to do away with government. It is, rather, to make it work—work with us, not over us; to stand by our sides, not ride on our backs. Government can and must provide opportunity, not smother it—foster productivity, not stifle it.

If we look to the answer as to why, for so many years, we achieved so much, prospered as no other people on earth, it was because here, in this land, we unleashed the energy and individual genius of man to a greater extent than has ever been done before. Freedom and the dignity of the individual have been more available and assured here than in any other place on earth. The price for this freedom has been high at times. But we have never been unwilling to pay that price.

It is no coincidence that our present troubles parallel and are proportionate to the intervention and intrusion in our lives that result from unnecessary and excessive growth of government. . . .

So with all the creative energy at our command, let us begin an era of national renewal. Let us renew our determination, our courage, and our strength. And let us renew our faith and our hope. We have every right to dream heroic dreams. . . .

In the days ahead, I will propose removing the roadblocks that have slowed our economy and reduced productivity. Steps will be taken aimed at restoring the balance between the various levels of government. Progress may be slow—measured in inches and feet, not miles—but we will progress. It is time to reawaken this industrial giant, to get government back within its means, and to lighten our punitive tax burden. And these will be our first priorities; on these principles there will be no compromise.

45

THE EVIL EMPIRE

The main theme of Ronald Reagan's first inaugural address was the need to stimulate the American economy by cutting taxes and getting the government "off our backs." This position was dear to the hearts of the "Old Right"—traditional business conservatives concerned chiefly with economic policies. But Reagan's triumphant campaign of 1980 had also energized the so-called "New Right"—groups concerned chiefly with restoring traditional morality by combating abortion, pornography, homosexuality, and women's liberation and by returning prayer to the public schools and the death penalty to American justice.

The heartland of the New Right was the Old South, where the liberalism of the Democratic party had alienated white voters and where Protestant fundamentalism, strengthened by television evangelists, was growing rapidly. Long a target of Republican strategists, the South became a natural base for Ronald Reagan, who skillfully tailored his appeals to the region by couching them in terms of morality rather than race. Such appeals would in turn attract all voters wanting to restore traditional authority and morals. One of Reagan's great political achievements was to bring these New Right voters decisively into the Republican camp.

Increasingly, moreover, the president linked the new morality to the old struggle against Communism. In part, he did this to forge a connection between his domestic agenda and the immense military build-up undertaken during his administration. He also knew that both old and new conservatives could unite behind an aggressive foreign policy. Perhaps the most famous instance of his linking diplomacy with moral conservatism came in a speech, excerpted below, to the National Association of Evangelicals. In this speech Reagan called Soviet Communism "the focus of evil in the modern world." Ironically, during his second administration Ronald Reagan met with Soviet Premier Mikhail Gorbachev on several occasions and signed a path-breaking treaty with the USSR banning intermediate-range nuclear forces in Europe.

Questions to Consider. What were the "tried and time-tested values" Reagan referred to early in his speech? Were they only the "concern for others and respect for the rule of law under God" that he had mentioned earlier, or did he mean something more? How did he think government support for birth-control services for girls would undermine the values of concern for others and the rule of law under God? What did Reagan's efforts to cut funds for teenage birth control share with the struggle against abortion? What did he mean when he called the Soviets the "focus of evil in the modern world"? Do you think Reagan really meant to imply that proponents of a freeze on building and deploying nuclear weapons were under the influence of Satan ("old Screwtape")?

★━━★━━★

Speech to the National Association of Evangelicals (1983)

RONALD REAGAN

This administration is motivated by a political philosophy that sees the greatness of America in you, her people, and in your families, churches, neighborhoods, communities—the institutions that foster and nourish values like concern for others and respect for the rule of law under God.

Now, I don't have to tell you that this puts us in opposition to, or at least out of step with, a prevailing attitude of many who have turned to a modern-day secularism, discarding the tried and time-tested values upon which our very civilization is based. No matter how well intentioned, their value system is radically different from that of most Americans. And while they proclaim that they're freeing us from superstitions of the past, they've taken upon themselves the job of superintending us by government rule and regulation. Sometimes their voices are louder than ours, but they are not yet a majority.

An example of that vocal superiority is evident in a controversy now going on in Washington. And since I'm involved, I've been waiting to hear from the parents of young America. How far are they willing to go in giving to government their prerogatives as parents?

Let me state the case as briefly and simply as I can. An organization of citizens, sincerely motivated and deeply concerned about the increase in illegitimate births and abortions involving girls well below the age of consent, sometime ago established a nationwide network of clinics to offer help to these girls and, hopefully, alleviate this situation. Now, again, let me say, I do not fault their intent. However, in their well-intentioned effort, these clinics have decided to provide advice and birth control drugs and devices to underage girls without the knowledge of their parents.

For some years now, the Federal Government has helped with funds to

The New York Times, March 9, 1983.

subsidize these clinics. In providing for this, the Congress decreed that every effort would be made to maximize parental participation. Nevertheless, the drugs and devices are prescribed without getting parental consent or giving notification after they've done so. Girls termed "sexually active"—and that has replaced the word "promiscuous"—are given this help in order to prevent illegitimate birth or abortion.

Well, we have ordered clinics receiving Federal funds to notify the parents such help has been given. One of the nation's leading newspapers has created the term "squeal rule" in editorializing against us for doing this, and we're being criticized for violating the privacy of young people. A judge has recently granted an injunction against an enforcement of our rule. I've watched TV panel shows discuss this issue, seen columnists pontificating on our error, but no one seems to mention morality as playing a part in the subject of sex.

Is all of Judeo-Christian tradition wrong? Are we to believe that something so sacred can be looked upon as a purely physical thing with no potential for emotional and psychological harm? And isn't it the parents' right to give counsel and advice to keep their children from making mistakes that may affect their entire lives? . . .

More than a decade ago, a Supreme Court decision literally wiped off the books of fifty States statutes protecting the rights of unborn children. Abortion on demand now takes the lives of up to 1.5 million unborn children a year. Human life legislation ending this tragedy will some day pass the Congress, and you and I must never rest until it does. Unless and until it can be proven that the unborn child is not a living entity, then its right to life, liberty, and the pursuit of happiness must be protected.

You may remember that when abortion on demand began, many, and, indeed, I'm sure many of you, warned that the practice would lead to a decline in respect for human life, that the philosophical premises used to justify abortion on demand would ultimately be used to justify other attacks on the sacredness of human life—infanticide or mercy killing. Tragically enough, those warnings proved all too true. Only last year a court permitted the death by starvation of a handicapped infant. . . .

Now, I'm sure that you must get discouraged at times, but you've done better than you know, perhaps. There's a great spiritual awakening in America, a renewal of the traditional values that have been the bedrock of America's goodness and greatness.

One recent survey by a Washington-based research council concluded that Americans were far more religious than the people of other nations; 95 percent of those surveyed expressed a belief in God and a huge majority believed the Ten Commandments had real meaning in their lives. And another study has found that an overwhelming majority of Americans disapprove of adultery, teenage sex, pornography, abortion, and hard drugs. And this same study showed a deep reverence for the importance of family ties and religious belief. . . .

And this brings me to my final point today. During my first press conference as President, in answer to a direct question, I pointed out that, as good
Marxist-Leninists, the Soviet leaders have openly and publicly declared that
the only morality they recognize is that which will further their cause, which
is world revolution. I think I should point out I was only quoting Lenin, their
guiding spirit, who said in 1920 that they repudiate all morality that pro-
ceeds from supernatural ideas—that's their name for religion—or ideas that
are outside class conceptions. Morality is entirely subordinate to the interests
of class war. . . .

They must be made to understand we will never compromise our principles and standards. We will never give away our freedom. We will never
abandon our belief in God. And we will never stop searching for a genuine
peace. But we can assure none of these things America stands for through the
so-called nuclear freeze solutions proposed by some.

The truth is that a freeze now would be a very dangerous fraud, for
that is merely the illusion of peace. The reality is that we must find peace
through strength. . . .

Yes, let us pray for the salvation of all of those who live in that totalitarian
darkness—pray they will discover the joy of knowing God. But until they do,
let us be aware that while they preach the supremacy of the state, declare its
omnipotence over individual man, and predict its eventual domination of all
peoples on the Earth, they are the focus of evil in the modern world. . . .

So, I urge you to speak out against those who would place the United
States in a position of military and moral inferiority. You know, I've always
believed that old Screwtape reserved his best efforts for those of you in the
church. So, in your discussions of the nuclear freeze proposals, I urge you to
beware the temptation of pride—the temptation of blithely declaring yourselves above it all and label both sides equally at fault, to ignore the facts of
history and the aggressive impulses of an evil empire, to simply call the arms
race a giant misunderstanding and thereby remove yourself from the struggle between right and wrong and good and evil.

46

RESPONSE TO TERROR

On September 11, 2001, terrorists belonging to Al Qaeda, a global network of Islamic extremists, crashed hijacked passenger planes into the World Trade Center in New York City and the Pentagon in Washington, D.C. The attacks killed nearly 3,000 people, most of them U.S. citizens, making this the most deadly attack on continental American soil since the days of the Civil War. With Afghanistan as a command and training base, Al Qaeda had cells in dozens of countries from North America to the Philippines. There was therefore no "return address" on this attack; no nation was responsible, so there was no nation on which to declare war.

President George W. Bush, in office less than a year, made this clear in a radio message shortly after the assault, asserting that "this is a conflict without battlefields or beachheads," against opponents "who believe they are invisible." Victory, said the president, would come in a series of actions against terrorist organizations "and those who harbor and support them." Bush quickly mobilized U.S. military strength and deployed it successfully against the ruling Taliban regime in Afghanistan—a radical Islamic theocracy that provided training and staging areas for Al Qaeda. American special forces and air power, supported by dissident Afghan warlords, overthrew the Taliban in a matter of weeks and restored a more sympathetic government in the capital, Kabul.

The president's objective to "eradicate the evil of terrorism" meant that the conflict did not end with the Afghan campaign, since neither Al Qaeda nor its leader, Osama bin Laden, a wealthy Saudi citizen, had been entirely eliminated. There were other Islamic militants in Lebanon, Palestine, Chechnya, Indonesia, Pakistan, and elsewhere who posed threats to the United States and its interests. Bush specifically denounced three other countries—Iran, Iraq, and North Korea—as an "axis of evil" that hid terrorists or presented other threats. Iraq became a particular focus of administration enmity. Bush accused Iraq—against which his father had waged a limited war a decade earlier to safeguard Middle Eastern oil reserves—of assisting Al Qaeda and possessing biological, chemical, and nuclear weapons of mass destruction. He threatened American military intervention, alone if necessary, to cripple terrorism and eliminate the weapons.

In September 2002, Bush enunciated a new foreign policy doctrine, framed by the war on terror and the confrontation with Iraq—but with broader significance. This "Bush Doctrine," excerpted below, stressed a commitment to human rights and free trade as well as opposition to terrorism. More profoundly, it asserted a right to strike preemptively, or preventively, against "rogue states and their terrorist clients before they are able to threaten or use weapons of mass destruction," a claim that no previous administration had ever made. It further committed the United States to building a military force that no potential adversary could hope to equal, a decision that abandoned the "sufficiency" or "parity" doctrines that had long guided American military policy. In referencing the need for "homeland security," the Bush Doctrine had clear domestic implications as well, as shown with the passage of the U.S.A. Patriot Act, permitting the collection of immense amounts of data—from bank transactions to library use to air travel to medical records—on both U.S. citizens and visitors to the United States, and the establishment of a new federal Department of Homeland Security.

Acting on his newly enunciated preemptive strategy, in 2003 Bush ordered the invasion of Iraq, without United Nations authorization, for the purpose of unseating the dictator Saddam Hussein. Some 150,000 U.S. troops, assisted by 45,000 British and Australians, waged the three-week campaign, which shattered the power of the government and drove Saddam into hiding. Between 11,000 and 15,000 Iraqi soldiers and up to 20,000 civilians died; the U.S. lost just 150 dead. The occupation of the country did not go well, however, with more Americans dying after the end of formal combat operations than before. Most European countries, many of whom had opposed unilateral U.S. action, refused to send supporting occupation troops, as did allies such as Turkey, Pakistan, and Canada. Significant parts of the country remained both dangerous to U.S. occupying troops and dysfunctional as of the end of the year. The U.S. forces found numerous torture chambers and mass graves attesting to Saddam Hussein's brutal rule—but no evidence of Iraqi weapons of mass destruction or ties to Al Qaeda. This led some to question the Bush administration's wisdom, even its honesty, in justifying the invasion. Others saw invasion as a natural extension of the Bush security strategy articulated in the document below.

George W. Bush was born in New Haven, Connecticut, in 1946. The eldest son of President George H. W. Bush and the grandson of U.S. Senator Prescott Bush, George W. grew up in Texas and, like his father, attended Phillips Andover Academy in Massachusetts and then Yale University, where he graduated in 1968. After serving as a fighter pilot in the Texas Air National Guard during the Vietnam War, Bush earned a

Harvard MBA in 1975, worked in the Texas oil and gas industry for a decade, and helped manage his father's successful presidential campaign in 1988. From 1989 to 1994 he was managing partner of the Texas Rangers baseball team. He was the first Texas governor to be elected to two four-year terms and in 2000 became the second son of a president to win the presidency, in part through a contested ballot situation in Florida, where his brother Jeb was governor. Bush, a Methodist, has been called the most religious president in American history and also the most conservative since the nineteenth century.

Questions to Consider. Of the seven main parts of the doctrine given below, which strike you as the most original or novel? Which seem to mark the biggest break from previous U.S. doctrine? In the part on "Terror Alliance," the final sentence has raised alarms among other countries' leaders. Why might they have concerns about the formulation? How is "terrorism" defined here? In the "Deadliest Weapons" section, how does the doctrine differentiate between trustworthy and "rogue" regimes possessing weapons of mass destruction? The section seems to equate the possessing of such weapons with seeking to possess them. Is this reasonable? The section on "Strike First" has become one of the most controversial parts of the Bush Doctrine. Why do you think this is so? Similarly controversial is the final section, "Military," which argues that no "potential adversary" should equal the United States in military power, implying a permanent objective of military supremacy. Again, why might this have raised such concern? Does this section further suggest that the intelligence community as well as the military would need to grow dramatically, and perhaps even expand its surveillance to within the United States itself? If so, would this represent a dramatic departure?

★══★══★

The Bush Strategic Doctrine (2002)

GEORGE W. BUSH

The United States possesses unprecedented and unequaled strength and influence in the world. Sustained by faith in the principles of liberty, and the value of a free society, this position comes with unparalleled responsibilities, obligations, and opportunity. The great strength of this nation must be used to promote a balance of power that favors freedom.

The Boston Globe, September 21, 2002.

Human Rights: In pursuit of our goals, our first imperative is to clarify what we stand for: The United States must defend liberty and justice because these principles are right and true for all people everywhere. No nation owns these aspirations and no nation is exempt from them. Fathers and mothers in all societies want their children to be educated and to live free from poverty and violence. No people on earth yearn to be oppressed, aspire to servitude, or eagerly await the midnight knock of the secret police.

America must stand firmly for the nonnegotiable demands of human dignity: the role of law, limits on the absolute power of the state, free speech, freedom of worship, equal justice, respect for women, religious and ethnic tolerance, and respect for private property.

Terror Alliance: The enemy is not a single political regime or person or religion or ideology. The enemy is terrorism premeditated, politically motivated violence perpetrated against innocents. In many regions, legitimate grievances prevent the emergence of a lasting peace. Such grievances deserve to be, and must be, addressed within a political process. But no cause justifies terror. The United States will make no concessions to terrorist demands and strike no deals with them. We make no distinction between terrorists and those who knowingly harbor or provide aid to them.

Regional Conflicts: Concerned nations must remain actively engaged in critical regional disputes to avoid explosive escalation and minimize human suffering. In an increasingly interconnected world, regional crisis can strain our alliances, rekindle rivalries among the major powers, and create horrifying affronts to human dignity. When violence erupts and states falter, the United States will work with friends and partners to alleviate suffering and restore stability. No doctrine can anticipate every circumstance in which U.S. action, direct or indirect, is warranted. We have finite political, economic, and military resources to meet our global priorities.

Deadliest Weapons: At the time of the Gulf War, we acquired irrefutable proof that Iraq's designs were not limited to the chemical weapons it had used against Iran and its own people, but also extended to the acquisition of nuclear weapons and biological agents. In the past decade North Korea has become the world's principal purveyor of ballistic missiles and has tested increasingly capable missiles while developing its own [weapons of mass destruction] arsenal. Other rogue regimes seek nuclear, biological, and chemical weapons as well. These states' pursuit of, and global trade in, such weapons has become a looming threat to all nations.

Strike First: We must be prepared to stop rogue states and their terrorist clients before they are able to threaten or use weapons of mass destruction against the United States and our allies and friends. Our response must take full advantage of strengthened alliances; the establishment of new partnerships with former adversaries; innovation in the use of military forces;

modern technologies, including the development of an effective missile-defense system; and increased emphasis on intelligence collection and analysis.

The United States will not use force in all cases to preempt emerging threats, nor should nations use preemption as a pretext for aggression. Yet in an age where the enemies of civilization openly and actively seek the world's most destructive technologies, the United States cannot remain idle while dangers gather.

Global Economy: We will promote economic growth and economic freedom beyond America's shores. All governments are responsible for creating their own economic policies and responding to their own economic challenges. We will use our economic engagement with other countries to underscore the benefits.of policies that generate higher productivity and sustained economic growth.

Military: We will maintain the forces sufficient to support our obligations and to defend freedom. Our forces will be strong enough to dissuade potential adversaries from pursuing a military buildup in hopes of surpassing, or equaling, the power of the United States.

We must strengthen intelligence warning and analysis to provide integrated threat assessments for national and homeland security. Since the threats inspired by foreign governments and groups may be conducted inside the United States, we must also ensure the proper fusion of information between intelligence and law enforcement. Initiatives in this area will include strengthening the authority of the director of Central Intelligence to lead the development and actions of the nation's foreign intelligence capabilities.

47

GAY RIGHTS

The movement to overthrow and redress the historic oppression of African Americans inevitably spread to other hitherto excluded groups, including women, Native Americans, and, increasingly, homosexuals, whom state and federal laws had long stigmatized and excluded on the basis of their sexual preference. A "homophile" movement appeared in the 1950s to give support and encouragement to the small, discreet gay and lesbian urban communities that had emerged in the wake of the great population shifts of World War II, and to protest (sometimes successfully) for the right to mail literature and hold government jobs.

Already encountering much police and other hostility, including physical attacks, the movement provoked an even greater backlash in the 1970s when it blossomed into a full-fledged "liberation" struggle, demanding security of person, equal rights in the workplace, and the ability to live openly gay lives. Southern states and cities passed discriminatory legislation, "gay-bashing" occured frequently in small towns and suburbs, and the armed forces, even after an effort by President Bill Clinton to ease discrimination, constituted a particularly harsh environment for gays and lesbians. Conservative religious bodies, including the Roman Catholic Church and the Southern Baptist Convention, fed the intolerance.

Even so, there was progress, driven by several factors: increased public tolerance; the fact that sons and daughters of prominent political leaders, including President Reagan, Speaker of the House Richard Gephardt, and Vice-President Dick Cheney, "came out" as homosexuals; the appearance of gay and lesbian characters on television; and, as with the struggle for black and women's rights, aggressive political activism and the effective use of the court system. The Supreme Court, previously not altogether sympathetic to gay rights, became a major player with its decision in *Lawrence* v. *Texas* in June 2003.

The case originated when Houston, Texas, police responded to a reported weapons disturbance in a private residence, entered John Lawrence's apartment, observed Lawrence and another man, Tyron Garner, engaging in a sexual act, and arrested them for violating a Texas statute forbidding two persons of the same sex to engage in

(as the Supreme Court decision put it) "certain intimate sexual conduct." A Texas Court of Appeals affirmed the constitutionality of the
Texas law, whereupon Lawrence appealed to the Supreme Court. Below are the Court's majority opinion, written by Justice Anthony
Kennedy, and an important concurring opinion, written by Justice Sandra Day O'Connor.

Anthony Kennedy was born in 1936 in Sacramento, California,
worked as a youth in the state senate and in his father's law firm,
attended Stanford University and the London School of Economics,
and received a degree from Harvard Law School in 1961. Kennedy
practiced law for several years in California, teaching on the side, before helping Governor Ronald Reagan draft an anti-tax ballot initiative
that paved the way for the passage of "Proposition 13," California's
stringent anti-tax measure. President Reagan appointed Kennedy to
the U.S. Court of Appeals in 1974, where he proved himself conservative but non-confrontational. In 1987 Reagan named Kennedy to the
Supreme Court.

Born in El Paso, Texas, in 1930, Sandra Day O'Connor grew up on
the family ranch in Arizona, attended Stanford as an economics major,
received a Stanford law degree in 1952, and moved with her husband
to Phoenix, Arizona. She served in the state senate from 1969 to 1974.
In 1979 Governor Bruce Babbitt appointed her to the state Court of Appeals, and in 1981 President Reagan appointed her to fill a vacancy on
the Supreme Court, where she has frequently been a "swing vote" in
decisions on which the other justices were evenly divided. Generally
regarded as a tough conservative, O'Connor has nevertheless been in-
strumental in preserving the chief elements of *Roe* v. *Wade* governing
abortion rights and on other cases protecting the rights of women
and children.

Questions to Consider. Justice Kennedy and Justice O'Connor based
their opinions on different constitutional principles: due process in the
case of Kennedy and equal protection in the case of O'Connor. Which
principle, in your opinion, would afford the greatest future protection
to homosexuals? Given the language of the two justices, which of them
seems to have been most committed to the protection of gay rights?
Liberals applauded this decision as extending an overdue protection to
a besieged minority. Conservatives denounced it as a threat to the family and social order. Did the authors of the opinion seem to have perceived it that way—as a revolutionary decision, in either direction?

■══■══■

Lawrence v. Texas (2003)

ANTHONY KENNEDY

(For the majority)

Liberty protects the person from unwarranted government intrusions into a dwelling or other private places. In our tradition the state is not omnipresent in the home. And there are other spheres of our lives and existence, outside the home, where the state should not be a dominant presence. Freedom extends beyond spatial bounds. Liberty presumes an autonomy of self that includes freedom of thought, belief, expression, and certain intimate conduct. The instant case involves liberty of the person both in its spatial and more transcendent dimensions.

The question before the Court is the validity of a Texas statute making it a crime for two persons of the same sex to engage in certain intimate sexual conduct. . . .

Equality of treatment and the due process right to demand respect for conduct protected by the substantive guarantee of liberty are linked in important respects, and a decision on the latter point advances both interests. If protected conduct is made criminal and the law which does so remains unexamined for its substantive validity, its stigma might remain even if it were not enforceable as drawn for equal protection reasons. When homosexual conduct is made criminal by the law of the state, that declaration in and of itself is an invitation to subject homosexual persons to discrimination both in the public and in the private spheres. . . .

The stigma this criminal statute imposes, moreover, is not trivial. The offense, to be sure, is but a class C misdemeanor, a minor offense in the Texas legal system. Still, it remains a criminal offense with all that imports for the dignity of the persons charged. The petitioners will bear on their record the history of their criminal convictions. Just this term we rejected various challenges to state laws requiring the registration of sex offenders. We are advised that if Texas convicted an adult for private, consensual homosexual conduct under the statute here in question the convicted person would come within the registration laws of at least four states were he or she to be subject to their jurisdiction. This underscores the consequential nature of the punishment and the state-sponsored condemnation attendant to the criminal prohibition. Furthermore, the Texas criminal conviction carries with it the other collateral consequences always following a conviction, such as notations on job application forms, to mention but one example. . . .

The present case does not involve minors. It does not involve persons who

Lawrence v. Texas, 539 U.S. (2003).

might be injured or coerced or who are situated in relationships where consent might not easily be refused. It does not involve public conduct or prostitution. It does not involve whether the government must give formal recognition to any relationship that homosexual persons seek to enter. The case does involve two adults who, with full and mutual consent from each other, engaged in sexual practices common to a homosexual lifestyle. The petitioners are entitled to respect for their private lives. The state cannot demean their existence or control their destiny by making their private sexual conduct a crime. Their right to liberty under the Due Process Clause gives them the full right to engage in their conduct without intervention of the government. "It is a promise of the Constitution that there is a realm of personal liberty which the government may not enter." The Texas statute furthers no legitimate state interest which can justify its intrusion into the personal and private life of the individual.

Had those who drew and ratified the Due Process Clauses of the Fifth Amendment or the Fourteenth Amendment known the components of liberty in its manifold possibilities, they might have been more specific. They did not presume to have this insight. They knew times can blind us to certain truths and later generations can see that laws once thought necessary and proper in fact serve only to oppress. As the Constitution endures, persons in every generation can invoke its principles in their own search for greater freedom.

SANDRA DAY O'CONNOR

(A concurrence)

I agree with the Court that Texas' statute banning same-sex sodomy is unconstitutional. Rather than relying on the substantive component of the Fourteenth Amendment's Due Process Clause, as the Court does, I base my conclusion on the Fourteenth Amendment's Equal Protection Clause.

The statute at issue here makes sodomy a crime only if a person "engages in deviate sexual intercourse with another individual of the same sex." Sodomy between opposite-sex partners, however, is not a crime in Texas. That is, Texas treats the same conduct differently based solely on the participants. Those harmed by this law are people who have a same-sex sexual orientation and thus are more likely to engage in behavior prohibited by 21.06.

The Texas statute makes homosexuals unequal in the eyes of the law by making particular conduct—and only that conduct—subject to criminal sanction. It appears that prosecutions under Texas' sodomy law are rare. This case shows, however, that prosecutions under 21.06 *do* occur. And while the penalty imposed on petitioners in this case was relatively minor, the consequences of conviction are not. . . .

This case raises an . . . issue . . . whether, under the Equal Protection Clause, moral disapproval is a legitimate state interest to justify by itself a statute that bans homosexual sodomy, but not heterosexual sodomy. It is not. Moral disapproval of this group, like a bare desire to harm the group, is an interest that is insufficient to satisfy rational basis review under the Equal Protection Clause. Indeed, we have never held that moral disapproval, without any other asserted state interest, is a sufficient rationale under the Equal Protection Clause to justify a law that discriminates among groups of persons. . . .

That this law as applied to private, consensual conduct is unconstitutional under the Equal Protection Clause does not mean that other laws distinguishing between heterosexuals and homosexuals would similarly fail under rational basis review. Texas cannot assert any legitimate state interest here, such as national security or preserving the traditional institution of marriage. Unlike the moral disapproval of same-sex relations—the asserted state interest in this case—other reasons exist to promote the institution of marriage beyond mere moral disapproval of an excluded group. . . .